"The notion of *home* has always been elusive. But as evidenced in these stories, poems, and testaments, perhaps home is not so much a place, but a feeling one embodies. I read this book and see my people—see us—and feel, in our collective outsiderhood, at home."

—OCEAN VUONG, author of
Night Sky with Exit Wounds

"There is a whole range of expression in this book, delving deeply into the manifold experiences of being a perpetual alien. To be from nowhere is the state of Asian diaspora, but there is also a wild humor and imagination that comes from being underestimated, rarely counted, hardly seen. Here, we begin to draw the hopeful outlines of a collective history for those so disparate yet often lumped together."

—JENNY ZHANG, author of *Sour Heart: Stories*

"*Go Home!* is a bold, eclectic chorus that provides an invigorating antidote to the xenophobia of our times."

—RUTH OZEKI, author of *A Tale for the Time Being*

"This anthology displays the colors of the liminal—half-tones and undertones mixing the wry, the irreverent, the outraged, the lyric, and the longing. A composite portrait of the Asian diasporic experience today."

—MONICA YOUN, author of *Blackacre: Poems*

"Hats off to Rowan Hisayo Buchanan for putting together such a rich and diverse anthology. In these dark we need these voices and stories more than

—JESSICA HAGEDOR

"In this new and daring collection, I find myself reliving moments of heartbreak that can only come from living in between two cultures—but also feeling profound relief in discovering I am not alone in these private burdens and joys. *Go Home!* should be celebrated, as reading it is a homecoming in itself."

—YUMI SAKUGAWA, author of *There Is No Right Way to Meditate: And Other Lessons*

"A stunning multigenre anthology of twenty-four writers that simultaneously conveys the inherent diversity of human experience, as well as humanity's most universal longing encapsulated in one endlessly unpacked word: *home*. We all need more books like this."

—KEATON PATTERSON, Brazos Bookstore

EDITED BY
ROWAN HISAYO
BUCHANAN

GO HOME!

FOREWORD BY
VIET THANH
NGUYEN

FEMINIST
PRESS
AT THE CITY UNIVERSITY
OF NEW YORK
NEW YORK CITY

ASIAN AMERICAN WRITERS' WORKSHOP

Published in 2018 by the Feminist Press
at the City University of New York
The Graduate Center
365 Fifth Avenue, Suite 5406
New York, NY 10016

feministpress.org

First Feminist Press edition 2018

 Go Home! was published in partnership with the Asian American Writers'
Workshop.

 This book was made possible thanks to a grant from New
York State Council on the Arts with the support of Governor
Andrew M. Cuomo and the New York State Legislature.

 This book is supported in part by an award from the National Endowment
for the Arts.

First printing March 2018

Cover design by Britt Gudas
Cover photo by Serena Vergano, courtesy of Ricardo Bofill
Text design by Suki Boynton

Library of Congress Cataloging-in-Publication Data
Names: Buchanan, Rowan Hisayo editor. | Nguyen, Viet Thanh, 1971- author of
foreword.
Title: Go home! / [compiled by Rowan Hisayo Buchanan ; foreword by Viet Thanh
Nguyen].
Description: First Feminist Press edition. | New York, NY : Feminist Press at
the City University of New York, 2018.
Identifiers: LCCN 2017012004 (print) | LCCN 2017032423 (ebook) | ISBN
9781936932030 (ebook) | ISBN 9781936932016 (trade pbk.)
Subjects: LCSH: American literature--Asian American authors. | American
literature--Women authors. | American literature--21st century.
Classification: LCC PS508.A8 (ebook) | LCC PS508.A8 G63 2017 (print) | DDC
810.9/928708995--dc23
LC record available at https://lccn.loc.gov/2017012004

CONTENTS

Editor's Note

Rowan Hisayo Buchanan

In Japanese there is a specific verb for traveling homeward: 帰る (kaeru). Going or coming home is its own enterprise, distinct from traveling to any other destination. There is something so particular about a journey made toward home. The word has a beauty and a comfort to it. But what does it mean to go home?

MY FRIEND AND I were standing in line for the New Museum. It was a lovely New York day and the light was low and violet. People ahead of us were eating food out of little paper boxes. Then we heard it: "Go home!" The man shouting at us was wearing a black plastic jacket and his beard was a blond-white scrawl. He slowed his pace only for the moment it took for the hatred to spill out of his mouth. The insult seemed so weak, like movie-villain stock dialogue. It was most of all ridiculous—because of the sheer impossibility of it.

My friend, let's call him T, grew up in Michigan. His family now lives in North Carolina. He was born in the north of China. The last time he went back to his birth-place, he was eight years old. We were waiting for our friend M to join us. She's half-Japanese, half-Sicilian and grew up in the Midwest. I was born in London. My grand-father was born in Tokyo and my grandmother in Shang-hai. My mother was born on the Upper West Side of New York. My father's side is a European hodgepodge. Where is it that Japanese-Chinese-Scottish-English-American people come from?

My idea of home is a verb. Home is a straining toward belonging. For me the feeling of wanting to go home is home. For others, home is a place they want to escape, a place that doesn't exist, a place that exists only in time, a place that exists in the breath of a parent, or the mouth of a lover. For some, home is geographical, but they cannot return because of political, financial, or personal reasons. Others are seen as foreigners in their chosen homes.

In my conversations with Jyothi Natarajan at the Asian American Writers' Workshop and Jisu Kim at the Feminist Press, we agreed we wanted to share many different visions of home. I began compiling this anthology after I moved from the United States to the United Kingdom. At the moment, both countries seem to be becoming less and less united. Xenophobic rhetoric gushes from political podiums. The ideal home they describe has locked doors—not letting anyone in or out. They want to decide who belongs where. But I have seen a pushback. Writers are amplifying each other's cries to kindness, to empathy, and to understanding.

I hope this anthology can participate in that work. This book binds together fiction writers, poets, and essayists. We reached out to established writers and to those starting out. We searched for stories of homes found and homes lost. It is full of joy and of sorrow. The writers in this book complicate and expand the idea of home. They tell new stories and break down old stereotypes. Each piece is different and each is its own definition of home.

But this one book can't contain all the vital voices. After you close the last page behind you, please open many more. Consider this book a doorway. The world presents ever-increasing ways in which we can be homed and unhomed. You may not see your own definition of home in these pages, but we hope you find resonances and use them as a starting point for your own writing and thinking.

Foreword

Viet Thanh Nguyen

When I was seventeen, I could not wait to leave home, even though I was more fortunate than many. My father and mother did nothing wrong in our home, which was in San Jose, California. Our first house was by a downtown freeway entrance ramp, the soaring taillights of the cars visible from my bedroom window. I dreamed of taking off with them. Our second house was in the quiet foothills, where my father still lives, his bedroom furnished with a computer and a photocopier manufactured in the 1980s.

There was no abuse, and there was always food, warmth, light, and religion. There was love, too, the quiet kind that expresses itself not through words and embraces but through acts of sacrifice, through the model of parental lives given to duty: the twelve-to-fourteen-hour days working at a grocery store with hardly a day off, the devotion to the church, the remittances sent home to desperate relatives in a postwar Vietnam—the typical grind of all refugee families.

And yet, despite not needing anything, I wanted

more, although exactly what, I did not know. I wanted to leave home because I wanted to find a home of my own creation. My parents' sacrifice allowed me to yearn for more than they could give, and for more than San Jose or the Vietnamese refugee community there could offer. To my teenage self, it was a bland city of routine desires for suburban homes and expensive goods, not of ideas or "culture." To me, culture meant the world I read about in books and saw in movies, the charming white fantasies of Paris and New York.

The culture of San Jose that I knew, the Vietnamese one, was neither charming nor fantastic. The Vietnamese community was marked by close bonds of kinship and identity but also by the fallout of war, demonstrated through anger, violence, and bitterness. It was the war that drove my parents to become shopkeepers toiling in their store, where they were shot one Christmas Eve. They were suspicious of their own countrymen and warned me never to open the door to Vietnamese people, for fear of them invading our home (when it happened, when the gun was pointed in all our faces, the hand holding it belonged to a white man). The closeness and the legacy of trauma meant, for me, an atmosphere of suffocation, confined by the walls and boundaries of my parents' home, of the Vietnamese community, and of San Jose.

I did not know it then, but what I wanted was a home without walls and boundaries. For some, walls and boundaries comfort rather than confine, keeping things out and keeping things in. As a refugee and an alien in the eyes of many Americans, I knew inarticulately that I was an outsider. At my mostly white high school, the handful of us who were Asian gathered in a corner for lunch and called ourselves the "Asian invasion." Growing up in San Jose, I might have become one of those outsiders and invaders who only wanted to get inside at any cost. But ever since I had seen a sign in a shop window near my parents' store that read "Another American driven out of business by the Vietnamese," I knew that the yearning to be inside—to be just another American—might also tempt people toward hatred and fear.

Comfortably ensconced at last within four walls and a mortgage, we may be tempted to close the door behind us and lock it shut. Some former Vietnamese refugees do so today when they say the United States should not take in new refugees from the Middle East. They are wrong, forgetting that once they were the outsiders whom the majority of Americans did not want to take in. They are not special or exceptional, only lucky to be the beneficiaries of American guilt (at having abandoned South Vietnam) and American political calculation (for taking in refugees from a formerly communist country was simply another strategic move of the so-called Cold War). In contrast to those who use homes to shut people out, I believe that we need to keep our doors open. Or knock down the walls altogether.

I found a home in language and storytelling. This home has walls of a kind. One needs to speak and read English to be in my home, which can be unwelcoming to some. But no one is locked out, beginning with me. I found my entryway in school, learning to read, and through librarians at the public library. The library was literally my second home and also the home of the books through which I found freedom and flight from a world that I found confining. Books offered adventure, the promise of new worlds, the sight of further horizons. While the San Jose library mostly offered the canon of colonizers, I nevertheless learned from this literature a love of language and storytelling, a desire for beauty in word and narrative. Through books and stories, the world became my home, a place from which I could never be dispossessed so long as I lived and my mind could roam. For a refugee like me who had lost his country of origin and his mother tongue, a home that could never be lost was a way to always feel safe.

It wasn't until I went to university that I discovered the powerful traditions of decolonization and minority writing, which emerged in part to contest the widely accepted literary canon. These traditions taught me defiance and the values of justice and solidarity, traditions that have their own beauty. Writers deployed them to stake their claim of being at home in literatures often written in the language of masters and colonizers.

The existence of *Go Home!* testifies to the power of language as a home open to all, albeit one that we must often fight for. Against the racist demand that we go back to where we came from, we say that we are already at home, not just in the United States, but in English.

While this preoccupation with home is a universal human concern, it becomes particularly dire for those whose identities make them vulnerable to the threat of never belonging. This has certainly been the case for Asian Americans, whose experience with racism in the United States has often times occurred through being painted as the perpetual foreigner, the yellow peril or brown terror, with unbreakable ties to a land of origin or ancestry.

But those who tell us to "go home" are no match for

those of us who can write back in the very language used against us. The beauty of a home in language is that it allows us to create a multiplicity of homes. The writers in this anthology talk about home as being found in family, history, food, love, place, body, memory, song, and religion. They describe homes filled with all kinds of emotions, from love to hate and everything in between. Their homes are places of comfort and discomfort, of belonging and alienation, of the beginning of life and its end. But if homes are not always idyllic and are often conflicted, and if in some cases it is impossible to go home because home no longer exists or is not a place one wishes to return to, then living with a degree of homelessness might be a necessity. There can be a danger in being too much at home, too secure, especially for writers. Feeling uncomfortable at times—feeling not at home—keeps us alert, empathetic, aware of how so many others are not at home or not allowed to feel at home.

Reading this collection, I visited all of these writers' homes and experienced their homelessness filtered through their stories and poems. All of their works were gifts to me, and I thought about how homes can be gifts too. While some gifts are given with the hope of receiving something in return, eventually, other gifts are given without any expectation of reciprocity. Stories exist along that spectrum as well. Sometimes writers write and hope for fame or fortune. Sometimes people create homes and expect to reap a return from those they house, a payment in love or at least obligation. But the best gifts, in my mind, are those that we give selflessly. As a writer, I aspire to be that kind of gift giver, hoping that my stories will affect readers I will never know and never hear from, just as I was affected by writers who never knew their words were a gift to me. As the recipient of generosity, I hope to give generously in turn, as I believe many of the writers in this collection are likewise giving of their words and stories.

As for my first home, I think of how my parents gave me so much and how I did not appreciate their gifts in my youth. If I had, would I have stayed home? If I had stayed home, would I have become a writer? Perhaps not. Probably not. And if so, then it was for the best that I left. In my case, as may be the case for many others, I had to leave home in order to go home. This was a figurative return, for I understood, over time, that the home they provided for me was not literally just a house. Their home was the act of giving itself, which is also to say the act of love. Going home, in my case, was then a matter of learning how not just to receive but to give, certainly to my own family but also to those who may be my readers.

Perhaps the writers in this collection also had to leave home in order to go home. Read them. Their gifts will show you the many shapes home can take, as well as the many ways we can leave and, maybe, return.

Release

Alexander Chee

In the fall of 1996, I moved into a sublet, a room in an apartment in the West Village of New York, at the corner of Greenwich Avenue and Seventh. The apartment belonged to someone I'd met through a friend. The rent was very cheap, and I had always wanted to live in the West Village. I had my eye on West Eleventh Street, and this was close.

The apartment was essentially a narrow hallway, and my room was a small room a little bigger than my bed. There was a bathroom, a kitchen, and his room, which was also the living room, and it had a door I couldn't go beyond if it was closed, as it meant my roommate was working, which is to say, giving a man a massage with the understanding that at the end he'd get release.

"Release?" I asked, when he first said it.

"A hand job," he answered. I nodded and then he nodded too, and laughed.

Release always struck me as a strangely hygienic term for it. I imagined men supplicant on the long table, afraid

1

they might not be allowed out of whatever the prison was of their lives. Leaping into the air afterward, maybe even capable of flight.

My roommate was tall, handsome, a former model, Amerasian like me—Dutch and Japanese—and he had a beautiful sleeve tattoo on his arm of a Japanese dragon, like a character out of a comic book. He was like a taller, prettier version of me, the older cousin I'd never had, the spitting image of Crying Freeman, from the manga of the same name about a Japanese assassin for the Chinese mafia—and while I think I mentioned the comics, I don't remember. I do remember how sometimes I had the uncanny feeling of having entered the comic, as if I'd loved it so much it had come true. Especially when he strode across his room, shirtless, the beautiful tattoo glowing on his pale skin.

He was smart and funny, and had literary aspirations that we sometimes talked about on the nights we drank wine late into the night in his room, which was also the living room. I was happy for a while there. I could count on one hand the number of hapa gay men I'd met back then, and of those, even fewer of them were literary. Each time I met one it was like we were from a homeland that had never existed, but that if we collected enough of each other, maybe it would. But we never said this, or, I never did, it was just something I felt. I liked being like him, and I wanted to be more like him, to be as sultry, as bitter, as funny in the same way—and as beautiful.

When I found out he wanted to be a writer, it made me proud somehow. As much as I wanted to be like him, it surprised me to learn he wanted to be a little like me too.

At times, while drinking wine, he would confess things

to me. The first confession was that he was terribly disfig-
ured. A motorcycle accident in Los Angeles, he assured
me, had ended his career as a model and actor. I couldn't
tell. His face and body were both still beautiful, as far as I
could see, and I could see no scars. When I told him, he
laughed bitterly. "You can see it in pictures," he assured
me. When he showed me photos of him as he had been, I
scrutinized them carefully, but he looked . . . the same. "A
really good plastic surgeon was at the emergency room,"
he then said. "You know. Thank God it was LA."

Yes, I remember thinking. *Thank LA too.*

NEXT HE TOLD me he had steroids he took to stay thin
without working out, as he hated working out, pills he
got from a doctor he saw in that room and who paid him
in prescriptions. Soon the doctor was revealed to be the
doctor who had worked on his face. Then I learned that
the friend who had recommended me to him was also a
client. There was a story he was telling me in installments,
but the installments felt like windows that could not show
the whole story—the real story was in what he did and
did not say.

The kitchen was right before his room. I never heard
much when it was happening, and he kept the door closed
if I was home while he had clients. As a courtesy to him I
tried not to be, though—and as the neighborhood was full
of bookstores, it was easy. His work didn't bother me—it
was a little funny to me, like living in the front room of a
brothel in the most boring way.

He was blithe about his work, as if it didn't matter
that he did this kind of work. As if it were only funny
that he did this—he liked to make jokes. But I soon un-

3

derstood, in his mind, the accident had foreclosed on a more lucrative modeling and acting career, and this work was what he could do now, the one way he could still make money off his looks. Most of the time he maintained an air of devilishness, but here and there, rage appeared, only in the eyes of the very still, very beautiful, allegedly destroyed face.

Every so often he would take out the photos of himself from before the accident, showing me, in something like a ritual, asking me again to see the difference that I could not see.

Gradually I understood that it didn't matter that he was still beautiful. Not to him. Not if every time he looked in the mirror he saw a stranger, someone who was going to fail him and his future. A replacement left behind by the accident.

HE BROUGHT HOME a dog a few months after I moved in, a short squat blond mutt, part Corgi, part terrier of some kind, golden and seemingly placid, going blind. I don't remember why, but soon after, he said he didn't want the dog anymore. By then the dog and I had grown attached to each other, and so I said I'd take the dog.

The dog woke from a nap on my bed one afternoon and snarled once before it leaped at me, attaching itself to my cheek, biting deep. I grabbed its throat reflexively, and it let go. At the nearby St. Vincent's Hospital, I waited in the emergency room to be told the wounds were puncture wounds and could not be sewn, only treated with salves and bandaged. So I was treated, given oral antibiotics and painkillers, an enormous bandage for my left cheek, and then I was released.

4

When I got home, my roommate had had it destroyed. He finally showed me the papers for the dog, which I'd not seen before the accident, with the word UNADOPTABLE stamped across them.

I DIDN'T STAY too much longer after that. I've never spoken to him again. I saw something of his in the *Village Voice* once, but by now only his face remains in my memory, his name lost to me.

The only other way I remember him is in my face. I can tell when it's going to rain now. I feel it in the scar, like a thumb pressing on the bone. When I do, I remember what the attending physician said. "It's good you caught him at the throat. This could have been much worse." Then he explained that if you're ever being attacked by a dog, try to catch and pull the front legs apart. This splits their breastbone open, incapacitating them. Though it seems to me to bring the dog's face unacceptably close. I am sure I could never do it, and I'm happy I've never had to try. But then I no longer, despite my love of dogs, let them lick my face.

My face is a stranger to me now, even all these years later. I tell people the story and ask if they can see the difference, and everyone says, "You can't tell." But I can. I never used to believe him about his face but I do now.

If I ever see him again, I'll tell him.

Things That Remind Me of Home

Kimiko Hahn

after Sei Shōnagon

moth balls
turpentine, curried chicken in the pressure cooker,
    gardenia—

From the living room, the sound of her Singer [Cast
Iron, 1895] [same year her father was born in Hiroshi-
ma-ken]. The speed of the tapping depended on her knee
pressure. Mother sewed doll clothes from her own dress
hems. *For me.*

the taste of sumi-e ink
kitty litter box nest to the black phone mulch
transistor radio, car radio, record player

My student misses home, a "res" out west. "Every boulder
and plant has a story and the story is about origin. About
home." I am never homesick for places—only people.

Mr. Cook—retired Chinese merchant marine so-named
by our super—sees me as I walk by an OTB on Ninth

Avenue. This is years after I've moved out of our shabby apartment building on West 105th St. but he immediately recognizes me. He waves and hurries up to me, saying, "My wife, she went home." Yes. Home. Ashes.

"Show me your green card."

Mr. C. stuffed his two-bedroom apartment full of newspapers, Playbills, photographs of stars and of himself, shoes from every photo shoot he'd been on, his wife's dresses over their thirty-two-year marriage, and so on. To meet him in the elevator, one would think, "A nice tidy eccentric who plays rabbis or wizards in adverts." Unless you looked at his limp black jacket, dandruff and mustard on his lapel. When the landlord told him to clean out or clear out, they got a dumpster. He died three months later.

A bar in Charleston, West Virginia, 1981, the man next to me says, "Where you from?" I say, "New York." He asks again and I smile and repeat, "I'm from New York." He says, "You look like a girl I knew in Saigon."

> "Home is the place where, when you have to go
>   there,
> They have to take you in."
>   "I should have called it
> Something you somehow haven't to deserve."[1]

お握り[2]

---

1. Excerpt of poetry from Robert Frost's "The Death of the Hired Man."
2. お握り—onigiri—rice balls

Trudy

Turpentine from those large orange and black cans. (But do these things convey home or homesick? I cannot tell the difference, it seems.)

This is the kitchen where mother lifted me onto the porcelain sink and sponge-bathed me. In the 105th Street kitchen, I gave sponge baths to our little girls. (The kitchen where the linoleum curled up and cockroaches nested and startled when the light was turned on, the constant smell of them, even with the window open to the sooty outdoors.)

Meggie and I cleared a space under the forsythia at the bottom of her driveway to eat Ritz crackers. Barbara and I dug out homes for our trolls in the gnarly hickory roots. Yesterday, Meena and I sipped martinis and she held my hand saying, "You must take care of yourself, dear Kimiko."

Deviled Ham

漬物[3]

stairwell, the Rittenhouse Hotel, the floor of his office, café, car, dogwood, shower stall

---

3. 漬物—tsukemono—Japanese pickles

Mothers, Lock Up Your Daughters Because They Are Terrifying

Alice Sola Kim

At midnight we parked by a Staples and tried some seriously dark fucking magic. We had been discussing it for weeks and could have stayed in that *wouldn't it be funny if* groove forever, zipping between yes, we should and no, we shouldn't until it became a joke so dumb that we would never. But that night Mini had said, "If we don't do it right now, I'm going to be so mad at you guys, and I'll know from now on that all you chickenheads can do is talk and not do," and the whole way she ranted at us like that, even though we were already doing and not talking, or at least about to. (We always let her do that, get all shirty and sharp with us, because she had the car, but perhaps we should have said something. Perhaps once everyone had cars, Mini would have to figure out how to not be a total bitch, and she would be leagues behind everyone else.)

The parking lot at night looked like the ocean, the black Atlantic as we imagined it, and in Mini's car we brought up the spell on our phones and Caroline read it first. She always had to be first to do anything, because she had the most to prove, being scared of everything. We couldn't help but tease her about that, even though we knew it wasn't her fault—her parents made her that way, but then again, if someone didn't get told for being a pill just because we could trace said pill-ness back to their parents, then where would it ever end?

We had an X-Acto knife and a lighter and antibacterial ointment and lard and a fat red candle still shrink-wrapped. A chipped saucer from Ronnie's dad's grandmother's wedding set, made of china that glowed even in dim light and sang when you rubbed your thumb along it, which she took because it was chipped and thought they wouldn't miss it, but we thought that was dumb because they would definitely miss the chipped one. The different one. We could have wrapped it all up and sold it as a Satanism starter kit.

Those were the things. What we did with them we'll never tell. For a moment, it seemed like it would work. The moment stayed the same, even though it should have changed. A real staring contest of a moment: Ronnie's face shining in the lunar light of her phone, the slow tick of the blood into the saucer, like a radiator settling. But Mini ruined it. "Do you feel anything?" asked Mini, too soon and too loudly. We glanced at each other, dismayed. We thought, perhaps if she had just waited a little longer—"I don't think so," said Ronnie. "I knew this was a dumb idea," said Mini. "Let's clean up this blood before it gets all over my car. So if one of you got murdered, they wouldn't blame me." Caroline handed out the Band-Aids. She put hers on and saw the blood well up instantly against the Band-Aid, not red or black or any color in particular, only a dark splotch like a shape under ice. So much for that, everyone thought, wrong.

MINI DROPPED CAROLINE off first, even though she lived closer to Mini, then Ronnie after. It had been this way always. At first Caroline had been hurt by this, had imagined that we were talking about her in the fifteen extra minutes of alone time that we shared. The truth was both a relief and an even greater insult. There was nothing to say about Caroline, no shit we would talk that wasn't right to her face. We loved Caroline, but her best jokes were unintentional. We loved Caroline, but she didn't know how to pretend to be cool and at home in strange places like we did; she was the one who always seemed like a pie-faced country girleen wearing a straw hat and holding a suitcase, asking obvious questions like, "Wait, which hand do you want to stamp?" or "Is that illegal?" Not that the answers were always obvious to us, but we knew what not to ask about. We knew how to be cool, so why didn't Caroline?

Usually, we liked to take a moment at the end of the night without Caroline, to discuss the events of the night without someone to remind us how young we were and how little we knew. But tonight we didn't really talk. We didn't talk about how we believed, and how our belief had been shattered. We didn't talk about the next time we would hang out. Ronnie snuck into her house. Her brother, Alex, had left the window open for her. Caroline was already in bed, wearing an ugly quilted headband that kept her bangs off her face so she wouldn't get forehead zits. Mini's mom wasn't home yet, so she microwaved some egg rolls. She put her feet up on the kitchen table, next to her homework, which had been completed hours ago. The egg rolls exploded tiny scalding droplets of water when she bit into them. She soothed her seared lips on a beer. This is the life, Mini thought.

We didn't go to the same school, and we wouldn't be friends if we had. We met at an event for Korean adoptees, a low-ceilinged party at a community center catered with the stinkiest food possible. Koreans, amirite?! That's how we/they roll.

Mini and Caroline were having fun. Ronnie was not having fun. Mini's fun was different from Caroline's fun, being a fake-jolly fun in which she was imagining telling her real friends about this doofus loser event later, although due to the fact that she was reminding them that she was adopted, they would either squirm with discomfort or stay very still and serious and stare her in the pupils with great intensity, nodding all the while. Caroline was having fun—the pure uncut stuff, nothing ironic about it. She liked talking earnestly with people her age about basic biographical details because there was a safety in conversational topics that no one cared about all that much. Talking about which high school you go to? Great! Which activities you did at aforementioned school? Raaaad. Talking about the neighborhood where you live? How was it possible that they weren't all dead of fun! Caroline already knew and liked the K-pop soundtracking the evening, the taste of the marinated beef and the clear noodles, dishes that her family recreated on a regular basis.

Ronnie rooted herself by a giant cut-glass bowl full of kimchi, which looked exactly like a big wet pile of fresh guts. She soon realized that (1) the area by the kimchi was very high traffic, and (2) the kimchi emitted a powerful vinegar-poop-death stench. As Ronnie edged away from the food table, Mini and Caroline were walking toward it. Caroline saw a lost and lonely soul and immediately said, "Hi! Is this your first time at a meet-up?"

At this Ronnie experienced split consciousness, feeling annoyed that she was about to be sucked into wearying small talk, in addition to a nearly sacramental sense of gratitude about being saved from standing alone at a gathering. You could even say that Ronnie was experiencing quadruple consciousness if you counted the fact that she was both judging and admiring Mini and Caroline—Mini for being the kind of girl who tries to look ugly on purpose and thinks it looks so great (ooh, except it did look kinda great), her torn sneakers and one thousand silver earrings and chewed-up hair, and Caroline of the sweetly tilted eyes and cashmere sweater dress and ballet flats like she was some pampered cat turned human.

Mini had a stainless-steel water bottle full of ice and vodka cut with the minimal amount of orange juice. She shared it with Ronnie and Caroline. And Caroline drank it. Caroline ate and drank like she was a laughing two-dimensional cutout and everything she consumed just went through her face and evaporated behind her, affecting her not at all.

Ronnie could not stop staring at Caroline, who was a one-woman band of laughing and drinking and ferrying food to her mouth and nodding and asking skin-rippingly boring questions that nevertheless got them talking. Ronnie went from laughing at Caroline to being incredibly jealous of her. People got drunk just to be like Caroline!

Crap, Ronnie thought. Social graces are actually worth something.

But Caroline was getting drunk, and since she was already Caroline, she went too far with the whole being Caroline thing and asked if she could tell us a joke. Only if we promised not to get offended!

Mini threw her head back, smiled condescendingly at an imaginary person to her left, and said, "Of course." She frowned to hide a burp that was, if not exactly a solid, still alarmingly substantial, and passed the water bottle to Ronnie.

Caroline wound up. This had the potential to be long. "So, you know how—oh wait, no, okay, this is how it starts. Okay, so white people play the violin like this." She made some movements. "Black people play it like this." She made some more movements. "And then Korean people play it like th—" and began to bend at the waist but suddenly farted so loudly that it was like the fart had bent her, had then jet-packed her into the air and crumpled her to the ground. She tried to talk over it, but Ronnie and Mini were ended by their laughter. They fell out of themselves. They were puking laughter, the laughter was a thick brambly painful rope being pulled out of their faces, but they couldn't stop it, and finally Caroline stopped trying to finish the joke and we were all laughing.

CONSEQUENCES: FOR DAYS after, we would think that we had exhausted the joke and sanded off all the funniness, rubbing it so often with our sweaty fingers, but then we would remember again and, whoa, there we went again, off to the races.

Consequences: summer arrived. Decoupled from school, we were free to see one another, to feel happy misfitting with one another because we knew we were peas from different pods—we delighted in being such different kinds of girls from one another.

Consequences: for weeks after, we'd end sentences with, "Korean people do it like ppppbbbbbbbttth."

THERE ARE SO many ways to miss your mother. Your real mother—the one who looks like you, the one who has to love you because she grew you from her own body, the one who hates you so much that she dumped you in the garbage for white people to pick up and dust off. In Mini's case, it manifested as some weird gothy shit. She had been engaging in a shady flirtation with a clerk at an antiquarian bookshop. We did not approve. We thought this clerk wore thick-rimmed hipster glasses to hide his crow's feet and hoodies to hide his man boobs so that weird high school chicks would still want to flirt with him. We hoped that Mini mostly only liked him because he was willing to trade clammy glances with her and go no further. Unlike us, Mini was not a fan of going far. When the manager wasn't around, this guy let her go into the room with the padlock on it, where all of the really expensive stuff was. That's where she found the book with the spell. That's where she took a photo of the spell with her phone. That's where she immediately texted it to us without any explanation attached, confident that the symbols were so powerful they would tentacle through our screens and into our hearts, and that we would know it for what it was.

Each of us had had that same moment where we saw ourselves in a photo, caught one of those wonky glances in the mirror that tricks you into thinking that you're seeing someone else, and it's electric. Kapow boom sizzle, you got slapped upside the head with the Korean wand, and now you felt weird at family gatherings that veered blond, you felt weird when your friends replaced their Facebook profile photos with pictures of the celebrities they look like and all you had was, say, Mulan or Jackie Chan, ha-ha-ha, hahahahaha.

You felt like you could do one thing wrong, one stupid thing, and the sight of you would become a terrible taste in your parents' mouths. "I'll tell you this," Mini had said. "None of us actually knows what happened to our mothers. None of our parents tell us anything. We don't have the cool parents who'll tell us about our backgrounds and shit like that." For Mini, this extended to everything else. When her parents decided to get a divorce, Mini felt like she had a hive of bees in her head (her brain was both the bees and the brain that the bees were stinging). She searched online for articles about adoptees with divorced parents. The gist of the articles was that she would be going through an awfully hard time, as in, chick already felt kind of weird and dislocated when it came to family and belonging and now it was just going to be worse. Internet, you asshole, thought Mini. I already knew that. The articles for the parents told them to reassure their children. Make them feel secure and safe. She waited for the parents to try so she could flame-throw scorn all over them. They did not try. She waited longer. And she had given up on them long before Mom finally arrived.

WE WERE HANGING out in Mini's room, not talking about our unsuccessful attempt at magic. Caroline was painting Ronnie's nails with a color called Balsamic.

"I love this color," said Caroline. "I wish my parents would let me wear it."

"Why wouldn't they?"

"I can't wear dark nail polish until I'm eighteen."

"Wait—they really said that?"

"How many things have they promised you when you turn eighteen?"

"You know they're just going to change the terms of the agreement when you actually turn eighteen, and then you'll be forty and still wearing clear nail polish and taking ballet and not being able to date."

"And not being able to have posters up in your room. Although I guess you won't need posters when you're forty."

"Fuck that! No one's taking away my posters when I get old."

Caroline didn't say anything. She shrugged, keeping her eyes on Ronnie's nails. When we first started hanging out with Caroline, we wondered if we shouldn't shit-talk Caroline's parents, because she never joined in, but we realized that she liked it. It helped her, and it helped her to not have to say anything.

"You're all set. Just let it dry."

"I don't know," said Ronnie. "It doesn't go with anything. It just looks random on me."

Mini said, "Well." She squinted and cocked her head back until she had a double chin, taking all of Ronnie in. "You kind of look like you're in prison and you traded a pack of cigarettes for nail polish because you wanted to feel glamorous again."

"Wow, thanks!"

"No, come on. You know what I mean. It's great. You look tough. You look like a normal girl, but you still look tough. Look at me. I'll never look tough." And she so wanted to, we knew. "I'd have to get a face tattoo, like a face tattoo of someone else's face over my face. Maybe I should get your face."

"Makeover montage," said Caroline. "Koreans do make-overs like pppppbbbbbbth," we said. Caroline laughed and the nail polish brush veered and swiped Ronnie's knuckle. We saw Ronnie get a little pissed. She didn't like physical insults. Once she wouldn't speak to us for an hour when Mini flicked her in the face with water in a movie theater bathroom. "Sorry," Caroline said. She coughed. Something had gone down wrong. She coughed some more and started to retch, and we were stuck between looking away politely and staring at her with our hands held out in this Jesus-looking way, figuring out how to help. There was a wet burr to her coughing that became a growl, and the growl rose and rose until it became a voice, a fluted voice, like silver flutes, like flutes of bubbly champagne, a beautiful voice full of rich people things.

MY DAUGHTERS

MY GIRLS

MY MY MINE MINE

Mom skipped around. When she spoke, she didn't move our mouths. We only felt the vibration of her voice rumbling through us.

"Did you come to us because we called for you?" asked Mini. Mom liked to jump into the mouth of the person asking the question. Mini's mouth popped open. Her eyes darted down, to the side, like she was trying to get a glimpse of herself talking.

I HEARD YOU, MY DAUGHTERS

"You speak really good English," Caroline said.

I LEARNED IT WHEN I WAS DEAD

We wanted to talk to one another but it felt rude with Mom in the room. If Mom was still in the room.

LOOK AT YOU, SO BEAUTIFUL

THE MOST BEAUTIFUL GIRL IN THE WORLD

Who was beautiful? Which one of us was she talking about? We asked and she did not answer directly. She only said that we were all beautiful, and any mother would be proud to have us. We thought we might work it out later.

OH, I LEFT YOU

AND OH

I'LL NEVER DO IT AGAIN

AT FIRST WE found Mom highly scary. At first we were scared of her voice and the way she used our faces to speak her words, and we were scared about how she loved us already and found us beautiful without knowing a thing about us. That is what parents are supposed to do, and we found it incredibly stressful and a little bit creepy. *Our* parents *love* us, thought Caroline and Mini. They do, they do, they do, but every so often we cannot help but feel that we have to earn our places in our homes. Caroline did it by being perfect and PG rated, though her mind boiled with filthy, outrageous thoughts, though she often got so frustrated at meals with her family during her performances of perfection that she wanted to bite the dining room table in half. *I'm not the way you think I am, and you're dumb to be so fooled.* Mini did it by never asking for anything. Never complaining. Though she could sulk and stew at the Olympic level. Girl's got to have an outlet.

Mom took turns with us, and in this way we got used to her. A few days after Mom's first appearance, Caroline woke herself up singing softly, a song she had never before heard. It sounded a little like: *baaaaaachudaaaaa/neeeeed-eowadaaaa*. Peaceful, droning. She sang it again, and then Mom said:

THIS IS A SONG MY MOTHER SANG TO ME WHEN I DIDN'T WANT TO WAKE UP FOR SCHOOL. IT CALLS THE VINES DOWN TO LIFT YOU UP AND—

"Mom?" said Caroline.

YES, SWEETIE

"Could you speak more quietly? It gets pretty loud in my head."

Oh, Of Course. Yes. This Song Is What My Mother Sang In The Mornings. And Her Hands Were Vines And She Would Lift Lift Lift Me Up, Mom said.

Caroline's stomach muscles stiffened as she sat up by degrees, like a mummy. Caroline's entire body ached, from her toenails to her temples, but that wasn't Mom's fault. It was her other mom's fault. Summers were almost worse for Caroline than the school year was. There was more ballet, for one thing, including a pointe intensive that made her feet twinge like loose teeth, and this really cheesed her off most of all, because her parents didn't even like ballet. They were bored into microsleeps by it, their heads drifting forward, their heads jumping back. What they liked was the idea of a daughter who did ballet, and who would therefore be skinny and not a lesbian. She volunteered at their church and attended youth group, where everyone mostly played foosball. She worked a few shifts at a chocolate shop, where she got to try every kind of chocolate they sold once and then never again. *But what if she forgot how they tasted?* She was tutored in calculus and biology, not because she needed any help with those subjects, but because her parents didn't

20

want to wait to find out whether she was the best or not at them—they wanted best and *they wanted it now.*

Once Ronnie said, "Caroline, your parents are like Asian parents," and Mini said, "Sucks to be you," and Caroline answered, "That's not what you're going to say in a few years when you're bagging my groceries," which sounded mean, but we knew she really only said it because she was confident that we wouldn't be bagging her groceries. Except for Ronnie, actually. We were worried about Ronnie, who wasn't academically motivated like Caroline or even *c'mon, c'mon, c'mon, what's next* motivated like Mini.

That first day Caroline enjoyed ballet class as she never had before, and she knew it was because Mom was there. She felt her chin tipped upward by Mom, arranging her daughter like a flower, a sleek and sinuous flower that would be admired until it died and even afterward. Mom had learned to speak quietly, and she murmured to Caroline to stand taller and suck in her stomach and become grace itself. The ballet teacher nodded her approval.

Though You Are A Little Bit Too Fat For Ballet, Mom murmured. Caroline cringed. She said, "Yeah, but Mom, I'm not going to be a ballerina." But Mom told her that it was important to try her best at everything and not be motivated by pure careerism only.

Mom told us we were beautiful and special and loved, but that is not to say that she was afraid to criticize the fuck out of us. Once Caroline tried to sing the song about getting up in the morning to please Mom, and Mom just laughed. *Ha-Ha-Ha-Ha-Ha-Ha, Oh Sweetie, Ha-Ha-Ha-Ha-Ha-Ha!*

"Mom," said Caroline. "I know the words."

You Don't Speak Korean, Mom told Caroline. *You Will Never Speak Real Korean.*

"You speak real English, though. How come you get both?"

I Told You. I'm Your Mother And I Know A Lot More Than You And I'm Dead.

It was true, though, about Caroline. The words came out of Caroline's mouth all sideways and awkward, like someone pushing a couch through a hallway. Worst of all, she didn't sound like someone speaking Korean—she sounded like someone making fun of it.

But if we knew Caroline, we knew that this was also what she wanted. Because she wanted to be perfect, so she also wanted to be told about the ways in which she was imperfect.

MINI WAS THE first to actually see Mom. She made herself Jell-O for dinner, which was taking too long because she kept opening the refrigerator door to poke at it. Mini's brain: c'mon, c'mon, c'mon, c'mon. She walked around the dining room table. She tried to read the *New Yorker* that her mother had been neglecting, but it was all tiny-print listings of events that happened anywhere but where she was about five months ago. She came back to the fridge to check on the Jell-O. Its condition seemed improved from the last time she checked, and anyhow she was getting hungrier, and it wasn't like Jell-O soup was the worst thing she'd ever eaten since her mom stopped cooking after the divorce. She looked down at the Jell-O, as any of us would do before breaking that perfect jeweled surface with the spoon, and saw reflected upon it the face of another. The face was on Mini, made up of the Mini material but everything tweaked and adjusted, made longer and thinner and sadder. Mini was awed. "Is that what you look like?" Mini asked. When she spoke she realized how loose her jaw felt.

"Ouch," she said. Mom said, *Oh, Honey, I Apologize. I Just Wanted You To See What Mom Looked Like. I'll Stop Now.*

"It's okay," said Mini.

Mom thought that Mini should be eating healthier food, and what do you know, Mini agreed. She told us about the dinner that Mom had Mini make. "I ate vegetables, you guys, and I kind of liked it." She did not tell us that her mother came home near the end of preparations, and Mini told her that she could not have any of it. She did not tell us that she frightened her mother with her cold, slack expression and the way she laughed at nothing in particular as she went up to her room. Caroline would have said: "I can't believe your mom had the nerve to ask if she could!"

Ronnie would have thought: there's being butt-hurt about your parents' divorce, and then there's being epically, unfairly butt-hurt about your parents' divorce, and you are veering toward the latter, Mini my friend. But what did Ronnie know? She was still scared of Mom. She probably hated her family more than any of us—we knew something was wrong but not what was wrong—but she wouldn't let Mom come too close either.

"HAVE YOU BEEN hanging out with Mom?"

"Yeah. We went shopping yesterday."

"I haven't seen her in a long time."

"Caroline, that's not fair! You had her first."

"I just miss her."

"Don't be jealous."

We would wake up with braids in our hair, complicated little tiny braids that we didn't know how to do. We would find ourselves making food that we didn't know how to make, stews and porridges and little sweet hotcakes. Ronnie pulled the braids out. Ronnie did not eat the food. We knew that Mom didn't like that. We knew Mom would want to have a serious talk with Ronnie soon.

We knew and we allowed ourselves to forget that we already had people in our lives who wanted to parent us, who had already been parenting us for years. But we found it impossible to accept them as our parents, now that our real mother was back. Someone's real mother. Sometimes we were sisters. Sometimes we were competitors.

Our parents didn't know us anymore. They couldn't do anything right, if they ever had in the first place. This is one problem with having another set of parents. *A dotted outline of parents.* For every time your parents forget to pick you up from soccer practice, there is the other set that would have picked you up. They—she—would have been perfect at all of it.

RONNIE WAS WASHING the dishes when a terrible pain gripped her head. She shouted and fell to her knees. Water ran over the broken glass in the sink.

Honey, said Mom, *You Won't Let Me Get To Know You. Ronnie, Don't You Love Me? Don't You Like The Food I Make For You? Don't You Miss Your Mother?*

Ronnie shook her head.

Ronnie, I Am Going To Knock First—

Someone was putting hot, tiny little fingers in her head

like her head was a glove, up her nose, in her eyes, against the roof of her mouth. And then they squeezed. Ronnie started crying.

—*And Then I'm Coming In.*

She didn't want this; she didn't want for Mom to know her like Mom had gotten to know Caroline and Mini; she didn't want to become these weird monosyllabic love-zombies like them, them with their wonderful families—how dare they complain so much, how dare they abandon them for this creature? And perhaps Ronnie was just stronger and more skeptical, but she had another reason for wanting to keep Mom away. She was ashamed. The truth was that there was already someone inside her head. It was her brother, Alex. He was the tumor that rolled and pressed on her brain to shift her moods between dreamy and horrified.

Ronnie first became infected with the wrong kind of love for Alex on a school-day morning, when she stood in front of the bathroom mirror brushing her teeth. He had stood there not a minute before her, shaving. On school-day mornings, they were on the same schedule, nearly on top of each other. His hot footprints pressed up into hers. And then he was pressing up against her, and it was confusing, and she forgot now whose idea all of this was in the first place, but there was no mistake about the fact that she instigated everything now. Everything she did and felt, Alex returned, and this troubled Ronnie, that he never started it anymore, so that she was definitively the sole foreign element and corrupting influence in this household of Scandinavian blonds.

("Do you want to do this?") ("Okay. Then I want to do this too.")

Ronnie hated it and liked it when they did stuff in the bathroom. Having the mirror there was horrible. She didn't need to see all that to know it was wrong. Having the mirror there helped. It reassured her to see how different they looked—everything opposed and chiaroscuro—no laws were being broken and triggering alarms from deep inside their DNA.

Sometimes Alex told her that they could get married. Or if not married, they could just leave the state or the country and be together in some nameless elsewhere. The thought filled Ronnie with a vicious horror. If the Halversons weren't her parents, if Mrs. Halverson wasn't her mother, then who was to be her mother? Alex would still have his family. He wasn't the adopted one, after all. Ronnie would be alone in the world, with only fake companions—a blond husband who used to be her brother, and a ghost who would rest its hands on Ronnie's shoulders until the weight was unbearable, a ghost that couldn't even tell different Asian girls apart to recognize its own daughter.

Mom was silent. Ronnie stayed on the floor. She collected her limbs to herself and laced her fingers behind her neck. She felt it: something terrible approached. It was too far away to see or hear or feel, but when it finally arrived, it would shake her hard enough to break her in half. Freeing a hand, Ronnie pulled out her phone and called Mini. She told her to come quickly and to bring Caroline and it was about Mom, and before she could finish, Mom squeezed the phone and slammed Ronnie's hand hard against the kitchen cabinet.

YOU ARE A DIRTY GIRL
NEVER

HAVE I EVER
SLUT SLUT
FILTHY SLUT
Ronnie's ears rang. Mom was crying now too. *You Do This To These People Who Took You In And Care For You*, Mom sobbed. *I Don't Know You At All. I Don't Know Any Of You.*
YOU'RE NOT NICE GIRLS
NO DAUGHTERS OF MINE

WHEN MINI AND Caroline came into the kitchen, Ronnie was sitting on the floor. Her hand was bleeding and swollen, but otherwise she was fine, her face calm, her back straight. She looked up at us. "We have to go reverse the spell. We have to send her back. I made her hate us. I'm sorry. She's going to kill us."

"Oh, no," said Caroline.

Mini's head turned to look at Caroline, then the rest of her body followed. She slapped Caroline neatly across the face. *You I Don't Like So Much Either*, Mom said, using Mini's mouth to speak. *I Know What You Think About At Night, During The Day, All Day. You Can't Fool Me. I Tried And Tried—*

Mini covered her mouth, and then Mom switched to Caroline. *—And Tried To Make You Good. But Ronnie Showed Me It Was All Useless. You Are All Worthless.* Caroline shook her head until Mom left, and we pulled Ronnie up and ran out to the car together, gripping one another's hands the whole way.

We drove, or just Mini drove, but we were rearing forward in our seats, and it was as though we were all driving, strenuously, horsewhippingly, like there was an away to get to, as if what we were trying to escape was behind us and not inside of us. We were screaming and shouting louder and louder until Mini was suddenly seized again. We saw it and we waited. Mini's jaw unhinged, and we only didn't scream because this had happened many times—certainly we didn't like it when it happened to us, but that way at least we didn't have to look at it, the way that it was only skin holding the moving parts of her skull together, skin becoming liquid like glass in heat, and then her mouth opened beyond everything we knew to be possible, and the words that came out—oh, the words. Mini began to speak and then we did, we did scream, even though we should have been used to it by now.

DRIVE SAFE

DRIVE SAFE

DO YOU WANT TO DIE BEFORE I TEACH YOU EVERYTHING THERE IS TO KNOW

The car veered, a tree loomed, and we were garlanded in glass, and a branch insinuated itself into Mini's ribs and encircled her heart, and Ronnie sprang forth and broke against the tree, and in the backseat Caroline was marveling at how her brain became unmoored and seesawed forward into the jagged coastline of the front of her skull and back again, until she was no longer herself, and it was all so mortifying that we could have just died, and we did, we did die, we watched every second of it happen until we realized that we were back on the road, driving, and all of the preceding was just a little movie that Mom had played inside of our heads.

"Stop," said Ronnie. "Stop the car."

"No way," said Mini. "That's what she wants."

Mom sobs again. *I Killed Myself For Love. I Killed My-*

self For You, she said. *I Came Back For Girls Who Wanted Parents But You Already Had Parents.*

"Mini, listen to me," said Ronnie. "I said it because it seemed like a thing to say, and it would have been nice to have, but there is no way to reverse the spell, is there?"

"We can try it. We can go back to the parking lot and do everything but backward."

"We can change the words. We have to try," Caroline said.

"Mom," said Ronnie. "If you're still here, I want to tell you that I want you. I'm the one who needs a mother. You saw."

"Ronnie," said Caroline, "what are you talking about?"

From Mini, Mom said, *You Girls Lie To One Another. All The Things You Don't Tell Your Friends.*

Ronnie thought she already sounded less angry. Just sad and a little petulant. Maybe showing all of them their deaths by car crash got it out of her system.

"The thing I'm doing," said Ronnie, "that's a thing they would kick me out of the family for doing. I need my real family. I need you." She didn't want to say the rest out loud, so she waited. She felt Mom open up her head, take one cautious step inside with one foot and then the other. Ronnie knew that she didn't want to be this way or do those things anymore. Ronnie knew that she couldn't find a way to stop or escape Alex's gaze from across the room when everyone else was watching TV. Stop looking at me. *If you could stop looking at me for just one second, then I could stop too.*

Mom, while we're speaking honestly, I don't think you're any of our mothers. I don't think you're Korean. I don't even think you come from any country on this planet.

(Don't tell me either way.)

But I don't care. I need your help, Mom. Please, are you still there? I'll be your daughter. I love your strength. I'm not scared anymore. You can sleep inside my bone marrow, and you can eat my thoughts for dinner, and I promise, I promise I'll always listen to you. Just make me good.

They didn't see Ronnie for a few months. Mini did see Alex at a concert pretty soon after everything that happened. He had a black eye and his arm in a sling. She hid behind a pillar until he passed out of sight. Mini, at least, had sort of figured it out. First she wondered why Ronnie had never told them, but then, immediately, she wondered how Ronnie could do such a thing. She wondered how Alex could do such a thing. Her thoughts shuttled back and forth between both of those stops and would not rest on one, so she made herself stop thinking about it.

As for Mini and Caroline, their hair grew out or they got haircuts, and everything was different, and Caroline's parents had allowed her to quit ballet and Mini's parents were still leaving her alone too much but she grew to like it. And when they were around, they weren't so bad. These days they could even be in the same room without screaming at each other. There was another meet-up for Korean adoptees. They decided to go. School had started up again, and Mini and Caroline were on the wane. Mini and Caroline thought, maybe, bringing it all back full circle would help? But they knew it wouldn't be the same without Ronnie. Mini and Caroline saw us first before we saw them. They saw us emerge from a crowd of people, people that even Caroline hadn't befriended already. They saw our skin and hair, skin and eyes, hair and teeth. The way we seemed to exist in more dimensions than other people did. How something was going on with us—something was shakin' it—on the fourth, fifth, and possibly sixth dimensions. Space and time and space-time and skin and hair and teeth. You can't say "pretty" to describe us. You can't say "beautiful." You can, however, look upon us and know true terror. The Halversons know. All of our friends and admirers know. Who are we? We are Ronnie and someone standing behind her, with hands on my shoulders, a voice in her ear, and sometimes we are someone standing inside her, with feet in her shoes, moving her around. We are Ronnie and we are her mom and we are every magazine clipping on how to charm and beautify, the tickle of a mascara wand on a tear duct, the burn of a waxed armpit. We watched Mini and Caroline, observed how shocked they were. Afraid, too. Ronnie could tell that they would not come up to her first. No? she said to her mother. No, she said. For a moment Ronnie considered rebellion. She rejected the idea. Those girls were from the bad old days. Look at her now. She would never go back. Mom was pushing us away from them. She was telling Ronnie to let them go. Ronnie watched Mini and Caroline recede. The tables, the tables of food and the chairs on either side of them, rushed toward us as their two skinny figures pinned and blurred. We both felt a moment of regret. She once loved them too, you know. Then her mother turned our head and we walked away.

Ramadan Red White and Blue

Mohja Kahf

Ramadan in the West
'll put hair on your chest
No sleeping in, fool
Boss here won't invest
in your Ramadan slouch

It's not your limp-wrist
Saudi-soft Ramadan
It's Ramadan, Shaker school
It's Medina-meets-Sparta
Get your Abu Dharr on

No clatch of women kin
cooking fancy-frill food
No shopping till dawn
No diners closed days
so temptation's removed

Your dumbed-down Muslimland
shortcuts don't play
This is Ramadan, USA—
hardcore and hungry,
the old Prophet way

My Grandmother Washes Her Feet in the Sink of the Bathroom at Sears

Mohja Kahf

My grandmother puts her feet in the sink
of the bathroom at Sears
to wash them in the ritual washing for prayer,
wudu,
because she has to pray in the store or miss
the mandatory prayer time for Muslims
She does it with great poise, balancing
herself with one plump matronly arm
against the automated hot-air hand dryer,
after having removed her support knee-highs
and laid them aside, folded in thirds,
and given me her purse and her packages to hold
so she can accomplish this august ritual
and get back to the ritual of shopping for housewares

Respectable Sears matrons shake their heads and frown
as they notice what my grandmother is doing,
an affront to American porcelain,
a contamination of American Standards

by something foreign and unhygienic
requiring civic action and possible use of disinfectant spray
They fluster about and flutter their hands and I can see
a clash of civilizations brewing in the Sears bathroom

My grandmother, though she speaks no English,
catches their meaning and her look in the mirror says,
I have washed my feet over Iznik tile in Istanbul
with water from the world's ancient irrigation systems
I have washed my feet in the bathhouses of Damascus
over painted bowls imported from China
among the best families of Aleppo
And if you Americans knew anything
about civilization and cleanliness,
you'd make wider washbins, anyway
My grandmother knows one culture—the right one,

as do these matrons of the Middle West. For them,
my grandmother might as well have been squatting
in the mud over a rusty tin in vaguely tropical squalor,
Mexican or Middle Eastern, it doesn't matter which,
when she lifts her well-groomed foot and puts it over the
    edge.
"You can't do that," one of the women protests,
turning to me, "Tell her she can't do that."
"We wash our feet five times a day,"
my grandmother declares hotly in Arabic.
"My feet are cleaner than their sink.
Worried about their sink, are they? I
should worry about my feet!"
My grandmother nudges me, "Go on, tell them."

Standing between the door and the mirror, I can see
at multiple angles, my grandmother and the other
    shoppers,
all of them decent and good-hearted women, diligent
in cleanliness, grooming, and decorum
Even now my grandmother, not to be rushed,
is delicately drying her pumps with tissues from her purse
For my grandmother always wears well-turned pumps
that match her purse, I think in case someone
from one of the best families of Aleppo
should run into her—here, in front of the Kenmore display

I smile at the Midwestern women
as if my grandmother has just said something lovely about
    them
and shrug at my grandmother as if they
had just apologized through me
No one is fooled, but I

hold the door open for everyone
and we all emerge on the sales floor
and lose ourselves in the great common ground
of housewares on markdown.

The Place Where I Live Is Different Because I Live There

Wendy Xu

On Friday all anybody did was talk
about waffles. When other people want
a thing I want it a lot too. Other people
wanted to save kittens from trees
while the trees maybe wanted
some saving also from the dark sort
of rain that fills a gutter. That shook out
some people from beds trying
to be happy. That caused a train full
of complicated ideas to stop near
my house which was great. I pay
attention to things that push
back. I muster up the energy to sit
through very important presentations.
One way to be amazed is to be
less amazing and then pay
attention. Don't ask any questions
about waffle-science. Believe that there
was only ever one kitten whimpering

in the tree and how great
are you. Admire how things wait
to push up through
the earth until the earth
is beautiful enough. I think
about painting my house. Then
I think about other houses.

Sit Bones

Sharlene Teo

–Lady in the blue top. Over there. Stack your shoulder over your wrist, the yoga teacher said. She was in her forties, English, with a helmet of chestnut-brown hair and Madonna biceps.

Chloe in the light-blue top tried to picture her body as a pile of rocks, rumbling into place. But that wasn't quite right. To "stack" reminded her of pancakes. The high-beamed studio was hot. The skylight burned her skin. Because her hair was black it attracted even more heat. Her left wrist hurt. She checked her alignment in the mirror. She wobbled all wrong. To her left posed a compact, half-Asian woman of indeterminate age, bathed in sunlight and maintaining a perfect side plank. The woman's gaze in the mirror was blameless and blank. They locked eyes for a moment but Chloe was the one to wince, to look away first.

ASHTANGA YOGA WAS one of two new routines Chloe adopted in her new life. The other was intensive therapy. Her old life in Singapore was a sullied thing to be talked out of, shucked and discarded. Less than a year ago she had fallen in love with her first serious boyfriend, a man two decades her senior named Alvin, or Ah Bock or Chicken Chok, depending who you asked. They met at a bus stop. 165 was taking forever. He stared at her for ages, with a bare-bulb intensity that would have been frightening coming from anyone else. But Alvin was handsome in just that sad and storied way that allowed him to get away with it. He looked younger than thirty-eight. He reminded her of *Crouching Tiger*–era Chang Chen, all sinewy and graceful. He asked for her number. She was so taken aback by his directness that she gave it to him straightaway.

That year, Chloe went from knowing demurely little to learning lots about men, firsthand, with an anthropological accuracy. Unlike the puppyish amateur boys in her junior college, Alvin was measured and patient. He drove her around in an unwashed Subaru with drink-carton boxes strewn across the back seat. He wooed her with long conversations on rooftop car parks and walks around the sloping neighborhood where she lived. Dalvey Estate was all sleepy bungalows and tall metal gates shielding immaculate gardens. Some houses even had their own security guards because ministers lived there.

Alvin told her about growing up so poor that his parents often left him alone for days with nothing to eat but a squashed packet of white bread. And long-ago things she didn't consider before then. Like how the Internet was a skill to him, not a habit. And how he used to meet his friends at the A&W drive-in at Dunearn Road just to chat shit, but that had shut down long ago, and this city was changing faster than he could even think. It was getting stuffed to the brim with ang moh expats and PRC and Bangladeshi immigrants and he didn't like that. His fingers circled the back of her neck as he spoke, sending electric tickles down her limbs that lingered for days afterward.

She was almost nineteen and had been with nobody before then. She wondered how other girls in relationships had the self-control, the decorum not to just relent. Religion was a big factor. But she had never been particularly devout. Within the stuffy metallic confines of the Subaru, things progressed quickly, entirely of Chloe's own volition. It stank of shoes and mothballs in there, but she didn't mind. They tried everything but, and then the whole works.

—It's always the quiet ones, he said to her.

The car juddered like a filthy cannon. She developed a crick in her neck from straining against the car door, trying not to fall off the slope of the seat. As a bonding experience, her mother brought her for a monthly manicure and pedicure. Subtle French tips to keep within school restrictions. Chloe's demure hands looked small and unlikely around Alvin's cock. She had expected a penis to be cruder close up, but instead she was surprised by the grotesque vulnerability of it, its neutral taste, her lack of disgust. He made her feel grown-up yet sensually silly and more comfortable in her own body.

Some weekends he drove to Malaysia. Mostly he was bound for KL, other times Ipoh. The trips always left him exhausted and slightly irate. He handled the import and export of packet drinks. Chrysanthemum tea, lemon barley, red longan.

—Just one of those nothing businesses you fall into, he muttered sadly into her neck. I'll bore you to death if we talk about it. All these long hours for small rewards. Everyone trying to shortchange each other.

Alvin wanted to move into vending machines, not drinks. The long-term plan was to go from packet drinks into big machines. He was vague about how and when. His teeth were straight and yellowed. He smoked like a chimney and his breath smelled the same, but she didn't mind. She kissed him with cannibalistic vigor. One time she dislodged a piece of food from his back tooth and ate it. It tasted like morning. It was impossible for him to disgust her.

—Sometimes I wish I was born twenty years earlier, on the same day as you, she told him one evening. So that I could spend more time with you and get all your references. And be totally alike.

—You're romantic, little Chloe, he replied. He had that hazy, forlorn look in his eyes that indicated his thoughts were elsewhere. They had been together for seven months. Sometimes she felt like she understood him better than she understood herself. She paid closer attention to his mannerisms and likes and dislikes than her own.

One day he stopped returning her calls. Chloe kept messaging him. Her parents, irritated, told her to put her phone away at dinner. After dinner her fifty calls clanged straight to voicemail. She rang so many times she memorized the cadences of the Singtel robot telling her the mobile user was unavailable. A week and a half passed. Now she knew why people called it radio silence. It was everywhere. She couldn't tune out the questions. Mostly, she blamed herself. She bit her knuckles until they chafed and bled, and wept until her eyes puffed up and she looked like a different person.

In college her best friends Choon See and Iris complained that she was going crazy for nothing, wrapped up in this old ah beng who had likely been married the entire time. He probably had three kids and a swollen, nothing-faced wife who posted housekeeping hacks, xenophobic memes, and alarmist product scares on Facebook all day. Although they conceded that he was cute "in an uncle way," they had never trusted him.

The following Monday, Iris thrust a copy of the *Straits Times* in front of Chloe's face. There was Alvin's photo on page ten. He looked old and misplaced. The newspaper referred to him simply as Lim Bock Ho, Alvin not included. So the boxes in the back seat and in the trunk didn't just contain wrapping and red longan tea. When two plainclothes officers from the Central Narcotics Bureau stopped his car, they found 1.8 kilograms of pure grade Vietnamese heroin, hidden in the lining of the trunk, concealed in packaging. The law stated that being found in possession of anything above 2 grams was considered trafficking. And anything above 15 grams resulted in the mandatory death penalty. Alvin was over 120 times that limit. He was going to be hanged. This was Singapore. There would be no arguing around it.

She couldn't even visit him. Not even through thick glass like she'd seen on television. The prison authorities didn't approve her request for a visit card. She couldn't focus on revision. Her A Levels were in three weeks.

–You're completely losing yourself, Choon See said.

He's a druggie and a dealer and a criminal, and you guys are pretty much done. Plus, he's got a death sentence! Wake up your idea! Don't you care about the A Levels?

Chloe clenched her fists and turned away from her. She had known Choon See since kindergarten, but now she felt like she didn't even want to be friends with this smartass for a minute longer. She muttered her goodbyes, citing that she was late for tuition, and stalked out of the leafy junior college campus. Back home, in the privacy of her bedroom she rang Changi Prison again. His face-to-face and televisit rights were temporarily suspended. They told her to check back again, wouldn't disclose anything further. Maybe he was in solitary confinement.

The CNB officers turned up at her house the next day, asking for Chloe Cheong. Her parents would not have known about her connection to Alvin otherwise; before then he had been a sloppy secret, one they were happy to leave unturned. Now the harsh and torrid reality of their daughter's love life was parked across their driveway. Her mother shriveled at the possibility of their neighbors spying from second-story windows.

–Were you aware of Lim Bock Ho's criminal activities? the officer asked her in the station. Did he ever ask you to transport anything for him?

–No sir, Chloe answered sadly. I had no idea.

–Then what did you think he sold?

–Packet drinks.

The officer sighed and took off his spectacles. She could tell he'd had a long day, and also that he was assessing her. He studied Chloe's features. She looked like a gormless, sexy stingray with her widely spaced eyes and chalky complexion. After three hours of questioning both officers seemed satisfied. She went into a side room and peed into a cup. She was clean as a whistle. She was free to go. Outside, it was late and dark. Her parents pulled up, ashen faced. Once she was buckled in the back seat, her father started talking.

–You're only eighteen, he said. Which is too young to throw everything away. Or even to know what's good for you. You gave us a real scare today. And we've made some serious decisions. Don't even try arguing about it. Be lucky that we can support you.

They were worried about the newspapers. Her father ran an insurance business. It couldn't afford to be compromised. What would their friends think? The day after Chloe's final A Level exam (economics) her parents sent her off to the airport. She had no idea how well or badly she was going to do for her exams. They had flown by in a fog.

And now she was going to England for ten weeks, or two and a half months. Her uncle Chua Bock Tin owned two luxury flats in central London. Her parents arranged for her to stay in the one-bed a floor under where her uncle's business associate Mr. Goh lived with his wife. This couple would "make sure she was settled in" (keep an eye on her). Chloe was being exiled to a safe, respectable place. Her mother found a holistic therapist who specialized in "the recovery and rehabilitation of toxic dependencies/ toxic relationships, low self-esteem, eating/emotional disorders, lowness of spirit."

–You're not being punished. We do this because we love you, her mother said. Chloe nodded gravely and walked through the departure gates. She felt her parent's eyes on her. She turned around and waved at them from behind the counters of plasticky purple, the same color as cherry yogurt.

England was punishment. England didn't excite her. And it was very far from Alvin. Now there would be thousands of miles and a couple of oceans that separated them, instead of just concrete and metal. Everybody else judged wrongly. She was more than just his stupid teenaged girlfriend. And he was not just some heroin dealer bound for the gallows. So what if heroin was one of the baddest of the bad drugs, the king bad drug, the life ruiner? She'd never tried it, wasn't interested, and did not even like alcohol or cigarettes. Why did the consequences have to be so super serious? Some babies and puppies were heavier than two kilograms. Ditto rice. Ditto her rucksack. Nobody got hung for possessing those. She wished, uselessly, that it had been salt in there, or soybean milk, like he said.

THE FLIGHT TOOK over twelve hours. She cricked her neck from sleeping funny, stuck between a fat Australian man and an auntie with a severe perm who sucked the air through her teeth every time their arms brushed. When the plane landed it did a balletic hop on the runway that made Chloe jump. Half-awake she thought that the plane had been sucked into a vortex, or shot into the sea by Russians or North Koreans. And this would be the end of her, the same way it would be the end for Alvin on whatever date the higher-ups decided. This thought brought her heart rate down and seemed to unite them.

The airport taxi pulled up onto an unimpressive brick building. She unloaded her suitcase blearily. London was freezing in such a charmless way. Less "Christmas-movie ice-cream special" and more "get inside, tropical foreigner, or you'll die out." The one-bed flat was just off Bond Street. Even totally unfamiliar with the city she thought, who lives around here? It was a soulless area that was more commercial than residential, and on weekdays and weekends alike, the streets below her window thronged with tourists and businessmen. The building had a concierge, a portly old man with a clipped accent and reptilian eyes. She often just nodded and hurried past him.

It was hard to tell those first days apart, or to find any comfort. But maybe that was the point. Her parents had said this stint was "for her own good." But she wasn't sure what her own good was. This seemed more like her parents' polished, carpeted brand of good. For the first week she had terrible jet lag and a mild tummy ache. Even the water didn't agree with her. Pushed through her letter box one day was a flyer for yoga classes in a Soho studio. She had always been curious about yoga. So she signed up. Her parents were pleased to hear about this new development, although they cautioned her not to get involved in any "cult, yogi Hare Krishna stuff."

Her appointment was on a Monday. The therapy center was a huge cake-white Regency building by a canal. It had a grand painted stucco facade and two huge columns by the entryway. The first time she visited, she thought she had come to the wrong place. A small sign indicated to press for the bell. She was buzzed in after a pause. Inside, it was very confusing. There was a reception area with polished wooden floors, and a labyrinth of narrow hallways and numbered doors.

She knocked on her designated door and entered a small, sepulchral room with bare shelves and a plant dying in the corner. The therapist was in her late thirties, with a shock of red hair and hazel eyes. Chloe couldn't tell regional English accents apart but assumed this woman had the same sort of clipped BBC diction as newscasters. Her name was Shona. She looked like the sort of person who showered with bar soaps and never embarrassed herself.

–Why do you think you're here, Chloe?

–Because I've been stupid. Even though I've done well at school, I have poor judgment.

–Why do you think that?

–Because my parents say so.

During the first session, she found it awkward to talk about herself initially but after just fifteen minutes private things tumbled from her mouth. Shona had a way about her. It was like she was playing games with Chloe, and the objective was to give as little of herself away as possible whilst using stares and silence to squeeze feelings out from the girl. At some points Chloe's words got tangled up in big hungry fish tears, like she was a fish that had just been taken out of a tank and laid out on a board to be gutted.

–You see, that's how I feel all the time, Chloe said. Like I'm about to be gutted.

–Or you're in prison with a death sentence, Shona added.

–Well, yeah. I never connected it like that. But you're right.

When Chloe reemerged into the street outside she didn't feel purged so much as empty. The two feelings were not the same, although they overlapped substantially.

WHEN SHE GOT home she flicked through terrestrial television. There was the usual gamut of trade deficits and interior decorating shows and police procedurals, which hit a little too close to home. She finally settled on a movie from the early nineties about a phlebotomist who spent her wild teenaged years as a groupie for a rock band. The woman looked like if you took Demi Moore and photoshopped her less hot. She had a rebellious teenage daughter, blond with a sour-cream face. The whole film structured itself around their clashes. The freewheeling, wisecracking rock-star father got off pretty lightly, in Chloe's opinion. Toward the end of the movie demi-Demi wept and said to her daughter:

—So what if you think drawing blood for a living is boring? So what if you think I'm a cop-out? Well, Kimberley, I've got news for you! You're sucking the blood out of me! Don't be like that! Don't make the same mistakes I did!

The actresses were standing by some interstate highway, shouting at each other. This depressed Chloe, both the American highway and the impassioned speech of last resort. She was near the end of her Singaporean teenhood and couldn't even imagine being fifty. Was this all she had to look forward to, the histrionic unraveling of hope into regret? Everything fun retrospectively frowned upon? If so maybe it was better to die young. It's just a dumb, trashy movie I hadn't even heard of, she sulked to herself, and stared at her silent phone.

—How would you describe your parents? Shona asked.

—That's so the sort of question a therapist would pose in a movie, Chloe replied.

Shona just smiled a safe close-lipped smile.

—Well, I've been wrong to them once, Chloe began. She always started speaking first, and felt in some small way that because of this Shona always won.

–Wrong like how?

–I made the wrong assessment, according to them, about my boyfriend. Didn't see that he was a criminal. And my parents have the memory of elephants. So now that I've been wrong in my judgment once, to them, I'll always be wrong.

–That must be very hard for you.

–It's okay, Chloe said. She looked out of the window and bit her lip.

–Let's go back to your ex-boyfriend, Shona said. This reminded Chloe that Shona was one of them. She was just like (and indeed getting paid by) her parents, or Choon See and Iris, any of the mean faceless people who read the newspapers and believed what they condemned.

Because of this, Chloe didn't mention that on the four days that she didn't have yoga or therapy, she stayed indoors and surfed the Internet. She read about prison life all day and thought of Alvin. In prison, inmates had to squat a lot of the time; it was less of a security risk if they were closer to the ground. Executions were always scheduled on Fridays at 6:00 a.m. Nobody watched. She stored these nuggets of information with a dreadful protectiveness, like ammunition, as if knowing details could possibly change anything. She didn't talk to anyone and only left the flat to get food. Christmas came and went. She watched the snow through the old sash windows without wonderment. When she emerged to the small Tesco around the corner, the real world, with its weather, felt like virtual reality. In a way, everything did.

In yoga class, the helmet-haired teacher constantly came over and adjusted her. This made Chloe feel very self-conscious, and demoralized that no matter how closely she thought she was following instructions she was still wrong. Nonetheless, she kept returning. There was something tortuous yet calming about how every minute in class seemed to stretch for a supernaturally long time. The other regulars were all better than her, and she suspected they attended every day, whereas she only went twice a week. The half-Asian woman was the best student. She always took the mat to the front left of the class, never sweated or had a hair out of place. When she caught Chloe trying to emulate her in the mirror, she always returned a neutral gaze. What did women like her and Shona do at the end of the day, after they had unmasked their perfect, proper selves? What little rituals did they perform before bedtime, what did they binge-watch? Chloe felt like the only unruly person in the world who pondered these questions.

SHE WROTE TO Alvin every fortnight. In the first letter she recommended yoga, complained about England. The prison regulations forbade her, if not she would have enclosed a selfie they took just before he got arrested. In the picture she pouted and he looked at her with open-faced adoration. She wanted to keep that feeling fresh in his memory but could only describe. Because the letters were screened she found her tone stilted and formal, as if she were writing essays. Clichés and platitudes were unavoidable, because they did the closest job. *I love you; I miss you, I think about you all the time, etc.* She could never get it right. Then again, who wrote letters anymore? Not even her grandparents. She wished she could email or WhatsApp him or even call.

In the two months she had been there, Chloe had met

her uncle's business associate in passing only a few times. Mr. Goh was predictable enough: a typical Singaporean businessman in his early fifties with a sparse pate of hair, a driving-range tan, and a quiet manner. But the identity of Mrs. Goh remained an open question. Chloe had expected a docile, amiable tai tai in a silk blouse and designer slacks or a maternal busybody of the soup-offering variety. Instead a bevy of different but equally unobtrusive fortysomething Asian women trailed Mr. Goh across the gloomy marble lobby, sometimes followed by one or two men, in both super casual and business attire. The concierge, who was Egyptian and intimidated her, noted all these comings and goings with his milky eyes. She wondered if he had cataracts, and if he had been working at that front desk for a hundred years.

–It's a cold and impersonal place, and my neighbors are weird, Chloe said to Shona. Sometimes I feel like I'm living in a mafia den. There's something shady going on. Maybe everyone is a criminal. If most people in the world are criminals, then what is the point of punishing someone to death for doing one thing wrong?

–You're referring to Alvin, Shona said. Have you heard from him?

–No, Chloe said. Well, actually, yeah. But I don't want to talk about it.

–You can talk about whatever you want, Shona said.

Chloe's face clouded. She smiled benignly and stared at the empty shelf behind her therapist's shoulder. She had finally received a reply from Alvin the morning before and was still getting used to it.

Dear Chloe, it is so good to hear from you. Thank you for your letters. Time really drags here, it began. The handwriting was like tidy chicken-claw scratching, exactly like how she'd imagined. She pictured him taking a long time to make it legible. The alphabet swooped and curved almost like simplified Chinese characters. He wasn't allowed to discuss any details of his case. But he, too, missed her. *So sick of the food. Lunch was fried bee hoon with one sacred piece of fish cake. Rice and sardines for dinner.* When she reached the last paragraph the handwriting turned to scrawl. *Chloe, you already know this won't work. You're still young. If I'm lucky I get life in here. It's not really a life. Don't waste your time. I can't keep this up. I didn't take your calls because it's easier this way. I'm sorry. Please take care of yourself.* He signed it LIM BOCK HO in block capitals.

Chloe's eyes smarted. She drew her knees up onto the chair and held them close with her hands.

—Over here, it's easy for me to just think about him all day, Chloe said after a pause, when I have nothing else to do in my flat. It's my first time on my own. And this city is so scary and boring. I think about him all the time, Shona. And I miss home and miss him. We didn't even get to say goodbye properly. How am I supposed to let it go like that?

Shona handed her a tissue. Chloe cried and gulped, gulped and cried in helpless waves, kept saying sorry as her shoulders shook. She was aware of Shona watching her, aware that she looked nineteen, and stricken, that feelings so consuming were considered normal for her age, even expected, even trite. She wished she were older to validate the heaviness she felt, this worn weight in the hollow of her throat.

—Take your time, we've got five more minutes in this session, Shona said, and handed her another tissue.

WHEN CHLOE EMERGED into the reception area her eyes hurt and she was totally drained. She stumbled toward the double doors like a drunk. Her head pulsed. She cried so hard in Shona's room that now she saw stars. She glanced toward the waiting room to the left of the reception, and was alarmed to see a woman kneeling, hunched down on the musty carpet. The woman had her hair in a bun and wore a long green coat. She had her hands over her face. She almost resembled a dancer in repose.

–Are you okay? Chloe asked.

The woman turned and looked up at her with raw red eyes. Chloe experienced a moment of is-that-who-I-think-it-is before her vision affirmed that yes, it was, there was no mistake about it. Here was the woman from the yoga studio who always held perfect poses, the star student.

The woman shook her head at Chloe at the same time that she recognized her back. She did a half-wave with her hands that seemed like a dismissal and apology at the same time, and then she wiped her eyes and looked away decisively.

–Chloe backed away, flummoxed, and left the building.

IN THREE DAYS' time she was flying home. Her exile had stretched and stretched and it was hard and good to believe that it was finally coming to an end. As Chloe packed she looked around the sparsely decorated flat with its amnesiac beige carpet and terrible paintings of fruit. The afternoon before, Shona said that she had shown great growth and progress over the course of their work together and that she should be proud of herself. They shook hands and this last time Shona escorted her all the way out of reception. Chloe didn't feel proud or changed so much as newly afraid. Like there were little pinpricks in her awareness of herself and the world and things might rupture anytime. She had gotten used to solitude, as well as the bus stop by her flat and the rowdiness and bustle of the shops and the roaring street outside, but she felt no fondness for London, she didn't agree with its often-feted charms. Her mother called to see how she was doing with the packing.

—And how's Mr. Goh and his wife?

—Barely seen him. And he seems to have a number of female companions, Chloe said.

—Aiyoh, don't gossip, her mother replied. Anyway, we'll see you soon. I'll come pick you from the airport and we can go for ban mian.

—Sounds really great, Chloe said.

She missed the food from home, had even started to miss Choon See and Iris again. It was bitingly cold here. She couldn't wait for the familiar, comforting humidity of the night air around her neighborhood, her bedroom at home, the glass and gleam of Orchard Road that she still found superior to Oxford Circus. She even missed her parents, although now that was gnarled up in grudge. But maybe they had done the right thing for her and in time she would come to appreciate that, although that thought felt like their words in her mouth.

Chloe was five minutes late for her final yoga class. She hurriedly unrolled her mat in the nearest space in the room. Out of the corner of her eye she saw the woman in the front left glance over. She looked immaculate as ever in her yoga capris and fitted top. It was as if nothing had ever passed between them. The helmet-haired teacher gave Chloe a quick nod.

–Stand in Tadasana. Sweep your arms up toward the sky and press your palms facing together, join your fingers, the teacher said. Tip your head back and soften your gaze. Don't let your ribs stick out. Feel your tailbone lengthen toward the floor. Then lift your rib cage. Hold for a few breaths.

Chloe stared at her thumbs and the watery winter sun coming in through the glass-paned ceiling and held her breath.

magritte

Wo Chan

my mother's face eclipsed by a spray of fortune

cookies my mother's face eclipsed by the expiration

of passports and my mother's face in window

fans. in front of my mother's face

a brown paper bag seeped in the dark

dream of grease, car door of the '97 Camry blown off

my mother's face. stranger's

lipstick, sunglasses lost and found my mother's face

behind acrylic beach balls, behind whitewood popsicles,
every

dollar bill obscures my mother's face.

canopy and birdseeds, my mother's face a shadow

recessed in shadow, the hot globe before

ringing at my mother's face

a television, the whole vault of it—stars, and still

that shaft of water. my mother's face reflects

in the well it thrashes under

wet, immutable lid

what do i make of my face / except

Wo Chan

that it is on me

and its physicality)though not me(is how i've been
addressed
m y w h o l e b o r i n g l i f e

when i was 9
i watched aladdin and thought, after money
i wish for whiteness

*i didn't even have all my teeth—or vocabulary,
just two yellow hands trying to catch the basketball

my brother hurled at the my face

when
i was 19 my ( )

erupted / in nodular cysts
the bleeding jupiter kind

of sulfuric condensates
and an alien registration.

i had it all
a family, some secondhand sweatpants,

a gender
whose every sentence began

wheniwasaboy

i looked like my mother
now, more like Father, Baba, Dad

am a full yard of irony
waiting for lightning to lick me back ~

once
i was on a gay date (just once)
and a hunched-over-woman slipped me a white note

i thought it said "JESUS"
but instead

"mario badescu"

the skincare brand i would sell months later
when i learned to sm(other) the errata

of hormonal bludgeonings
to the surface—other children saw derm—

otologists at the sight of a curly pube
while my own mother

wheniwasaboy waited until her gallbladder exploded

to get her gallstones removed.
i watched her dimpled ass

blow in the wind of the hospital hallway
as she learned to walk again

and i slept in her bed and fed
her plain contraband congee

i am still talking about faces

the dented, fraxeled, mole-scarred, and trenched ones
i took a pill many times that induced apoptosis

"cell death"
i could barely afford 4 months of

my lips peeling like WWII wallpaper
the sex i was not supposed to have
did not happen anyways

as a nude-myself i am cratered irreversibly

so why
must i explain the thoughts i've had

on the things i never got to decide

they happened to me)(happen all the time
& i changed i learned i could keep changing

I must to keep myself

Aama, 1978

Muna Gurung

> *I could read my nonexistence in the clothes my mother had worn before I can remember her. There is a kind of stupefaction in seeing a familiar being dressed* differently.
>
> —*Roland Barthes*, Camera Lucida

"If we didn't wear a sari, word would reach the main office that 'so-and-so's wife was not wearing a sari today,'" Aama says to me between fits of laughter over the phone. "Then they would call our husbands to the office."

She's laughing now because she doesn't have to be afraid anymore. She isn't in Singapore, living in an all-Nepali camp, one of the hundreds of women taking care of their homes and children while their military husbands served the country as Gurkhas.

She's told me this story before, but never with such lightness. Aama and I don't often laugh together. It's not like we are serious all the time, but laughing together requires that we let ourselves be a little soft, a little silly.

"Later, the newer chyamas started wearing pants. To think that I used to be so shy in a maxi!"

A maxi is exactly what Aama is wearing in a photo, taken in their kitchen in Block A in 1978. The maxi wraps around the waist and stretches all the way to the ankles, sometimes even kissing the floor. Aama says she was probably making rice in the photo. She imagines it's 9:00 a.m. and that Baba is waiting for his packed meal for the day. When I ask her who took the photo, she shrugs and says, "I don't know." And then after a long pause, "Maybe your father?"

Aama is quick to start every answer with "I don't know" or "I forget." It is her way to keep me at a distance, to buy herself time so she can figure out just how much of the story she wants to allow. Of course the photographer is Baba. But the fact that Aama has to pretend to think, or pretend not to know (when she had just said that Baba was waiting for his lunch in the photo), irritates me. As a younger person, an exchange like this would be enough to set me off. I would storm past her while she reasoned with astrology: "Your planet and my planet, Muna, they just don't align."

Writer Marianne Hirsch once said, "To look is also, always, to be seen." And I sometimes wonder if Aama's pretend uncertainty about who the photographer is comes from a place of vulnerability. Maybe she can't bear to justify to her grown daughter the way she is looking at the photographer. Her mouth slightly open, starting or ending her protest of not wanting to be captured on film in the kitchen, in the middle of cooking, looking like that. But in this soft protest there is pleasure budding in her right cheek; a dimple is waiting to cave in.

It's not like Aama is unable to love. She is just careful about her loving—whom to love and how much. She doesn't show it in the way Baba and I do: with wide smiles, high-pitched voices and touch.

I have only seen Aama and Baba share affection—in the way I understand it—once. I was twelve and we had already moved back to Kathmandu from Singapore. It was late afternoon and I was coming home from school. I walked in through the door calling out "Aama!" as I always did. They groaned from their bedroom to tell me where to find them: Aama and Baba were lying in bed, fully clothed, arms around each other, sleep still lingering in the distance between his nose and her hair. They didn't get up when I walked in. I don't know how our conversation led to this, but as I was standing over them in my school uniform and they were talking to me with their eyes still closed, I remember asking them if theirs was an arranged or love marriage. Baba said, "Love, of course." To which Aama opened her eyes, got up to retie her hair, and said to Baba, "What nonsense!" Then turning to face me, she said to me, more as a reminder than anything, "We will always have arranged marriages. We are not those white people you see in movies who wear shoes to bed and marry whomever they want, only to get divorced."

Years later, Aama and I will battle over love and whom you choose to be with, why and how.

"IN THE CAMP, the women got together and taught each other how to sew or knit sweaters," Aama says. When I ask her who in the Singapore heat would wear sweaters, she says, "It wasn't ever for Singapore, silly. It was for Nepal. We would knit sweaters so that we could take them home as presents." I don't push. I don't tell her that if I were on the receiving end, I would much rather enjoy something made and bought in that foreign magical land than something handmade. Before I can say anything, Aama reminds me, "Singapore was always temporary. Everything we did, we did with Nepal on our minds."

But by the time Baba retired in 1994, my parents had saved up enough to return home in style. They buy a fridge, rice cookers, fans, foldable beds, mattresses, radio, TV, plates, forks, knives, spoons, pots, and pans. She clicks her tongue in regret when she thinks about it now. "We didn't have minds. We were like mules," she says. "We never thought Nepal would ever have any of these things. We should have saved up the money. You can get everything here now!" Aama gently taps her forehead. "But—maybe also, we never thought we would travel back to Singapore or visit any other place after we came back."

As a twelve-year-old moving back to Kathmandu, I remember being really excited about one piece of cargo. It was a sky-blue foldable picnic table and bench. We even had a rainbow-colored parasol for it. There was no green space in the first apartment we moved into, so I would ask Baba to take it out and place it in the garage so that I could do my homework. Aama would hear me and scream: "Don't do it! It'll get dirty! It's for when we build our home with a garden!"

WE HAVE A garden in our Kathmandu house now, but they still don't use that plastic table and bench. "It looks so small and cheap," Aama says.

"IN THE EARLY days though, I always asked myself: *Why Singapore? Why are we here?* There was nothing in the rooms they gave us: just a rusty spring bed with a flimsy wooden board. We had to buy everything. It took us years to put things together. Can you believe it, I would wash out the milk cans and use them as flower vases," Aama remembers. When I tell Aama that new hip restaurants in New York use milk cans as vases, there is a silence on the other end and then a "But why?"

The milk cans along with rice, daal, sugar, salt, pepper, bread, biscuits, tea, milk, veggies, and meat were all a part of our ration bag that appeared once every fifteen days. It was red and chubby. All the kids whose parents could buy them soft Gardenia bread ate that bread instead of ration bread. For the longest time, until Baba got promoted to inspector, we ate ration bread. But Aama would cut off the edges and say, "See, ration or Gardenia? No one will ever know."

But kids always know.

Aama was a repurposer like that.

The Milo tins and Johnnie Walker bottle on the shelf in another photo are familiar childhood objects. We reuse those square Johnnie Walker bottles to chill drinking water in the fridge. But Aama always made sure to set aside one or two bottles; she would make black tea in the perfect whiskey hue, pour it in these bottles, and with the labels still intact, close the caps and place them in the display case next to the TV. She wanted visitors to see that we had a fine line of drinks.

But Aama is a restless decorator. The sofa in the living room will be facing south one day, and just when we grow comfortable with the way the light from the balcony hits our legs but not our faces, Aama will change it up on us and move the sofa elsewhere. "I get bored," she reasons.

"I can't stand that about you," I tell her.

"I don't like it either," Aama says, and her agreement surprises me. With me, Aama has always found a way to disagree; even if we might be saying the same things, her words come from a place of *but*. "Nowadays, I can't find anything in this house," she says, referring to our Kathmandu home where she moves items from one cabinet to another and then forgets where she's moved them. "I'm getting old."

Her "boredom" also has made her get into the habit of throwing away things that are old or just sitting around harmless. "She is possessed on some days. She doesn't listen to me," Baba says. In his small complaint, you can tell that he's not trying to change her ways. If there is a photo she doesn't like, she cuts them into little pieces and throws them away. It's no secret that the photos in our family album only tell the stories that Aama wants to narrate; she doesn't think that anyone in the family would or should object.

"Do you have anything that is dear to you that you keep?" I ask her.

She shows me a coral piece strung in a red thread. "This one here's originally from my sister's necklace. Our mother gave it to her. There aren't corals anymore, they say. Is that true?" she asks me, with a look that translates vaguely into *you should know, I sent you to school*.

"And your blue slippers," she says, pulling them out from a trunk where she has spread two bags full of mothballs. They are fuzzy blue, closed-toe house slippers with a panda on them. "You used to love them so much. The soles are still good. I'll give this to your child."

It's cute, sure, but also arbitrary. Why the coral, the fuzzy slippers, and not that famous necklace Baba bought for her? "Oh, that! I loved that!" she exclaims. "Your Baba would buy a lottery ticket every Saturday and once he won seventy-five dollars! We were so happy we couldn't feel the ground, but when he won four thousand dollars . . . I don't think I've felt richer."

I remember this story because my brother said that the day Baba won that ticket, he didn't sleep the entire night. "So with that money, he bought me the necklace I am wearing here," she says, pointing to another photograph where she is seated with a friend wearing matching black sleeveless tops, printed maxis, long necklaces, hair parted in the middle with a baby boy each on their side. "I don't know where it is. Probably sold it and ate it."

When I ask her why they are wearing identical clothes, she says that when a friend in the camp bought something they liked, they would ask her where she bought it and then all of them would go to that place and buy the same thing.

"Well, that's annoying," I tell her.

I am a hypocrite, of course. Because I don't tell her about the matching tattoos I got with my girlfriends. Or the way we "accidentally" buy the same shoes. Or how we begin to listen to the same bands, like the same songs. Or how we eat the same things, like the same restaurants. Repeat the same expressions in the same manner. And sometimes how we fall in love with the same kinds of people, or long to be each other and have each other's lives.

"But there were other women in the camp who weren't like us," Aama says. "They were educated and gave private tuition lessons to our children if we could afford to send them there." Most of these women that Aama refers to were Nepalis born and educated in Darjeeling. "They used to call us pahadiyas, mountain people. To them, we were villagers who had no sense of taste and didn't know how to wear clothes. Maybe they were right."

She speaks about them not in disgust, but in admiration. She tells me how beautiful these women were, how perfectly their hair was made, how their homes looked like sets on Hindi films, and how they walked—straight with their chins up.

"In my next life, I want to be educated like them."

TODAY AT SIXTY-FOUR, Aama rests her reading glasses on her nose, and with a pen clutched tightly like chance between her index finger and thumb, she writes down the following sentences from her first English lesson: "I am a woman. I am Nepali. I am a mother."

I get out of bed. With eyes barely open, I follow the sound of Aama's voice and find her in the prayer room seated on the floor, her notebook on a small stool in front of her. I curl up on the floor, my head barely touching her lap. It's 6:00 a.m. Aama is doing her homework.

As I listen to her sound out each English word in the sentences, I wonder if she has ever had these thoughts in Nepali. She surely has never said them out loud. These sentences are protests. They are highly political. Only intellectuals and poets speak this way. But here she was, her first lesson, where she was identifying the "I" in her, and owning the "am." Softly, she was translating to me in Nepali, saying, "So Muna, listen: I am a woman, I am Nepali, I am a mother."

It is suddenly clear to me that for the most part of my life, I have failed to see Aama as a woman. I have never tried to see that young woman in the photo who was shy to wrap herself in a maxi, who left her village to go to a country where she didn't complain about how scary it was to turn on the gas stove, or how she didn't know what to wear, how to wear it, where she lived in fear of being watched and seen, where she raised three children who have now made homes far away from her.

"Yes, you are a woman, you are Nepali, and you are my mother," I say back to her.

"You my daughter," she says in English, giggling. Then in Nepali: "Uffff, I don't know. I am so old. What am I doing learning a new language at this age?"

AS A CHILD, I remember only wanting to be carried by Aama. Her skin was soft and always cool; she never sweat. But she was always sick and always weak and she'd tell me to go with Baba. "But Baba feels hot," I would complain. Eventually, Baba would grab me, and I'd protest and squirm and cry, finally placating myself by fiddling with the sharply folded tip of his shirt collar. My birth gave her gastric, she claims. Somedays, the gastric makes her legs boil, sometimes, it sends sharp pains like cold marbles rolling down her spine, and sometimes it causes her to burp fire. A mysterious disease that, to my knowledge, only plagues Gurung women in our family, where their stomachs ache but when they go to the doctor, there is nothing there.

"It's easy to remember how long I've had gastric," she says. "It's as old as you are."

Delicately, I Beg of You

Muhammad Amirul bin Muhamad

When we arrived at the middle of the flower field, I asked my parents if they would help me pluck some flowers, the lavender ones some distance away from where we stopped the car. They were probably actually lavenders, but you wouldn't know just by looking, and especially not from where I was standing. My parents told me to stay with the car. I had decided to stay anyway. And so I stayed, and sat on top of it.

They looked so delicate, my parents. I told them to be careful and they asked me why I wanted those particular flowers.

"No one else is going to see them if they stay there. I'd like for at least one other person to see them. Beautiful things, those flowers."

It was a lie, most definitely. It wasn't even about the flowers. I don't care for flowers—even in death, I don't think I'd care for people bringing me flowers. Heck, I didn't actually say that I wanted the flowers. I had just asked if they would help me pluck them. But they looked so delicate and as they stepped out of the car, I just wondered how much more delicate they would look plucking flowers. That's why I asked, I suppose. I wanted to see my parents plucking flowers.

I sat atop the car, listening to the wind breathing. It carried my parents' whispers, their sighs, their hums, their heart. Delicate. They looked so delicate I could have cried and not stopped and the earth would have made up for all the crying with even more flowers. There were so many flowers, but it didn't look that way, it looked like it could have had more flowers and still somehow look like there wasn't enough. I bet there were more lavenders that were more lavender than the lavenders that I had in sight, the ones my parents were plucking.

I didn't tell my parents how many flowers I wanted, but I knew they knew. They always knew. Even when their knowing was wrong. They would think they know. They wouldn't say anything, that's certain. They weren't saying anything at that moment either. They just kept plucking and plucking until they thought I'd be happy. Happy with what exactly, I didn't know, and neither did they. All by myself on top of the car. I sat and I watched them. One of me and two of them. One of each, and one in union, but two separate persons, much like me. One, each, delicate.

I wanted to whisper to them, "Why?" at which point they would look up and ask me to repeat what I had just said. They would look up, this I know. They wouldn't go about plucking the flowers and ask me without looking at me. They would look at me. I was looking at them. I looked at their faces. Tired, each different, but both delicate. Like something precious unearthed, with a little bit of dirt that needed brushing off, but clean and ancient and fragile underneath. "What did you say?" one of them would ask and I would tilt my head, feign some amount of ignorance, and let them carry on with their labor. Then I'd whisper, "Why?" again, this time, making the seemingly fleeting inquisition a little bit more weighted so that it didn't latch onto the wind. This time, just for my own ears. "Why?" I didn't have an answer to this and I loved the possibility that my parents would have the answers to this big question, each different, but somehow they would agree with each other anyway, very delicately, so it would appear like they're finishing each other's sentences. People in love did that a lot, surely.

I accepted, ever so delicately, that this was not true. That my parents didn't have the answers to a lot of things, to "Why?" Too delicate to hold all the world's knowledge in one lifetime. And that is fine. Being delicate. The flowers, my parents, sitting on top of the car, the wind, plucking the flowers, lavender as a color, as a flower, we're all so delicate. And I accepted that the wind would eventually sweep everything away anyway, delicately and definitely and "Why?" would not matter too much. At this moment, my parents were plucking flowers and I was watching them.

Then it was time to go and it was time to say goodbye.

But they were still plucking flowers. There were so many of them in their hands now. They looked beautiful. Delicate. I wanted to tell them that it was time to leave. That it was no longer like when I was a kid. I didn't want to have to ask if I could go, I wanted to tell them that I needed to go.

Plainly, I just wanted to tell them that it was okay, that the flowers were enough, that, finally, I was going.

But my words never could come out delicately enough when it came to speaking my heart. My words, they cry and they crush, and through the tumult, my words get lost and wrecked, and my parents are so delicate, I had no heart to speak. So I kept my heart. I kept my delicate heart from my delicate parents and I didn't say a delicate word. I didn't speak at all.

I let the wind carry me away, away from sitting on top of the car, away from the flowers, away from my parents plucking flowers, away delicately.

The Words *Honey* and *Moon*

Jennifer Tseng

Woo honked the horn lightly, unconvinced by his wife's urgings that it was an American custom. He was embarrassed as it was by the eight tin cans she had tied to the fender with string. Camille laughed at his timorous tapping and called it a "Chinese honk." Finally, when it was clear he would not soon Americanize its duration or intensity, Camille leaned over, put both her hands on the car's black apple, and pushed with all her willowy might. She'd never felt so American in her life. The street filled with the music of their German car's horn and someone nearby honked back. Though by this time, the pair (who had met at a dance and perhaps had *nothing but Samba in common*) was miles away from the church. The guests, who had stayed on the front steps to wave and to whistle their support, were out of earshot and the newlyweds were on their way west.

They drove, according to Woo's plan, directly from the church to Kenosha, Wisconsin, and arrived in plenty of time to visit the Kenosha County Zoo, first on their list of dazzling destinations. The Kenosha County Zoo was no petting zoo. It was the largest zoo in the state of Wisconsin and contained an endless array of exotic animals. There were, among other mammalian and ornithological treasures, a pair of giraffes from the African veld, a snow leopard from the mountains of central Asia, a Kivu highlands gorilla, a flock of Palmetto flamingos, an Arabian cheetah cub (though no adult cheetahs), three black Louisianan swans, a few New World monkeys, and a small family of zebras on loan from William Randolph Hearst's California ranch.

This multifarious collection met with Camille's instant approval and garnered for Woo a generous supply of bonus points in their slit eyes versus green eyes game. Her only grievance was that they did not have even one giant panda, the animal she most closely associated with China and therefore with Woo. He quickly appeased her with an optimistic allusion to an upcoming (petting) zoo in Nebraska. In his eagerness to please her, he too became excited and could almost see the dressy oversized bears in his mind's eye, munching on crisp branches of young bamboo, next to their horse and cow neighbors.

For dinner they ate in a pleasant lakefront restaurant whose only distinguishing feature seemed to be its inclusion of a separate menu for children twelve and under, no doubt the feature that had captivated his colleague Mac's darling Isabelle and earned the restaurant its place on their list. To Woo's delight, Camille confessed she had never tasted shellfish or steak. In the spirit of education, he recklessly ordered one of each for her, along with a prime rib for himself. She was more easily charmed by the shrimp, those C-shaped curls of coral flesh, than she was by the steak, which she greeted with confusion as a bloody, cabbage-less version of her mother's corned beef. Where were the peppercorns, she wanted to know. Didn't he agree that peppercorns and beef were perfect complements?

"Ah-ha, you are so gourmet for someone who never try gourmet before," he teased.

"I am?" she asked, and her eyes went greener and rounder than he had ever seen them.

Woo found dinner on the whole banal. He took solemn note of the frozen vegetables and canned fruits and thought wistfully of the day he would pick fresh corn and carrots from his own backyard, plump oranges from his own Valencia tree. He declined dessert, but watched Camille suck on a series of spoonfuls of "orange" sherbet. The carnival color of those soft sugary moons chilled him. He accepted a spoonful fed to him by her gemmed, ecstatic hand only to surprise her, with the hope that she might widen her eyes in response, which she did. To his palate, the taste was cloyingly sweet and artificial. He patiently kept this knowledge to himself, the way a parent might suppress the falsehood of Santa Claus for the sake of a child. Though he made plans to introduce her to something finer as soon as the opportunity presented itself. Belgian chocolate, he thought, or macaroons. Surely there would be no mung bean pastries or shaved ice with coconut milk en route to the western coast of the United States. And so he called to mind a list of all the superior European and American sweets he had tasted since his arrival in his wife's country.

"I'm still hungry," Camille said excitedly.

"That can't be," Woo laughed, while simultaneously calculating the bill so far. "Two appetizer, two entrée, one dessert! Holy Toledo!"

"It's true." She smiled. "I get really hungry when I'm happy. Does that happen to you?"

"No such a thing. I'm hungry when I don't have food. Work hard, eat more. Exercise, eat more. Happy, no happy, this is irrelevant."

"Well, I'm still hungry."

"Then you must be very happy," he said, looking at her directly.

"Mmmmhmmm," she hummed, her fingernail tapping the various dessert options in a jaunty dance on the laminated menu. "What do you think? A slice of apple pie with cheddar cheese or raspberry cheesecake?"

Woo brooded silently for a moment over Americans' preoccupation with cheese. It was his own pet theory that cheese was the culprit responsible for America's obesity problem. He entertained the thought of his leggy, slit-eyed child bride turned happy and voluptuous. He could get used to there being more of her, but if it meant eating out more often, whether or not his wallet could adjust was another story. Then he felt a pang of confusion. Had she ordered so much food because she was happy or was she happy because she had ordered so much?

"Tell me which one to get," she said. "You choose and we'll share."

"No, no, no. I don't want. Your favorite you pick."

"Are you sure? Is it okay? Am I eating too much?"

"My poor growing girl," he said. "You eat! You eat!" She ordered the cheesecake with a scoop of sherbet.

"Mother says I don't eat enough. But at home I'm never that hungry. It's not that I'm unhappy, just not happy enough to eat. Not like now with you. I'm so happy. Why do you think that is?"

Camille chattered away while Woo listened and interjected the occasional peppercorn of wisdom, to please her conversational palate.

"In China we have a saying, the best appetizer is hunger. Eating is like getting married. When you wait, when you are patient, it tastes good. When you are hungry, everything tastes like the best."

Later, when the waiter came to bring their dessert, he found the table so cluttered by the many dishes Camille had sampled that there was no place to slip the bill except next to her right elbow. Woo reached awkwardly over the dirty plates to take the ticket.

It dawned on him that she did not have any money, probably not even a few coins in her small beaded purse. What sort of girlish things did she store in there? Lipsticks and tissues, perfumes and picture postcards of places she had never been? Now and in the future he must pay for her. He pulled two blue twenty-dollar traveler's checks from his wallet and signed them carefully. A Chicago bank had issued them to him; he knew they were valid, but the blue, almost purple color of the notes was so different than the green of American currency. It looked to him more like play money, extracted from a children's game.

THE MILKY WAY Motel was situated like a mole on Kenosha's high eastern cheekbone. Contrary to its illuminated sign, which promised a buxom, braided blond girl pouring a pitcher of glowing, milk-colored stars into the night sky, its small lobby contained a gaunt, spidery man with bruised eyes seated at a metal desk. Woo surmised that the girl from the billboard sign must have been born of this man's imagination, a girl from the world that existed behind the lids of his bruised eyes while he slept. It was dusk and the man looked as if he might doze off momentarily. He was wearing square, plastic reading glasses that magnified the shadows on his face as he scanned the classified section of a newspaper and sipped from a small tumbler of milk. There was a poster of the solar system on the wall behind him and a Swiss-cheese-block paperweight on the desk. The green glass lamp by which he read was the only light in the room other than the moon. Had either newlywed known of such a thing, they might have thought the office looked like that of a California fortune-teller's.

When Woo stepped into the dim, milk-scented lobby, the man held up a room key and continued scanning the classifieds.

"Good evening," Woo said, stepping up to the desk. "Pardon me please. I am Joseph Woo. I have tonight reservations. Two people. Husband and wife."

The man continued reading and took a sip of milk. Woo wondered if he was to reach out and take the key from the man's hand. He didn't think it a wise idea.

"You're supposed to take the key," Camille whispered in his ear. "He's busy."

Something was wrong, Woo thought. He was sure this was not the custom. The man was supposed to take their names, signatures, identity verification. What kind of establishment was this?

He pulled out his wallet and found the three-by-three card that he had cut from a three-by-five to fit. There in his own Royal typescript were the words:

The Milky Way Motel
725 Lake Dr.
Kenosha, WI 53141

81

THERE WERE NO Motel 6s in Wisconsin. Woo had hesitated each time he had booked a non-6 reservation. It was likely that independent motel keepers were not regulated to the extent that chain motel keepers were. There was no systematic quality control, no centralized power to enforce high standards. The man at the Milky Way Motel was precisely the type Woo had feared: a lazy, unregulated clerk with no consideration for the customer.

He longed to be in Iowa—their next destination—where a Motel 6 clerk named Candy had not only given him clear directions to the motel but to the state fair as well. She'd recommended the apple fritters and told him to have a safe trip.

He thought that if they stood in front of the reading man long enough, he would have to look up, that shame or self-consciousness or both would force him, but the man continued reading and sipping like a machine. In fact, he seemed so undisturbed that had he not been holding out the key, Woo would have thought he hadn't noticed them. Had he not been reading, Woo might have thought he was blind. Finally the man finished his milk. As he tilted his head back toward the solar system to allow the last drops to fall on his tongue, Woo snatched the key angrily out of his hand. Woo was defeated. His fantasy of driving through the night to Iowa had been brief. Their day had seemed as long as his stay in America, a small lifetime. His new wife was tired and he noted with affection that her green eyes were sleepy, verging on accidental slits. Such pale skin, such thin arms, such a long and fragile neck. So tired. They could not go back and they could not proceed. They must stay.

Woo carried both the suitcases upstairs to their room.

Camille followed him like a sleepwalker. He fumbled with the key in the dark (surely Motel 6 would have lights burning near the doors at night), checked once more to see that it was room 8, and then opened the door. The sight of the double bed filled his startled, exhausted body with a jolt of electricity.

"Woo Tai Tai," he said brightly, trying to maintain his composure. "Welcome to your bridal room."

"Woo Xiansheng," she said, climbing into the bed. "Your wife is very happy."

Woo turned the bedside lamp on and switched off the overhead light. Perhaps she would fall asleep immediately and he would not be faced with the frightening prospect of seducing her. Which was stronger? His desire to touch her or his desire to avoid touching her? He didn't know. She seemed to have fallen deeply, prophetically asleep.

He leaned his face close to hers the way he had seen her do with the names of the smallest towns on the maps. Her orange-blond hair smelled of green apples and of the German wood of his father's rolltop desk. He had thought it would smell of persimmons. This is not to say he was disappointed, no, not even mildly. He was fond of the un-expected fragrance, but it was yet another indicator of his lack of ability to calculate and predict in matters of Ca-mille and/or in matters of the body. He continued to look at her face without touching it. He tried to understand its many parts, which moved, even in sleep. The happy slits of her eyes quivered as she slept and he could see the strange marbles of her eyeballs beneath the lids, crossing back and forth as if reading a hidden book.

There was a light dusting of freckles on either side of her elfin nose, so few in each sprinkle that the marks seemed like a mistake or an afterthought on the part of her maker. Between her nose and her lips was a slight valley dotted with fine downy hair, so pale in color that they were visible to him now for the first time. Her lower lip was larger than the upper; it looked almost swollen and he wondered if she was feverish. But her face was not flushed and he could feel without touching it that its temperature was cooler than that of his own. Her ears, which also surprised him by not detecting his approach, had lobes that were attached to the side of her face, so that the outline of the ear was one long continuous curve, unlike his own whose curves were interrupted by the separation of the lobe from the rest of the ear. He thought hers a less formed and simplified version of his own. His discovery of this recessive trait pleased him in some way and emboldened him to touch her.

Of all her many girlish and alien traits, he found her eyebrows to be the most exquisite. Made of the same persimmon color as her hair, the brows were orderly, as if their maker had measured and cut and counted each feathery piece by hand, assembled the arcs and then trimmed and combed them with a mechanical device. Woo touched each brow once with the tip of his middle finger as if painting them on. Ruan de, he thought. How soft. Softer than he could have predicted. Their softness made him all the more curious about the down valley above her lips. The fine pale hairs must be softer there in that ethereal slope, that tiny shadow. He thought to drag his tongue across the delicious ditch, but then Camille sighed heavily as if to warn him away. Better to let her sleep.

He took off his shoes and began to pad around the carpeted room in his socks. Through the picture window, he could see the dark shine of Lake Michigan. There were several boats in the dock and each one had a small light at its helm. The sight of the boats waiting to sail, the black water, filled him with sad thoughts and so he walked away from the window and set to unpacking their things.

He would leave the curtains open so that his wife might see the water when she woke up. All through dinner she had looked at it and pleaded with him to take her to the beach the next day. She wanted to see everything in daylight. She wanted to lie on the sand. Was it like the ocean? She'd wanted to know. Though he'd planned to take her to a penny arcade, he deferred to please her and to defray costs.

He opened her suitcase without thinking for a moment that she might see it as an invasion of privacy. He had nothing to hide. Why should she? He hung up her dresses and brought her yellow-and-white toiletry bag to the bathroom. He unzipped the bag and began rooting through its contents for her toothbrush, which he thought ought to be allowed to air-dry, to protect it and the bag from mildew. Camille had the good habit of brushing her teeth after meals, but he suspected that she seldom remembered to shake the brush after rinsing, and when she did, it was not with much vigor. Of course he had never witnessed her in the act of brushing, but he had made subtle inquiries.

He found her white plastic brush and its wet bristles without difficulty, though not before leafing past several other items including a tube of lipstick, two paper packages each marked "slender regular tampon," a pair of tweezers, a beige compact, and a box of prophylactics still wrapped in cellophane, all of which electrified him. Though it was the sinister cellophaned box that delivered the deepest bolt to his body's core. This was very bold of her. She had been thinking something about him. The most maddening currents of fear and electricity crept through his fingers as he studied the box. It contained twelve prophylactics and among the many words printed on its modest back were "pleasure," "contact," and "sexual intercourse." Woo threw the box back in the bag, zipped the bag and pulled his hands away in haste, as if the items might electrocute him.

He stepped back into the bedroom carefully, afraid, now more than ever, to wake her. He hung his own clothes up next to hers, pulled out a few more necessary items (a fresh bar of Dove soap, a washcloth, a jar of peanuts, an orange, a Chinese-English dictionary, the latest issue of *Reader's Digest*, and a pair of gray pajamas), and then stowed the suitcases in the closet. Then, as quietly as he could, he arranged the peanuts, reading materials, and orange on his nightstand and sat on the side of the bed that was farthest from Camille. Perhaps he should double-check the lock on the door, he thought. This he did swiftly. And the window. Was there one in the bathroom? He couldn't remember. He brought his personal belongings into the bathroom and closed the door. Locked it. Leaned into the shower to look for a window and found nothing but a minty expanse of tile.

Woo ran the faucet until the water was hot and then began turning the bar of soap over and over in his hands in order to produce a generous lather. He carried a bar of Dove with him wherever he went—to the University, to the library, to the movie house. Whenever he felt anxious, he excused himself from the anxious-making situation and went to the nearest restroom to wash his face. The strong smell of the soap calmed him and the emollients left his skin feeling clean and elastic. Now he massaged the bubbles into his cheeks, breathed deeply and waited for the familiar sensation to relieve him. What was wrong with him? The Dove trick had failed. He checked the bathroom lock and then changed into his gray pajamas. The light cotton trousers that were usually so comfortable made him feel exposed. The fabric was quite thin, almost sheer! Could she possibly see through it? No such a thing. Ridiculous. Time for bed. You'll feel more relaxed tomorrow if you sleep.

Woo slipped into the bedroom. He turned off the lamp and climbed as stealthily as he could into the bed. He closed his eyes and tried to quiet his breathing. The sheets were cold and slick, though his bride's body emanated warmth from its brief distance. When he opened his eyes the room was filled with light and he was overcome by dread, thinking that morning had come. But only two minutes had passed. A large boat that he could now see was docking, its lights flooding their room. He closed his eyes again and when it was dark again, he opened them.

Without moving his body, he turned his head to look at Camille. Her head was turned away from him, her hair a silky, messy flame on the white pillow. Slowly, slowly he lifted the covers up so that he might look at her. It was then that he was reminded she had climbed into bed fully clothed. This fact relaxed him somewhat, for now he was comfortably occupied with how wrinkled her clothes were becoming. Without a hint of irony, he said to himself that he should remove her clothing immediately and hang it up at once. There was the removal of clothing for the purpose of hanging it up and there was the removal of clothing for other purposes. Each form of clothing removal was, in

Woo's mind, easily compartmentalized, neither threatening to undermine the other, until, however, he reached out to unbutton the top button of his wife's blouse. He paused and boldly pulled the covers down to the foot of the bed so that he might see everything, only then beginning to understand his own truest motives.

To his utter fright and delight there were only four buttons on her blouse, so that once he had unbuttoned two, he was already halfway to ecstasy or dread, he didn't know which. He unbuttoned the third and fourth quickly, afraid again of waking her, and then realized that the real terror would be in pulling the blouse open to expose her. This he did and almost choked on the air that was racing to reach his lungs. By a much-needed brand of newlywed's luck, he transformed the beginning of the choke into a subtle, even elegant throat clearing. He was determined to not wake her—not for fear that she would unwrap her sinister cellophane box, for that was swiftly seeming less and less sinister, but for fear that he might not complete his heavenly task of saving her wardrobe from wrinkles.

The skirt went next, side zipper, hook, eye, and then her red leather sandals with their crossed straps each fastened by a single sharp tooth of steel, and a red tongue of leather, easy to release. As he arranged her sandals next to his own black shoes, his restless child bride pedaled her bare feet twice as if on a dream-manufactured bicycle, and made a gurgling little dove noise. Was she cold, he suddenly wondered? To him the room seemed warm, it was summer after all, but he could not presume to know how she felt then. Should he leave her underclothes intact and cover her? The wrinkles, unfortunately, were no longer an issue.

He scanned the room for a thermostat and was overcome with gratitude to the motel staff, to even the blind reader downstairs, for furnishing such a luxury, when he spotted a compact silver box mounted next to the bathroom door. He raised the thermostat to eighty degrees and turned to his love.

She was in what is called by sleep experts the "runner's position." Though Woo was no Freudian and he interpreted this change simply as an opportunity to unlatch and remove the elastic contraption that persisted in keeping her upper half secret from him. Her arms were languid and soft as he pulled them this way and that through the straps. His poor girl was being so good. Whether it was his accurate assessment of the depth of her sleep or his raving desire's rationale, Woo became convinced that Camille would never wake. He moved quickly to her lower half and unrolled her lemon-yellow underpants slowly out and down over her plump curve. He fumbled during the final moments of untangling the yellow bonds from her ankles and feet. When the bonds were free from her body and her body free from its bonds, he turned her from the runner's position so that she was on her back.

He looked at her. He watched her grow cold and stiff and then warm and soft again. He watched her return to the runner's position and pedal her feet and turn her head. He grew self-conscious and tried to read his magazine in the near dark. This cycle lasted throughout most of the night. He would watch her sleep and then grow self-conscious. He would read his magazine and then grow impatient with its drab articles and idiotic cartoons. He would curse the insufficient light and then as if to punish himself, he would read on until he thought he would hurl the magazine at the picture window and then he would set it quietly down on the nightstand and resume looking at his nubile wife.

During these intervals he was ravenous and ate both the entire jar of peanuts and the orange, along with a roll of different-colored hard candies that he had found in Camille's toiletry bag. Any chance he may have had of falling asleep was quickly reversed by this massive intake of protein and sugar. The room was hot and smelled of peanuts. In Woo's opinion, a pleasant smell, a comfy cocoon. His pajamas were damp with sweat but he did not dare remove them. Between his lovely bride and his tasty snacks, his jangled nerves and his exhaustion, the night provided him with a seemingly endless supply of tortured insomniacal bliss. It was not until the sun began to rise over the lake and Camille began to stir, that Woo's eyes closed at last. As he fought and then failed to stay awake, he pored over the maps in his head, revised his budget, and thought of the strangeness of the words *honey* and *moon*, were they two words or one? He reviewed the many words he had recently learned—*snow leopard, zebra, flamingo, raspberry, sherbet, Milky Way, prophylactic, Maidenform*—and thought it unlikely that he could possibly remember them all.

HE WOKE AT 11:00 a.m. and his first thought was of Pang and the terrible morning he'd slept past 8:00 a.m., a story he'd never told Camille. And then, corroborating his fear that laziness leads to disaster, he heard the sound of his child bride vomiting in the bathroom. Eat too much, he thought. Maybe learn her lesson.

"Camille." He knocked softly on the bathroom door. "You need some help? Can I get you anything?"

"No," she said, whispering. "Please go away. I don't want you to see me. I'm sick."

"Silly girl talking nonsense. Daddy doesn't mind. His poor girl is sick, maybe need something, eh?"

"No thanks, please go away!"

Woo dressed quickly and went out to buy her some ginger ale, which he found for sale by the can in a vending machine behind the building. He returned to find her in an orange sundress on the floor, tracing the strawberry-red line of the map with her finger. She looked as ripe and as healthy as she had the night before.

"I'm better now," she said, springing up and kissing his cheek. "I just ate too much. I think that's all it was."

"Drink anyway." He opened the can, wiped its aluminum lip, inserted a straw (one of ten he had taken from the restaurant), and handed her the ginger drink.

She sucked on the straw obediently, collapsing her cheeks and puckering her mouth until her sucking noise resonated as air and droplets in the empty can. She was cured.

They spent the day at the beach, on Milky Way Motel towels. Camille lay in her white two-piece bathing suit watching the water, while Woo, hatted and in slacks, sat reading the last of his Chinese newspapers. He refrained from looking at her sun-lotioned body and concentrated instead on conjuring images of her he had on file from the previous night.

The kiss on the cheek this morning had been a puzzle to him. They were not in the habit of touching each other. He thought with pleasure of the possibility that Camille had been awake for part of or even all of his late night roamings and that the kiss had been a clue to him, an affirmative peck. Now he longed for Iowa, if not for Candy the clerk, then for the day to end and the night to arrive so that he might have a second chance.

"Joseph." Camille pulled her hair back with a silver barrette. "Thank you for hanging my clothes up last night. I was so tired."

"Sure, sure. Sleep in your clothes no good. Not comfortable. Too many wrinkles."

"I really like that you did that."

"You did?" He was alarmed at the possible meanings she intended. "Were you able to sleep?"

"Mmm, like a baby." She tilted her face up to the sky and closed her eyes. "I thought you might be upset with me," she said with her eyes still closed.

"Why upset?"

"Well, you know, it being our honeymoon and all. I sort of slept through it."

"Sleepy girls need their rest, no problem."

"Can I ask you a personal question?"

"You talk nonsense. Anytime ask questions."

"Did I like it?" she asked, sounding intrigued.

"Shenme like it? What's the meaning of this question?"

"Do I have to say it? I just mean, you know, did I like *it*?"

"Shenme *it*? What is *it*?"

"What you did to me while I was sleeping."

"Oh my golly, you're some kind of crazy girl! Number one, while you're sleeping I'm reading magazine, have some snacks. No such a thing do to you anything. Number two, you like something you tell me, I'm not telling you! Huh!" he grunted, mildly offended.

"You mean you really just hung my clothes up?" Camille started to laugh.

"What's funny?" Woo demanded. "Of course I'm hanging your clothes up for you. What do you expect?" He sounded shocked, as if the reckless thought of making love to her while she slept had never crossed his ancient, puritanical mind.

THERE ARE WOMEN who can articulate their wants quite clearly so that for even the most inexperienced of husbands, supplying those wants becomes easier. And there are men who can, without their wives' lucid articulations, intuit their wants and expertly supply them. Neither Camille nor Woo were quite so fortunate. If just one or the other had been one of these types, the matter of their lovemaking would have been greatly simplified. But as it was, Camille had never been counted on to articulate anything before, much less something as embarrassingly intimate as her own physical wants, and Woo, a bachelor in the truest, deepest sense of the word, had never before supplied anyone's wants but his own.

This they quickly learned during the series of long nights that unfolded in variously sized Motel 6s across the country. Each was patient with the other afterward. Their nights were tender even as they failed to satisfy. But the continuous lack of known demands coupled with the continuous lack of successful supply led to a relational revolt that took a toll on their waking hours. Each injured party responded in a different way to the crisis.

Woo lost interest in their evening ritual entirely. That is, he began by feigning a loss of interest that then conveniently turned genuine. Certainly at first, the electrical sensation he'd been experiencing in Camille's presence threatened to derail his celibate mission, but eventually he found that the longer he ignored his own electricity, the less frequently the voltage flared up. He'd never felt quite so manly and utterly in control before and was relieved to be rid of that dangerous tangle of wires—so many variable bolts and sparks and invisible force fields exploding and firing without his permission. Better to maintain control of the charge, to ignite it and snuff it out for his own benefit only.

Camille, on the other hand, became insatiable. Her eyes were fierce slits more often than not and the many attractions that had delighted Mac's easy Isabelle did not satisfy Woo's impossible bride. No roller coaster was fast enough, no carousel horse the right color. He won carnival game after carnival game, but none of the fun prizes caught her eye. The cotton candy was too sweet, the popcorn too salty, the petting zoo full of nothing but farm animals. "Where are the pandas?" she cried. "Why can't we go dancing?"

She began demanding more and more—she wanted dinners out and movies, museum tickets and dancing—a number of items that were not on their itinerary nor part of their detailed budget. She wanted Iowa City instead of Des Moines, Badger Creek instead of Lake Anita, Kansas instead of Nebraska. All of it arbitrary, Woo was convinced. All of it designed to madden him. The more she asked for, the more he refused. This he did not out of spite but on principle. There were times when he adored her fierceness and longed to turn the car in any direction she wanted to go, but his principles outweighed his adoration for her and he drove on.

When they arrived at the Motel 6 in Des Moines, she refused to get out of the car. "Why do we always have to stay at Motel 6? I don't want to stay at another one." She had her sandaled feet on the dash to spite him and was looking at the map through the slits of her eyes as if plotting an alternate route.

"Motel 6, what's the problem? We have reservations." Woo didn't understand. What a nice clean motel! The night before had been particularly tender and unsatisfying and their daytime personalities were revolting.

"I don't mind staying in a few here and there, but every single time? What will people think?"

"What people?!" Woo shouted, incredulous.

And then, for the first time since their journey west had begun, Camille understood that she was stranded. There were no other people. No Heartland, no mother, no father, no movie dates or trinkets, white rabbits or dried plums—just a husband. She began to cry.

There was nothing, aside from sex and communism, that frightened Woo more than tears and so while Camille wept over the road atlas, he went into the Motel 6 office and canceled their reservations. He got on Interstate 80 going west and began searching for signs to Lake Anita.

It was at Lake Anita (for which he had silently sacrificed the highly touted Badger Creek) that Woo and Camille encountered a handful of those "people" whom Camille had unwittingly referred to, just thirty miles earlier, as if her naming of them had made them exist. The incident, which Woo was loath to recall in detail, involved a group of four ten-year-old boys who suddenly and in symphony threw wet stones at Woo's sweatered back while he was at the edge of what he thought was a desolate thicket, relieving himself. He was in midstream when the first stone struck, though his sweater cushioned the stone's impact and distracted him from seriously considering its source. Ping! Ping! The second and third struck in quick succession and then a shower of smaller stones, also wet, hit him like rain. The usual racial epithets were hurled as well and then as quickly as they had ambushed their man, the boys vanished into the thicket. Ha ha, ha, he could hear them, heh, heh, heh.

Woo did not let the incident disrupt him. He finished out the stream, shook and tucked himself in, button, then zipper, then belt.

Camille, who had watched through the car windshield, sprang up out of the car when he returned. She rushed up to him and kissed him on the cheek. It was a kiss of the same variety as the kiss in the hotel room, the sort she spontaneously doled out on rare occasions.

"Why didn't you yell at those lousy jerks?" she asked.

"This is minor incident. Too much trouble for nothing," he said, alluding to a wider spectrum of incidents she knew nothing about.

"Why didn't you at least tell them you aren't Japanese?"

"Why didn't you?" he asked.

She bit her thumbnail and looked down at his sweater, which he had taken off and folded.

"Why were you wearing that sweater? It's so hot! If I was a man, I'd take my shirt off."

"No such a thing. It is unsafe to expose oneself in an isolated location. Hot, cold, doesn't matter."

"Gosh, that's so paranoid," she said. He had looked so funny in that sweater, standing in the August sun.

After the two of them were in the car again, she watched his black eyes scan not just the unknown road in front of them but both mirrors and the shoulders too. From time to time he looked briefly at her face. She saw that he too was stranded. No Chinatown, no bachelors, no newspaper, no plums. In the cities and towns to come, who would understand him? Who, if not she, would keep him safe?

SO IT WAS that the newlyweds, each marooned in their own way, made of the time remaining a temporary life. He drove the car he had given her that she was incapable of driving and she held in her small lap the many maps he had purchased for his own private pleasure. They ate fresh fruit and dry cereal for breakfast, according to his taste, and they stopped at McDonald's for lunch, according to hers. They adhered to Mac Celan's list of restaurants for dinner, less because their tastes correlated with his or Isabelle's and more to prevent disagreement between them. Woo misplaced Celan's list of favorite destinations and it was just as well.

In Nebraska, he bought her a set of checkers and it became their habit to play in the motel room after dinner. Sometimes while they played, they sipped ginger ale poured from cans into complimentary tumblers filled with complimentary ice. The ring-shaped pieces of ice, which Camille loved to slide on her fingers, Woo retrieved from a metal machine every evening. It was Camille's duty to take as many complimentary postcards from the Motel 6 lobby as was appropriate, according to the number available and the clerk's disposition. When she was bored, which was seldom, she shined his shoes, for he loved his shoes to be shiny but disliked blackening his hands. And when he was feeling tender (also seldom) he ran her a bath.

Their German engine rumbled and coughed and dust

flew through the open windows. They were always in the car unless it was evening and because of this, Woo felt dirty at the end of each day. She learned that his sweat, like water, had almost no discernible odor; he learned that she hummed while she ate. He sensed at times that she was homesick; she began to suspect that he dyed his hair. Both grew accustomed to the sound of traffic roaring past them, the sounds of "people" motoring swiftly and mysteriously past them, even as they slept. The bright red-orange 6 became a beacon to both, though it meant something different to each of them. They exhausted their supply of prophylactics and did not buy more. It was difficult to connect that which they did in the dark with their nomadic sunlit selves.

Their conversations quieted and then ceased and that was for both of them an unexpected comfort. And then one morning they crossed the California state line and Woo said, "Tonight we will be home." And Camille said, not without a sadness, that she had lost track of the days and in so doing, had almost forgotten where it was they were going.

Post Trauma

Rajiv Mohabir

I spent the summer wearing the stink into the soles until the bottom of my loafers dropped out under the big toe's heel. O Corona, Corona, the black crows ties to my feet—I flew the 7 train to Junction Boulevard into the mariachi of chili and lime on corn on the cob to peck the grains along the rails. Until February's slush tumbled white first then a black wet; I was born in February my afterbirth a murder lifting like a could in caws. That winter my mother refused closed-toe shoes. Rats froze in Queens gutters, blanketed, cell walls broken by ice, and starved. I didn't have much to eat, just a bag of beans and basmati, just cumin without other spices. Somewhere in Queens my aunts curled their lips, sneered my name, drew their curtains tight, the eyes of their homes shut and blind to me. The lentil grains broke into mush then grew cold, crows in the daal, my feet black and aching.

Costero

Rajiv Mohabir

Also called a Guiana dolphin
because of its coast hugging
and riverine disposition,
the Costero's shape echoes
a bottlenose except
it's 6.9 feet long and so terrified
of humans it flees from boats
at the slightest whir
despite being a true
Delphinidae: estuarine and
electroreceptive from Nicaragua
to Brazil. Its cousin the Tucuxi
may be more of a sister
or faggoty brother: pink skin
to the Costero's blue. In fact
scientists only recently began
rent these two subspecies
into two distinct kinds—
but who knows if they breed

or produce viable offspring?
There is no "true" of any hyper-
sexual order. It's easy
to be mistaken for something
you're not. People think
I am Indian when I am clearly
Guyanese. When I say Guyana
they repeat the colonial name
Guiana or even *Ghana*. Few know
about Indians abroad and read
foreignness for queerness, assuming
I am straight when clearly
borders are only asymptotes.

Pygmy Right Whale

Rajiv Mohabir

*It's the last survivor of quite an ancient lineage that
until now no one thought was around.*

  —Felix Marx, of the University of Otago, Aotearoa

So much is not clear
of ancient lineage. Is the ocean
too rich with nutrients or
is the whale's molecular
makeup and bone structure
not echoed in any other
species? A question puzzles
scientists for many years.
This smallest of baleen
whales they assumed it to belong
to the Right Whale's taxonomic
category despite its falcate
dorsal fin, its mouth's curve
serving as a shibboleth.
What we can't make out

at first sight our brains
assimilate like how once
Justin imitated what he thought
an "Indian" sounds like
to mock my mother, whose
actual speech, like hurricane
or storm-bird, is from continents
away. *I don't like Muslims*
he said. What did he know
of kinds: coolie or desi, or
what foreignness obscured
my desire for the neighbor boy?
He could have called me many
convenient things. Come to find out
all of the Pygmy Right Whale's
genus have died out leaving no
trace of family Cetotheriidae—
its name scientists call
a "wastebasket" genus like the term
"South Asian" or "Middle
Eastern" or "faggot"
a category used to classify
what brown they see
and do not understand.

कालापानी

Rajiv Mohabir

का मतलब पानी है काला
या वे पार करने वाले
पार करके काला हो जाते हैं
का मतलब राज़ रिवाज़ भूलना
का मतलब बदलाव
का मतलब अंधेरा, का
मतलब रात का मत
लब सूर्यास्त, का मतलब जनम
छोड़ना, का मतलब खो जाना
अपने आपको, का मतलब पानी
सांस में, का मतलब नाम
खोना, का मतलब अनाथ बनना, का
मतलब कुली नाम लेना, का
मतलब पीठ तोड़ने की महनत,
का मतलब नाना नानी आजा आजी
की पसीना, का मतलब
गयाना, का मतलब नया दिन, का
मतलब अमरीका का
मतलब जलयात्रा का

मतलब ज़िंदा रहना, का मतलब
कला जो पूर्वज के माथे का कालापानी से
आयी है, का मतलब
कहानी का शुरूआत, का
मतलब सूर्योदय

Kalapani

Rajiv Mohabir

means water's black
or that sea crossers
blacken, means to forget
secrets and rituals, means
conversion, means darkness,
means night means
sunset, means giving up
this life, means to lose
yourself, means water
in the breath, means losing
your name, means being orphaned means
taking the name "coolie" means
breaking your back from work,
means your grandparents' sweat, means
Guyana, means a new day, means
America, means sea voyage,
means to remain living, means
art from your ancestors' sweat

which was its own
kind of kalapani, means
the story's beginning, means
sunrise

The Unintended

Gina Apostol

21. Magsalin, translator (and aspiring mystery writer), tardily mourns the death

Magsalin, uncertain of her future in a Third World order, had grown up with intense though scattered academic desire. It does not help that her childhood included the streets of Harvard, in Cubao, and New York, in Cubao, two dark corners of cartographic humor that, as is often the case in the Philippines, actually exist.

Poststructuralist paganisms, the homonymic humor of Waray tongue twisters (which descend, as always, into scatology), French novelists, Argentine soccer players, Indonesian shadow puppets, Indo-European linguists, Dutch cheeses, Japanese court fictions, and mythopoeic animals in obscure Ilocano epics indiscriminately gobbled up her soul.

It is not an uncommon condition, this feeling of being constructed out of some ambient, floating parts of the Internet. (So glum scholars of the Anthropocene appraise this unsettled, textual state.)

Some of her youthful attachments were fetishistic, while others were just symptoms of malnutrition.

She adored the concept of signs, without acknowledging the need to understand it.

On a Tumblr blog, now deactivated, Magsalin notes that her youth in Manila is lost, and sadly she now only annotates a past paved with sacral relics of bookish bones merged with atrocities of "daily praxis" (a kind of evil, undefined).

I will list here only a partial list of her old Tumblr *tristesses*:

The retirement of Franco Baresi, sweeper, of AC Milan, in 1997 (she used to follow Serie A before the referee scandals and the monopoly of the sport in Asia by Sky TV);

Random apostrophes on giant Nestlé powdered milk advertising billboards that dominate the ride from Manila's airport;

The death of Wilfrido Nolledo, author of *But for the Lovers*, his Philippine masterpiece reissued too late by Dalkey Archive Press and out of print, of course, in his home country;

Brutal attacks by nice fellow writers at international writing workshops in Iowa, after which she drinks warm Bud Lights with the neoliberal fuckers filled with postcolonial melancholia anyhow;

Readers who declare you cannot truly understand the works of the novelist Jose Rizal if you read him only in translation—a bullshit excuse for not reading him at all;

Bloggers who keep announcing the end of print books while deploring print's extinction;

Finding the mismarked grave of Antonio Gramsci (the map said Giacometti) under the shade of outcasts in the Protestant Cemetery in Rome;

The word "praxis";
Readers who ask, Why do you always bring up Philippine history that no one knows anything about?
Good writers, even white males, who are prematurely dead.

Hirsute, looking practically flammable on his book jackets, Stéphane Réal died, so to speak, *in medias* script. One might say, dying of lung cancer, he vanished in a puff of smoke. One imagines the last sight of him was his demonic beard, a fey salt-and-pepper affair, the color of pumice or a crosswise shard of culvert (like those abstract tarred bits lying for months off of Café Adriatico, still unswept after the June rains). In the shape of a *scudetto*, the beard, like the Cheshire Cat's smile, is the last to disappear. A number of his works, journals, jottings, juvenilia, are illuminating, in a haphazard way. Réal's last novel, a mystery, remains a puzzle. It is unfinished. Having occurred before the diaspora of cultural philosophers to the World Wide Web, his death was a conundrum of the analog kind. His stack of papers, Magsalin imagined, would need dusting.

There is a sense that young Magsalin, a poor and underfed student in the eighties, would not have minded a ticket from Manila on Air France, or even Etihad or Emirates, straight to Nice or Cap d'Antibes, where she would first lie languid on the beach for a day, the sun being the best antidote to jet lag, then rent a cheap car to traverse horseback-riding campsites and haute corniches through the *vals* and *valses* of the middling Midi and on down the horrible French nuclear scenery into the bowels of Paris.

She would drop off at Pére Lachaise, with the help of

the TomTom® App for Finding Dead Writers Who Are Still Members of the Group Blank-Blank-Blank, and she would genuflect before his jar of ashes (or columbarium, as it is called in Wikipedia), in between staring at the not-so-subtle winged sphinx of Oscar Wilde's last riddle and Gertrude Stein's soothing, but pebbly, grave.

She would love to have helped organize the papers of his incomplete mystery, or checked out his obsessive annotations of Lady Murasaki (his bedside reading—a surprise, as the Japanese woman of the Heian period has a languid, dreamy expansion opposite to his terse, epigrammatic style); but to be honest, she does not even know the date he died.

First she consults a virtual encyclopedia. Not yet owning an iPad or even a MacBook Air, good for traveling, she sits before her uncles' clumsy, troglodytic iMac, the one that looks like an alien in the midst of an affecting lobotomy, its sweet bald head kind of droopy. But Magsalin cannot find the exact place and time of Réal's death. She surmises that no reader has minded that void, hence its disappearance online. The more likely reason, however, is that she misspells his name. Anyway, Magsalin has no patience with Google, not to mention Bing, in these moments of idling before getting back to work.

It is not writer's block. She is in writer's pause, engine humming, anticipating a turn in the plot, unknown but expected.

1. The story she wishes to tell

The story Magsalin wishes to tell is about loss. Any emblem will do: a dead French writer with an unfinished manuscript, an American obsessed with a Filipino war, a filmmaker's possible murder, a wife's sadness. Her work is not only about writers who have slipped from this realm, their ideas in melancholy arrest, though their notebooks are tidy; later one might see the analogy to real-life grief, or at least the pathos of inadequate homage, if one likes symbols. Of course the story will involve several layers of meaning. Chapter numbers will scramble, like letters in abandoned acrostics. Points of view will multiply. Allusions, ditto. There will be blood, a kidnapping, or a solution to a crime forgotten by history. That is, Magsalin hopes so.

28. The photographer at the heart of the script

The photographer at the heart of the script Magsalin has been asked to peruse is a woman. The infamous photographer of the Philippine-American War abandoned a restrictive, Henry James–type *Washington Square* existence (similar to the filmmaker Chiara's own, except with more Chantilly lace) to become a bold witness of the turn of her century. She is a disturbing beauty with a touching look that her otherwise embarrassingly pampered life fails to obscure. The protagonist's name, whether classical allusion, theatrical trope, or personal cryptogram, is still forthcoming—Calliope, or Camille, or Cassandra.

It is 1901.

She is not alone.

The great American commercial photographer Frances Benjamin Johnson has already scooped the men of her day with her photos of Admiral George Dewey, the victor of Manila sailing leisurely around the world in semiretirement. Admiral George Dewey is lounging on his battleship *Olympia*, docked in Amsterdam. In 1898, the *Olympia* had fired the salvos at Spain's empty ships on Manila Bay. Frances Benjamin Johnson's photographs of arresting domesticity on a battleship a year after are celebrated in *Ladies' Home Journal* and *Cosmopolitan*. The way she tames war for her nation is superb—Admiral George Dewey with his lazy dog, Bob, sailors dancing cheek to cheek on deck like foretold Jerome Robbins extras, pristine soldiers in dress whites on pristine white hammocks, and the admiral looking at photographs of himself with the Victorian photographer in white Chantilly lace by his side.

It is easy to imagine Chiara the filmmaker reading Joseph Schott's book *The Ordeal of Samar*, stumbling upon the idea of the photographer on the scene of the atrocities in Balangiga. It is the photographer's lens, after all, that astounds the courtroom in the four courts-martial that troubled America in 1902: the trial of General Jacob "Howling Wilderness" Smith; of his lieutenant, the daring marine, Augustus Littleton "Tony" Waller; of the passionate and voluble witness, Sergeant John Day; and of the water-cure innovator, Major Edwin Glenn. The rest of the men who slaughtered the citizens of Samar were untried.

America is riveted to the scandal, as pictures of the dead in the coconut fields of Samar are described in smuggled letters to the *New York Herald* and the *Springfield Republican*.

They are like bodies in mud dragged to death by a typhoon, landing far away from home.

Propriety bans the pictures' publication, but damage is done.

The pictures have no captions: *Women cradling their na-*

ked babies at their breasts. A woman's thighs spread open on a blanket, her baby's head thrust against her vagina. A dead child sprawled in the middle of a road. A beheaded, naked body splayed against a bamboo fence. The congressional hearings on the affairs of the Philippine islands, organized in January 1902 in the aftermath of the Samar scandal, hold a moment of silence.

True, the photographer's fame is split.

Senator Albert J. Beveridge, Republican of Indiana, the globe-trotting imperialist, calls Cassandra a traitor to her class.

She should highlight the Americans who are victims of slaughter, not their enemies!

She is a vulgar creature not fit to be called citizen, much less woman!

Senator George Frisbie Hoar, Republican of Massachusetts and nemesis of William McKinley, calls her a hero of her time.

Senator Hoar famously accuses his own party's president in the aftermath of the Samar trials: "You have devastated provinces. You have slain uncounted thousands of the people you desire to benefit. You have established reconcentration camps. Your generals are coming home from their harvest bringing sheaves with them, in the shape of other thousands of sick and wounded and insane to drag out miserable lives, wrecked in body and mind. You make the American flag in the eyes of a numerous people the emblem of sacrilege in Christian churches, and of the burning of human dwellings, and of the horror of the water torture."

Save for a few points of wishful thinking, his words are blunt.

"Your practical statesmanship has succeeded in converting a people who three years ago were ready to kiss the hem of the garment of the American and to welcome him as a liberator, who thronged after your men when they landed on those islands with benediction and gratitude, into sullen and irreconcilable enemies, possessed of a hatred which centuries cannot eradicate."

True that. (At least until 1944, and all is forgotten.)

It is easy for a reader to overlay this calamity with others, in which the notion of arriving as liberators turns out a delusion, or a lie.

And it is easy for Chiara to overlay montages of her own childhood with that of her possible heroine: the baby among maids brought out for display at lunch parties on Park Avenue; the birthday girl whose abundance of presents includes her mother's monsoon weeping. Objects of the heroine's desire in silent parade: rosewood stereographs, magic lanterns, praxinoscopes, and stereopairs from the photographic company with the aptly doubled name Underwood & Underwood. Her souvenir snapshots from hotels around the world and an antique set of collectible prints captioned "nature scenes": Mount Rushmore, waterfalls, black children, cockfights.

Her own aristocratic world can be seen as an easy stand-in, in sepia wash, for nineteenth-century Cassandras. The movie's white-petticoated protagonist clutches the old Brownie camera that is Chiara's prized possession.

The photographer will be one of those creatures beyond her time and yet so clearly of it, beloved of film and epic, with a commanding presence heightened more so by the backwaters in which she lives and oblivious of the trap in which she exists, that is, her womanhood.

The script, as Magsalin reads, creates that vexing sense of vertigo in stories within stories within stories that begin too abruptly, in the middle of things.

But Magsalin is a reader. She is the kind who takes five years to finish Marcel Proust, and by the time she is done her translation is out of fashion and the book has a different title; but the point is, she finishes. Every time she thinks of the book's ending, *Time Regained*, the memory of the experience of reading it persists; it makes her happy. She is a dying and annoying breed, with a sense of obligation now somewhat obsolete.

She is confused by the manuscript, but she keeps track of her confusion, annotating each mixed-up scene as she goes, taking out from her bag an actual notebook, of course a Moleskine, and a fountain pen, bought from eBay. She includes in her notebook problems of continuity, the ones not explained by the hopscotching chapters; issues of anachronism, given the short life span of the subject (1940–1977); words repeated as if they had been spilled and reconstituted, splattered and jumbled up then placed on another page; an unexplained switch of characters' names in one section; and, of course, the problem of lapsed time—in which twin (or is it quadruple?) simultaneous acts of writing are the illusions that sustain a story.

At times she hears rising up in her that quaver that readers have, her discomfort over matters she knows nothing about, as if the writer should be holding her hand as she is walked through the story.

But she rides the wave, she checks herself: a reader does not need to know everything.

How many times has she waded into someone's history, say Gustave Flaubert's Revolution of 1848 in what turns out to be a favorite book, *Sentimental Education,* and know absolutely nothing about the scenes, the background that drives them, and yet she dives in, to try to figure what it is he wishes to tell. It turns out her ignorance is part of her adventure. She calls those discomforting reader moments the quibbles—when she is stuck in the faulty notion that everything in a book must be grasped.

But still, against her quibbles, she scribbles her *Q*'s: her queries for the author to address later.

> *Cassandra Chase's presence in Samar is a quandary for the military officers. The enterprise of the Americans on the islands is so precarious, perilous, and uncertain, that the burden of the traveler's arrival in wind-driven bancas, rowed by two opportunists, a pair of local teenagers who hand off Cassandra's trunks to the porters with an exaggerated avidity that means she has overpaid them, gives Captain Thomas Connell in Balangiga a premonition of the inadequacy of his new letters of command.*
>
> *Who has jurisdiction in Samar if a mere slip of a woman in a billowing silk gown completely inappropriate to the weather and her situation flouts General Smith's orders in Tacloban and manages the journey across the strait and down the river anyway on her own steam, with her diplopia and diplomatic seals intact, a spiral of lace in her wake, a wavering tassel of white, complete with trunks full of cameras, and Zeiss lenses, and glass plates for her demoniacal, duplicating photographic prints?*

22. Magsalin does not get it

Magsalin shakes her head. Starting a movie with a voice-over by a society photographer who discovers her soul amid butchery will turn off local viewers. Anti-imperialists are touchy people. And as a polite trigger warning, the device is risky.

In a movie about a Philippine war, why use a nineteenth-century Daisy Buchanan, some socialite photographer who, unlike the truthful shallowness of the *Gatsby* original, will turn out to have a bleeding heart? That idea is so 1970s, when politics mattered, and even the heiress Patty Hearst had a cause. Or that journalist in *Reds*, the Diane Keaton character who nurses the Yankee commie John Reed back to life in the Warren Beatty epic—sure, it is nice to have a woman's voice in a time of war, but does she need to be so—*white?*

Whatever.

It is obvious that the upper-class WASP photographer, actually a mutated Ukrainian Jew, is a stand-in for the generic consumer being enticed to know the story.

And that soundtrack—Magsalin hates it.

It sticks in her head. *We're caught in a trap. I can't walk out. Shove it up your nose.* She has heard these songs, including the bovine marginal declensions—the *wo-ow-wo-ow-wo-ows*—all throughout her childhood.

A sad trick, this pop track.

That the soundtrack for the Philippine-American War is stuffed with bloated late Elvis, earworms of his crass decay, listened to over and over again in the benighted tropics—or at least, among her mother's generation—disappoints her.

Elvis is from her uncles' time.

Magsalin had never liked the songs, though it surprises her now how all the tunes she thought were absolutely Filipino, like "Are You Lonesome Tonight," an annoying kundiman if she ever heard one, turn out to be Elvis. Except "My Way." "My Way" is Frank. To sing "My Way," you are not allowed to deviate from the Frank-ish phrasings, or you will die. But Elvis has this phenomenal stature among local drunks, and no matter how anyone mangles his desperate songs, they always bring tears to someone's eyes.

Turns out the serenade songs, the kundiman that men used to sing to virgins in their gauzy camisas looking out from capiz-shell windows in thatched-roof trappings, nipa huts idealized as symbols of authenticity, of the genuine Filipino-ness of their lives, in the TV love dramas of the time—turns out all of the kundiman harana songs her uncles loved to sing were Elvis.

Or based on Elvis.

He was inescapable in her childhood, but at the time Magsalin had no clue. She grew up innocently with her uncles' drinking bouts, in which the songs seemed to spring from the bamboo groves, and grown men sang pitch-perfect versions of creepy ballads while sopping up bahalina tuba, their homegrown wine. Even now, her uncles in Manila bring in fresh gallons of this wine from cargo ships that look as if they had known the days of Magellan, and in Manila they have translated their provincial guitar fests into insomnia-inducing, mechanical nights of karaoke.

It strikes Magsalin that the congenital link between drunkenness and song in her uncles might be an ancient tumor, a fever of the islands beyond anyone's control, so that Elvis and Frank are daemons, or maybe cancers— forms of visceral necrosis, a genetic malady, and not necrotizing corporations. It was a shock when she arrived in America, and she recognized that the culture she had thought was hers to sneer at was, all along, not really. It was claimed by others. Worse, her own culture, of the fermented coconuts and the demented singers, was not visible at first in New York—except maybe in the vaga-bond diesel from hot dog trucks that gave off the whiff of jeepney smog: but even that missed the necessary attach-ment of the smell of fish balls.

"Sweet Caroline" was the Boston Red Sox song, not her uncle Tio Exequiel's signature anthem. No one, not even Tio Exequiel's oldest brother, Tio Nemesio, clearly a better tenor, was allowed to sing it. But to her confu-sion it was also owned by this humongous sports arena of phenomenal passion. In America, she kept confronting these doubles, repetitions of details from her homeland that have reverse or disjoint significance in this simul-taneous place, as if parallel universes of Elvises and Neil Diamonds were a dark matter of the cosmos that eludes theorists of the world's design.

That she has Elvis Presley in her bones, a secret me-tastasizing thing, just as she has nipa huts and the crazy graphics of jeepney designs, occurred to her as a blow. And once, on a visit to Nashville, when all she heard in this museum she stumbled into—which contained only El-vis's cars—was Elvis, all day, all the time—the idea struck her—oh gee, what if—

What if Manila is necrotized in America, too—scar tissue so deeply hidden and traumatizing no one needs to know about it. One is in the other and the other is in one, she thought, feeling ill in Nashville. Her self overdubbed, multiplied, intercut, and hyperlinked, but which is to be master, she wondered, feeling dizzy, about to fall (she also had too much bourbon). These realizations of *différance* comprised her surrender to her new world of signs. She does not mourn her dumb recognitions, though she curses the fact that it is her lot to note them.

In short, Magsalin became interested in alternity, to the misfortune of her friends in Queens, who hate to listen to her pontification at their historic ethnic dinners in which, with exaggerated gestures as they pick up mounds of rice, they like to eat in peace with their hands.

The alter-native.

Magsalin apologizes for the pun but has no willpower: she does not resist it.

Anyhow, she proclaims to her peers at one of their utensil-deficient dinners—it is a thought that strikes her as she strokes a mangled piece of pork with her manicured pinky—"Everybody is messed up and occupied by others! Even if you are not Filipino! We are all creatures of translation, parallel chapters repeating in a universal void!"

Dead silence amid pig's blood and the dregs of cow marrow.

Then they all go on clumsily scraping up dinuguan and bulalo, for after all none of them is any good at being indigenous out in Flushing—they order all of the wrong things for their homesick performance, this renegade act of eating without spoons.

Unquote.

18. Chiara meets the translator in Punta

Chiara in the taxi reads the email attachment from the translator.

121

She barely registers Magsalin's pleasantries, how nice it was to meet!, etc. She reads online in the cursory way she was never taught at school—in school she had to annotate, then look up words in the *OED*, then give a synopsis of her incomprehension. School drove her nuts. Slow reading is an art, her teachers kept saying, but their faith was no insurance against her indifference. School gave her migraines: she kept being told to expand on her thoughts when she had none that merited expanding. Her brain seemed more like a ball of hair in a bath drain, as miserably dense as it was inert. She dropped out without regret to go on a drug trip occasionally punctuated by luxury tourism. The result was her first movie, *Slouching toward Slovenia*, a study of tedium and apathy that became an indie sensation, though in truth all she wanted was to portray a certain patch of light on a beach in Ancona, against the Adriatic.

She scrolls through the attachment, barely reading the words but taking in without question the insult she is meant to feel—the normal way one reads on the Internet. Libel suits are a hazard of fast reading. She begins typing furiously on her iPad as the taxi careens. After all, Chiara has a right to be angry. After all, Chiara is already a crime statistic in Manila's traffic bulletins. And the last few hours of rest have not erased her feeling that the city of Manila wants her dead.

Punctuation is an ongoing online dilemma. Tacky exclamation marks provide rudiments of etiquette Chiara forgoes. She also scorns emoticons, stand-alone uses of colons with single parentheses, and illiterate shortcuts, such as *u* for *you*. She is an Internet prig in a world of online junkies. It is a black mark on her generation that the mindless adoption of the signifier *lol*, an insufficient proxy for the vagaries of the human voice, happened in her lifetime. She never uses it. Even with friends, she fails to sign off *xoxoxo*, as if her denial of trite, reciprocal affection were a mark of superiority. She never reads the offensive signals she has committed in her texts and is not bothered by the affection she fails to convey, resisting even the existence of the absurd term *emoji*.

She barely acknowledges the taxicab driver's deep bow as he pockets her tip. Her presence at midnight at the front door of Magsalin's home in the Punta district has the same substance as her online tone: unapologetic, admitting only of intentions relevant to herself.

If Chiara were not so tiny, wide-eyed, looking a bit troubled in her skewed, though still faintly perfumed, tank top (you see, the maid catches Chiara's naked expression of distress despite the arrogant blue eyes barely glancing at her—the servant, who could shut the door in her face), the latecomer would never have been welcomed into the Magsalin home—that is, the home of the three bachelor uncles from Magsalin's maternal line: Nemesio, Exequiel, and Ambrosio, drunkards all.

Midnight in Manila is no comfort for strangers. Servants in this section of Manila are justly wary of late-night knocks on the door. Corrupt barangay chairmen harass them for tong, doleful bandits pretend to be someone's long-lost nephew, serial drunks keep mistaking the same dark, shuttered home for their own. Chiara does not notice at first that the address Magsalin had scribbled on the bakeshop's napkin is a haunted avenue in leafy, cobblestoned disrepair, full of deciduous shadows, aging tenements of purposeless nostalgia amid wild, howling cats, and the occult strains, somehow, of stupid disco music.

Chiara registers that the location has a disjoint familiarity, like a film set in which she has carefully restored elements of a childhood by dispatching minions to gather her recollections, so that her memory becomes oddly replete, though only reconstructed through the inspired empathy of others. Such is the communality of a film's endeavor that magic of this sort never disconcerts Chiara. Life for Chiara has always been the imminent confabulation of her desires with the world's potential to fulfill them. So while the street and its sounds have an eerie sense of a past coming back to bite her, Chiara also dismisses the eerie feeling. She steps into the foyer of the old mahogany home without even a thank-you to the maid, who against her better judgment hurries away at the director's bidding to fetch the person she demands, Magsalin.

"I did not give you the manuscript in order for you to revise it," Chiara begins without introduction.

"Pleased to see you again, too," says Magsalin. She gestures Chiara to the rocking chair.

"I'm not here for pleasantries."

"You are in someone else's home, Miss Brasi. My uncles, who are still awake and, I am warning you, will soon be out to meet you and make you join the karaoke, would be disappointed if I did not treat you like a guest. Please sit."

Not looking at it, Chiara takes the ancient rocking chair, the one called a butaka, made for birthing. It creaks under her weight, but Chiara does not seem to hear the sound effect, a non sequitur in the night.

Now Magsalin is towering over the director, whose

small figure is swallowed up in the enormous length of the antique chair.

"I did not revise the manuscript," begins Magsalin, knowing she must choose her words carefully, "I presented a translation. A version, one might say."

"I did not ask for a translation." Chiara looks up at her. "I gave you the manuscript as a courtesy. It is the least I can do for the help you will give me."

"I have not yet offered that help."

"But you will."

"Yes, that is true. I have decided to help you get to Samar, to help you with your film. But not without extracting my pound of flesh."

"Coauthorship of my screenplay?" snorts Chiara. "That is unacceptable. You are only a reader, not an accomplice."

"Permission to make of it as I wish, seeing as my perspective offers its own matter."

"And desires that distort," says Chiara.

"Possibilities and corrections," murmurs Magsalin.

"Misunderstandings and corruptions," retorts Chiara.

"A mirror, perhaps," says Magsalin.

"A double-crossing agent," snaps Chiara.

"Yes," says Magsalin, "the existence of readers is your cross to bear."

Meet a Muslim

Fariha Róisín

My sister put on the hijab when she was twenty years old. I remember the color of her first scarf—a pale blue green, maybe chiffon, crinkling at the corners of her smiling eyes, enveloping the circumference of her perfect moon-shaped face. My sister was one of the most beautiful women I knew growing up. Perhaps challenged, in beauty, only by my own mother. She had plump lips, pale and pink like the color of figs, but full like plums, always chapped like creases behind knees in the warm summer heat. She was strong, smart, and terrifying.

I was thirteen when she put on the hijab. Two years after September 11.

The day she put it on we were sitting in her cul-de-sac room. The window overlooked our pristine blue pool with leaves dredging on the surface from our overarching mango tree, shedding its leaves with a tranquil languidness. But I did not feel calm. A feeling of dread panicked through my tiny little body. My stomach lay ill with concern, plummeting through all the reasons why she shouldn't do what she was about to do. My heart, emptied out, carved only by fear, thudded against the cavity of my chest. It was like watching someone about to take a vow, an oath—a samurai, putting on their armor. I felt scared for her.

Since then, she has explained to me that the hijab is much like armor. It acts as a shield against the world of men, meaning: by and large the patriarchy—where women are so often disposable. The hijab acts as a litmus test; it balances the playing field where men are encouraged to take women seriously not for their beauty, but for their intellect. The best explanation I've been given from my sister is that the hijab is like a second skin. It's protection from all of the earth's defenses and energetic toxicities.

THE FIRST TIME I realized I was Muslim, and thus different, was in grade school when I didn't know any of the words to the Christian hymns in religion class. I also knew that my religion—Islam—didn't have an assigned class dedicated to it. Back then it was considered acceptable for kids of other faiths to go to Bible Study. I used to think that this was because it bred religious tolerance, but as I got older I realized it was just out of laziness. Strangely, however, I liked going to religion class.

My sister was seven years older than me, and went to an all-girls private Catholic school in the suburbs of Brisbane. She wore a uniform that consisted of a pale yellow shirt and a forest-green checkered skirt and really ugly earth-brown socks and shoes. Every day, I would pick her up from school, my father in the front seat of the car waiting. In the interim I'd walk around the Christ-on-the-cross-laden halls and feel supremely content with my surroundings. Sometimes, if I was lucky, I'd watch the nuns mulling around the convent on campus, and even talk to Sister Catherine, my favorite sister—who was particularly zealous and enthusiastic. I developed a love of religion and spirituality in those halls, a love of the religious iconography, the gravity and significance of religious worship. It *felt* like a house of God, and I was deeply grounded by that feeling, the feeling of being embraced.

My parents weren't religious, though they weren't particularly nonreligious either. My mother is a painter and works with kids on the side, she's prayed five times a day since I've been alive. My father is a Marxist with a fondness for international development and Islamic philanthropy. He is inspired deeply by the Quran, though he never imposed it on either my sister or me. In fact, he taught me all things that I love and hold dear about Islam.

Together, we'd watch documentaries about Islamic architecture; or he would take me to exhibitions dedicated to Islamic art. I learned early on about Islamic science—and how it was responsible for so many historic findings, such as the removal of cataracts, or even the inventions of hospitals and pharmacies as we know them today. From philosophy to astronomy—from Ibn Battuta (a historic Islamic traveler) to Avicenna (the OG Renaissance man who was both a medical doctor and philosopher)—I read obsessively about Baghdad in its prime, the poet Rumi, and would listen to Nusrat Fateh Ali Khan and dream of the universe and galaxies ahead of, and beyond, me.

It's a Mohsin Hamid quote where he says that the day before 9/11 he was just ostensibly another American—just one with a strange name—then the day after 9/11 he was suddenly a loaded word: Muslim, a suspicion, a target.

I WOULD NOT be able to count on my hands the amount of times my sister has been harassed on the street for wearing a hijab. I've heard so many stories of the lewd sexual harassment of Muslim women or other forms of sexual abuse, and even in some extreme cases, death. Muslim women are murdered because they represent something that the West still refuses to understand. Ironically, the misogyny that fuels a person to kill a woman is overlooked because the deaths are warranted by how a Muslim woman chooses to represent herself. Which is an offense, to some—but apparently the harassment of women isn't.

A few years ago, Richard Dawkins, your resident atheist-science bro, suggested broadcasting "loving, gentle, woman-respecting erotic videos" into Islamic theocracies, like Iran, as a means of challenging the institutionalized religion that exists in those societies. This rhetoric—one of misguided sexual and "modern" interventionism—continues to other these cultures. And of course the narrative impales Muslims as unnatural creatures who know nothing of pleasure, and only of dogma. I'm so glad that he wants to save us from our boring sexless lives. The hubris it must take to be Richard Dawkins.

To him, and his trusty band of naysayers, science—or rather the absence of religiosity—is misapprehended as a trapping of intellect. Not only that, the fetishization of Islam as a guilty male-ego-driven monolith obscures and dismisses all the powerful women making so many strides in the Muslim world. Just read Isobel Coleman's *Paradise Beneath Her Feet*, which dissects feminism in the Muslim world from country to country (Pakistan and Malaysia are some case studies). This disavowal of Islam by the West pushes forward an entropic worldview that men—

especially white men without religion—are not corrupted by their bravados. Which is a farce. Dawkins probably doesn't believe in God because there's nothing that he could believe in more than himself.

Men like him are so consumed by their own egos that they assume that the position of women in the Western world is not lacking in anything. That on the altar of freedom and democracy we, as women, have been given all our rights and everything is fine. That intersectional identity doesn't exist. That, in America, women no longer experience sexual harassment just by walking down the street. That women receive equal pay for equal work. That between 40 to 70 percent of female murder victims are not killed by their intimate partners. That 83 percent of girls aged twelve to sixteen do not experience some form of sexual harassment in public schools.

AFTER CHARLIE HEBDO in 2015, the question of freedom of speech garnered much support. #JeSuisCharlie became an international phenomenon and world leaders even marched to support a concept of freedom that some of them haven't even institutionalized in their own countries. In 2010 the Senate of France banned the wearing of the niqab and burqa. They even employed Fadela Amara, a Muslim, who served as a junior minister in the French government, to state the following: "The veil is the visible symbol of the subjugation of women, and therefore has no place in the mixed, secular spaces of France's state school system." Thing is, what the French, or the West, don't understand is that it's an act of "subjugation" to a society that has a very specific idea of what a woman should and shouldn't wear.

To me, that's not the feminism that I take solace in. To me, feminism is open and brimming with diversity. I believe in a feminism for women of color, trans and queer women, nonbinary femme folk, and most definitely one for Muslim women. France's idea of secularism is based on homogeneity. The problem of that stance is that it only further negates and dismisses the identities that are more complicated than just the one prescription they have of a woman. It's a deeply limiting perspective.

I don't wear a hijab, nor do I plan on ever wearing one. But I do believe, and purport to believe, in the right of freedom for all. I, as a Muslim and a feminist, understand that feminism means comprehending that there are things outside of one's existence and frame of understanding that are just as valid as what we know for ourselves. In a post-9/11 world we have imposed so many restrictions on Muslims and yet expect dedication in return. With every drone that strikes a child in Pakistan, we refuse to comprehend the roots of Islamic terrorism; with every ban of religious freedom of expression, we tautologically debate the concept of freedom for the West; with every speech that is delivered that encourages love and compassion, we isolate a religion, and its mostly peace-loving majority because it supports our international, and national, narratives of what it means to be a nation.

MUSLIMS ARE HUMAN beings. There are over 1.5 billion of us.

It's been hard growing up in this world that has decided on what it means to be you. From every TSA checkpoint, to every nasty comment on the absurdity of the veil, Islamophobia is a very real thing. Making a concerted effort to understand Muslims is actually where it all begins.

THERE'S SOMETHING SACRED about a religious experience.

Recently, I participated in a debate at Trinity College in Dublin where the motion was "This House Believes Religion Does More Harm Than Good." I was on the opposition side, explaining that to say something is outright bad can't be applicable when it affects so many lives in such a deeply positive way. I don't really know if it's possible to describe the nuances and folds of Islam to those who've never wanted to understand it. How do you explain what it feels like to dive into something that feels embracing, all-encompassing, how Islam, like most religions, I'm sure, has great peaks that are undefinable? That it gives you meaning and hope in a glorious way. That it exalts you and revitalizes your being. How can we explain what that feels like? How do we define religion and its impact? Is it really quantifiable?

Things shift within a religious identity; since wearing the hijab my sister has experienced rapid changes in how she feels about herself and the world. There are times she's grappled with the weight of such a symbol, and she's come to terms with what she needed in those times. I've experienced that in my own way, embracing that all identities evolve and change and rupture and blossom. I've done things to myself I'd never comprehend doing as a young Muslim kid, like drinking or trying drugs—aiming to be honest and live with integrity within each moment has been key. Getting older has meant understanding that the limitations of my identity are abstract, and that faith is malleable, as is desire. Everything is complex.

I think back to the day when my sister wore that hijab, a day that things changed for her, but also inevitably for me. In many ways it was a humbling moment, a terrifying experience of understanding what it feels like to be openly hated, to witness others publicly disgusted. Through that, it was a day when I realized (though it took me years to *fully* understand) that there is something deeply powerful in subverting the norm. Pushing boundaries is how we learn, so with each step that I change a bigoted perspective, each time I allow someone to question and challenge their unfounded beliefs, I find some solace. If opening up about the nuances of life is eye-opening for others, then why not give words to your experience.

Truth is, there's no other way.

It's an act of survival to speak up, it's revolutionary to say: hey, here's my story, please listen.

Elegy

Esmé Weijun Wang

Something changes on the plane ride from San Francisco to Taipei. Inside the plane you are already molting into something else; the aluminum tube that holds you is an in-between space. The flight attendants who ask what kind of breakfast you want inquire by asking, "East or West? East or West?" They do not ask what kind of food you want. It is not a matter of congee or a gelatinous omelet. They want to know who you are and who you want to be.

I always say "East," even though I belong to the West. Food goes into the gullet, is digested, becomes blood.

THE IDEA OF "gluten" is foreign to my Taiwanese relatives. Even the doctors among them don't recognize what it means to be gluten allergic, gluten sensitive, or gluten intolerant—which is what I became three years ago, when my immune system began to attack my body willy-nilly and with great force. I was infected with late-stage Lyme disease; in response to the proliferating bacteria, my body took on a host of symptoms: moderate-to-severe bodily weakness, chronic fatigue, frequent fevers, joint and muscular pain, Raynaud's syndrome, peripheral neuropathy, cognitive dysfunction, and more, many of which were impacted by systemic inflammation. Any bite of food containing gluten, or even contaminated by gluten, now caused severe, full-body pain.

In Taiwan, spilling from my mother's mouth to restaurateurs and street-stall owners while I stand by: the attempt to explain what I can and cannot eat so that they might be able to point to which of their dishes I *can* eat, or to adjust their dishes to be gluten free. *Things with wheat . . . Yes, bread. Also things with soy sauce. And fish balls. Noodles. Rice noodles are okay . . .*

Her explanation hacks away at the foods formed from the hands of my grandmother, and from her hands, and from the hands of Taiwanese people at street stalls. The first time I returned to Taiwan after getting sick, I subsisted on protein bars and hard-boiled eggs for weeks. My mouth watered at the thought of oyster noodle soup brought home in metal pails. I once said that I'd eat Shanghai soup dumplings as my last meal—because I loved them so and because they tasted like joy. I was known in my family as the one most passionate about xiao long bao; we ordered them in restaurants as my own private dish. Five soup dumplings would come to the table in a bamboo basket; I tucked them one at a time into a deep soup spoon, bit a piece of the thin skin to let out the hot soup inside, and felt the steam rise against my face as I ate the rest.

I was born in America, but I was raised with my mother's Taiwanese cooking. Pork and eggs stewed in soy sauce. Fish from the Chinese supermarket, steamed with ginger and green onions. Pork chops with chopped mustard greens. I can still eat these things, but not from

Taiwan, cooks who serve food to Taiwanese first- and second-generation immigrants in Cupertino, or hip, Taiwanese Brooklyn eateries. Only my mother, who taught me to love these foods in the first place, knows which ingredients to use and which to lovingly replace. If I want to experience these gustatory experiences, they must once again occur in the home.

TWO YEARS AFTER my last trip to Taiwan, my brother and sister-in-law had a daughter: my first chance to be an aunt. For my niece's one-hundred-day celebration, a Hong Kong tradition celebrated by my sister-in-law's family, I ate almost everything but that which seemed obviously gluten filled. I avoided noodles, but devoured foods that likely had soy sauce—which does contain wheat—in them: chicken with crisp skin, gelatinous crab on greens. I wanted it all so badly that I descended into recklessness. I assumed that I'd know if I'd eaten something improper within five or ten minutes.

"It's been years since I had anything like this," I said to my husband.

He asked if I was okay. I told him that I'd waited for a reaction and hadn't had one. I ate until I was stuffed full of memories.

But at night in my bed, everything hurt. My stomach ached; my hips were shot through with pain like fire; wandering pain lit up my muscles and made my hands twitch. I lay in bed, trying to find an inch of skin that didn't hurt. Eventually, I took an emergency painkiller.

The next morning, I still hurt. I drank coffee and wrote prayers in my journal while nerves lit up throughout my body, reminding me of my transgressions. For that day and the next, I lay in bed, unable to decide whether I regretted what I'd done—yet the memory of that terrible pain has kept me from attempting similar culinary experiments, as much as I yearn for them.

A FEW MONTHS after the one-hundred-day debacle, and knowing how much I missed the food of my childhood, my husband made Taiwanese beef noodle soup with gluten-free noodles and gluten-free soy sauce. I was feeling unwell, and so he prepared the soup until our house smelled of the cramped, raucous noodle joints of my youth while I lay in bed, occasionally coming out to see what he was doing based on *The Food of Taiwan: Recipes from the Beautiful Island* by Cathy Erway. For the first time, I learned what actually went into the dish that I'd eaten almost all of my life: five-spice and star anise, stew beef, black-bean paste. Once the soup had simmered for a good, long while, I took a sip of the liquid from a wooden spoon and found that it tasted *correct*—it was not so much about the actual taste-on-tongue, but about the aromatics settling into the nostrils, filling one's head with properly scented steam; it was *correct* in my heart, filling the emptiness that had formed over the years through degeneration, creating the yawning spaces where my sense of home once lay. Before eating, I took photographs to seal the meal in my memory—this was the day my husband took the time to make me beef noodle soup, and the day I was able to eat beef noodle soup without pain.

We settled in for a reunion, the bowl and I. I gulped it down gladly, drank all the soup, and I smiled at him: happy, home.

Cul-de-sac

Chaya Babu

The day of the Post-it was like any other really. The house a lull, the pink-gold of gloam peering through the thin metal blinds everywhere. Ribbons setting the walls aflame. What happened before or after, I don't know—I just know that my fingertips grazed the grain of the wood on the banister before I left the bottom step and that the hush of the kitchen as I turned matched the whispering swells of my unsuspecting breath.

The pens, coins, tube of lip balm, and mini pads of paper emblazoned with pharmaceutical logos formed the only hint of clutter on the first floor. It was here that the sticky note hung askew, one side angled slightly north, the bottom edge flapping up. Why it caught my eye as I passed an unremarkable point on a path I had tread thousands of times is tough to call; it was as if some invisible thread tugged on my right cheek, as if some part of me knew the words would stand out from the usual mindless doodles my mom scribbled while talking to her friends. There was meaning laden in the message, which read: "Bradley had a baby girl Sophie."

It was unclear who the note was intended for, possibly a reminder to herself about something, or even who it was about, and I almost dismissed it and kept on my way. But then my mother appeared from behind the open door of the god closet, where she had been kneeling with her eyes closed in front of a large plastic Ganesh and silver oil lamps upon which twists of cotton sat immersed in ghee, one end of each burning a tiny teardrop-shaped fire. She glared at me, her thin lips clamped shut, tight.

Pausing in my tracks, I said, "Bradley Meyer?" more out of instinct than genuine curiosity.

We stood there in silence for a beat, and then she squinted a little, never taking her beady eyes off of me.

"Cheryl is so depressed; he hasn't even finished his education," she said, the words a verdict—slow, deliberate, tragic, a quiver emanating from the back of her throat. "The mother is some *girlfriend*."

I said nothing as the familiar chain of terror coiled hard and heavy in my belly, the truth, that I was to be held answerable for things untouched by me, clawing itself from the shadows. On that slip of paper and all over my mother's face was the scald of accusation, as if I had singlehandedly let the stain of wanton sex and out-of-wedlock children spread into our otherwise neatly bleached and pressed world.

The cul-de-sac was a vortex, and what was real and what was not was ever shifting. Someone was to be charged with carrying the mistakes, the messes, that did not, could not, fit here—and here, our roles held fast and blame rolled over to whomever had unwittingly assumed it in the first place.

CUL-DE-SAC IS FRENCH. In America it signifies a circular dead end or blind alley. Ours, Briars Corner, fell in order with the others like it. Strung at uneven intervals along Carlton Avenue, like charms hanging from an unclasped bracelet, no two are exactly the same yet they form a pattern nonetheless: up from Iron Ridge to Doxbury Lane, down to Fox Run and Woodsford Bend. Similar to its sisters, the cul-de-sac opens with reserve, tight at first, the constricted strait of a globular jug, making way then for what lies beyond the widening—the chiaroscuro of weathered asphalt, raised slightly in the center where a pewter disk covering a manhole serves as the anchor between four houses set back from the through street. The inner homes are partly shielded from view by numbers one and two, which sit perched on the corners facing Carlton at the inlet. Each comes with its black tin mailbox, affixed to the foot of a driveway paved smooth, and the gilding of verdant landscaping. Over time, the Meyers planted a rosebush at the cusp of their yard and the cement curb, the Callahans, a wall of white pines marking the rim of their property, and my parents, a short, solitary cherry tree that blooms and fades each spring and sheds its blossoms on an island of woodchips amidst a million spears of grass.

In kindergarten, before the flowering tree took root out front, I'd get off the minibus at noon and ring the doorbell at the mudroom. Every day, the housekeeper would answer the door. This was the woman my parents had hired to keep the house spotless while my mother wasn't there to wipe our fingerprints off of the cream-colored Formica cupboards. Every day, I'd ask, "Is my mom home?"

"She's at work," she'd say.

We'd stand like this for a moment, she in the doorframe, I a step down and still outside on the porous concrete stoop, clutching the straps of my backpack as if I might turn on my Converse high-top heels if her answer was no. Instead I'd look up at her, my face at her hip, both of us with blank stares. She'd shuffle aside so I could enter.

I spent a lot of time across the cul-de-sac at Jessica Meyer's. Her house was a mirror image of ours: contemporary eighties angular monstrosities that nobody wants now. Her mom stayed home during the day. It wasn't until years later that I realized how much time it must have taken Cheryl to coat her lashes in that lacquer and feather her big blond hair. And to go where? Her soft leather handbag, large enough to fit my mother's purse as well as the hard otoscope case she pulled down from the closet whenever I had a sore throat, had a rabbit's foot dangling from the zipper and sat on the kitchen table next to a ring of keys, lots of keys that jingled in tandem with the clack of her stilettos and opened who knows what, but there were so many that I inherently assumed her life was as large as the things she carried.

After school, Cheryl drove us places if we had places to go. In the car she listened to cassette tapes of Black Box and Technotronic and Janet Jackson. Jessica would dance in her seat to it, *PUUUUMP PUMP THE JAM, PUMP IT UP, WHILE YOUR FEET AAH STOMPING,* mouthing the words, her torso arching forward and back in sharp staccato movements to the beat, her seat belt pulling taut with the curve of her body. Together they went into the city some days to take classes at Broadway Dance Center.

"Chaya," her mom called to me in the back seat one day, glancing briefly in the rearview mirror through her gigantic tortoise-shell sunglasses. "What kind of music do you like, sweetie?"

"Ummm . . ." I said, trailing off. I didn't know. I was six.

THROUGH THE MEYERS I learned the ways I was wrong. In their yard, which Jessica's dad Jack tended to routinely, we ran through sprinklers and ate hard pretzels and drank pink lemonade with ice cubes clinking against the glasses. They ate salad before their meals and put salt and pepper on everything. I had never seen salad tongs before. The floors in their living room were silver-gray tile as opposed to warm cedar covered with oriental rugs like in our house, and the walls in Jessica's room were pale lavender. On her tufted carpet that reminded me of pussy willow catkins, her mother would blow-dry Jessica's hair after giving her a bath until it was fluffy, a halo of spun-gold cotton candy.

We were small and quiet compared to them. My father didn't take care of the lawn, which browned in patches and had haphazard sproutings of weeds. His hands didn't hold baseballs or wrenches or dirt; day and night, they scalpeled and sutured the flimsy walls of veins and sketched the vessels of the human body on sheets of white paper on Saturdays. He came home late, too late to tickle or joke. He sometimes read us *The Sneetches* in bed before sitting cross-legged with a tiny tattered prayer book in his dark-lined palms.

Jack got home by dinner, beaming, smelling like cigar smoke and suede from the factory he owned. He scooped up Bradley, still a baby, and roared, "WHO'S MY BOY!"

He built them a wooden swing set but also helped my sister Rekha with her math homework, though I'm not sure she needed it. Rekha who basked in the glory of the Meyers' easy sophistication, who joined jazz classes with recitals for which she wore sparkly midriff-bearing spandex, who liked Donnie Wahlberg just like Jessica and so the two of them shared that, my crush on Joey McIntyre signifying some obvious lack on my part.

She was my big sister and yet somehow Jessica took her. She declared, "REKHA IS MY SISTER." And nobody protested. Not even the parents. They just laughed. Despite the fact that Jessica and I swirled globs of paint on opposite sides of the easel at school to make identical puke-brown masterpieces and ran across the asphalt circle to each other the second the minibus drove off on most days, in the mornings she insisted on holding Rekha's hand. I walked alone.

When I soon discovered I was suited to neither gymnastics nor ballet—or rather, I sensed something erroneous about my brown body in a leotard—I excused myself from the carpool. My afternoons were passed dwarfed in the Briarcliff house, its high sloping ceilings and faint echo through the hollowness of the Green Carpet Room. I watched *Ghostwriter* on the television from my parents' bed, sat in awe as my grandfather built deft inventions out of discarded wires in the basement, or retreated into the pages of R. L. Stine books on the dense mauve cut pile in my room. To this, my mother said, "It's not that you're not talented, you're just lazy."

Still, if it was a bone-cutting New York winter, the kind that had the kids from all six houses walking backward to the bus stop in the mornings to keep the wind from whipping at our small faces, or if it was raining particularly hard, Cheryl would pick us up at the mouth of the cul-de-sac, where we got dropped off starting in first grade. We'd scurry out of the big bus's accordion doors and see the boxy white Volvo parked there with the smack of its black wipers in the wetness, waiting, just yards from the safe, dry havens of actual shelter. Once I just stood there. Only for a minute, but nonetheless. Rekha and Jessica tumbled into the car next to a bundled-up Bradley, slick, heaving, relieved to be under cover at last. "Well, Chaya? Are you getting in or what?" Cheryl asked, peering out with raised brows. The storm poured around me, splashing onto the plush floor of the Volvo. "You can stand here, but we're going to go." Drenched, I had a lurking worry she might not make the three-second detour along the arc of the cul-de-sac to take me home.

I MADE UP every excuse possible to go to work with my mom. We drove the forty minutes to the South Bronx in her mint-green Honda station wagon, a choice that deflected the wrong kind of attention in such poor parts, she explained, and then in the evening through the thick rush of taillights on the Sprain the opposite way toward Westchester. While she saw patients, I sat in her office off of what felt like a secret corridor in the behemoth that was Lincoln Medical Center. We always went through the ER entrance on Park Avenue near 148th Street, away from the noisy main roads that smelled like hot grease and fried food, but I never saw the actual ER. She described it for me once and then I envisioned trash littering its floors, the homeless loitering in its overcrowded lobby, and the smell of urine mingling with sounds of pain.

My mother, a pediatrician, left a private practice in Peekskill where she worked part-time while caring for my grandparents for full-time work at a pediatric AIDS clinic at the public city hospital. At this job, she spoke of how sometimes she didn't know if she was supposed to be examining a child or the child's mother, young women coming in at eleven and twelve years old with screaming babies. "Sometimes they will have many children," she'd say, having become the expert on not just her patients but a whole lot of Americans, "the blacks," as she put it. "And they don't know who the fathers are." Her universe existed like this: Briarcliff to the Bronx and back.

My parents picked the town—no, the *Village* of Briarcliff Manor—on the same basis as most of the other residents, for the public education system, ranked annually in news magazines eighteenth or sixth or eleventh best in the state for its allocation of some absurdly high number of tax dollars per student behind schools like Scarsdale and Horace Greeley. These were the ambrosial districts immigrants longed for from the other side, the hedges as manicured as the women's hands, the streets green and the people crisp, white. There were no chains or franchises welcome within these borders, only quaint mom-and-pop shops lining the brief commercial stretch we called "town"—a hardware store, delis with cured meats, an ice cream parlor, and boutique salons where the ladies tag-teamed me, openly fearful of touching the rough black ropes I had for hair. Here, Drs. Babu and Rao built a dream house numbered four with geometric skylights and a crystal chandelier that cast rainbows over the marble foyer in a development with the newer money of Jews and Italians, far—well, ten minutes tops—from a country club with rules of belonging writ large. Here, we lived in the ways we knew how.

On Sunday mornings my mom made a week's worth of food in the basement kitchen, an entire story dedicated to ensuring that the scents of coriander and cumin didn't seep into the fixtures. One set of Ajji and Tata lived down there too, with the other on the ground floor because of my mother's mother's worsening Alzheimer's. But that we had three refrigerators in our house, the back one stacked with pots of lentils, and none displaying our earnest drawings from Ms. Linville's art class because my parents thought "it doesn't look nice," was a detail that did not go without notice on my part. I chopped vegetables while my mom sat on the cold yet sticky floor with the coconut grater and as mustard seeds popped in bubbling oil over a blue flame on the second stove. Each night she lay at the foot of my bed singing "shuddha brahma paratpara rama kalatmaka parameshwara rama" and patting my leg tenderly off-beat.

THROUGH SOME ODD stroke of fate, Cheryl's last name was Babu. Romanian roots apparently. For years, Jessica obsessed over this fact, staking her claim to some sort of meaningful connection to us, or, more accurately, to Rekha, that ran deeper than the cul-de-sac. "We're family," is what the adults would say. And since Bradley wandered through our front door frequently to have my mom feed him a bowl of cereal and I sat with the Meyers at the town pool in the summers drinking Capri Sun from their cooler, it's not so much that I found this family a false construct as much as I could not fathom my belonging to it.

By fourth grade, even these ties felt tenuous, at least as far as Jessica and I were concerned. We were not friends. Things had started to matter, like fair, wispy hair and whether your clothes were picked by certain kinds of moms. Mine wore white coats and, if something more formal was called for, saris that smelled like suitcases. No matter the occasion, her long ponytail, tied loosely at the nape of her neck, was held in place by clear colorful balls that only kids should wear.

Walking to our respective homes one day after getting off of the bus, Jessica quipped, hardly looking at me, "You're wearing *that?*" as if we were getting dressed to go somewhere and I was weighing outfit options versus it being the end of a school day. This caught me off guard. Yes, I was awkward and unpopular, and she had succeeded from the get-go in securing the affection of a cool older girl who just happened to be my sister. But this. It was something else.

I wondered how it had grown. I knew the seeds were planted early, nurtured by my silence and the shame they all heaped upon me for my coarse unruly mane, ashy knees darker than Rekha's, a unibrow, and a dusky shadow over my top lip even when I should have been too little to be ugly. But when had it borne such fruit?

I had on magenta jeans and a white button-down shirt with little cowboy boots sewn along the placket. In what I thought was a clever move, I wore my own brown cowboy boots with a stitched design on the toe to match. Under Jessica's gaze, I wished I had chosen something else. What, I couldn't be sure. Just not the Western-themed getup.

She still ended up at our house sometimes.

"Rekha, will you do my makeup?" she asked one night.

They crouched together in the narrow alcove near the door of the bedroom that Rekha and I shared, just enough light reaching the full-length mirror through their huddled bodies.

"Oh my god, I'm going to make your blue eyes look so pretty," Rekha said.

Jessica sat with her legs folded beneath her, frozen, looking up and her mouth stretched downward as if her cheekbones were in the way. Rekha, thirteen then, tried to draw a line along or through Jessica's bottom lashes in a way that I thought must be painful. In this moment, the redness of the area immediately around her eyes reminded me of how raw her mother looked in the few fleeting instances I had caught her barefaced in the morning, once with what I swore was a bandage over her nose and the surrounding area puffed and purple.

When Rekha finished with the pencil, she took out the mascara. I was used to this part, but it got me every time.

"You have *such* long eyelashes," she told Jessica. "They're, like, perfect."

Rekha glanced at me so quickly it was almost imperceptible. But she did, and I knew why. Jessica might have been the pretty Maureen Peal to my position as the cul-de-sac's Pecola Breedlove with her shimmering hair and even the way her top lip didn't fully exist or touch the bottom one if she didn't make a concerted effort—the opposite of what my sister called my big black-people lips—but she did not have eyelashes. They were short, sparse, and the same color as her skin. I was the hairy one. And along with this gross misfortune, I was also the one with the lashes, ones you could actually see. But I swallowed the tide of bile that welled in my core: even I wasn't stupid enough to believe that such a concession was grantable.

JESSICA HAD LOST most of her friends come middle school, and she needed to get back in with me. I can't remember how or why, but she found her way into my circle. I think people like her were just good at that. Plus in a sixth grade class of sixty-odd students, the burnt-out mean girls had to be put somewhere. Briarcliff, as shrouded as we were by the many trappings of innocence afforded by wealth, was the kind of place where a young woman could hit peak it-girl status by twelve. In Jessica's case, I probably got her because of the cul-de-sac.

Some things stayed the same or otherwise just evolved from their earlier iterations. The same guys we'd known since kindergarten who now provided Jessica and the other girls I hung out with a steady rotation of boyfriends were also the ones who etched GO BACK TO INDIA BABU into the desks at school for me to find after the period changed. We had both grown up some, but I did not grow out of my difference. Her hair was colored like Angela Chase from box dye labeled "Chestnut," a hue that brought out the harsh pallor of her skin; I rocked chola bangs, curled each morning with high heat and a round brush, with silver hoop earrings that matched my braces. I admit that, for a little while, I still had a moustache.

When I was alone, I obsessively monitored the radio to make mixtapes of AZ with Miss Jones, Lauryn and Erykah, The Lost Boyz, Gina Thompson with Missy, and for the first time I imagined I could be a person in the world. But since I got in trouble for breathing or walking while Rekha studied for the SATs, much less turning up the bass on Hot 97, I once again found myself in Jessica's room overlooking low hills of freshly cut lawn and the rock wall that separated the vast splay of her backyard from the intermittent whoosh of the Taconic. We lay on the floor listening to Biggie and Wu-Tang, pressing our fingers into molten candle wax and thinking we were really gangster.

It was during these years that I learned the word "exotic." Jessica would tell me, with the blind confidence of her toddlerhood preciousness, that this quality, this bird-of-paradise-esque thing I supposedly possessed, is what had the guys at the Westchester Mall gawking and, if they were older, trying out their game.

"They fucking love you," she said, *they* delineating a specific set of boys, with names like Chauncey and Terrell instead of the Jakes and Scotts we knew and coming from places like Sleepy Hollow or Ardsley, surrounding towns with a broader mix of people and closer, by mere miles, to the city. "It's because you're so exotic. You have these big almond eyes and tan skin. You're just so exotic." I guessed she'd failed to notice from our childhood baths together and all the subsequent years of knowing me that my skin was just plain brown. I hadn't, like, gone to the beach.

It remained apparent through high school that to be desired, and to desire, were rights I had no business exercising within the confines of my own existence: home, the brick buildings of school, and a Friday night house party here and there, many of such gatherings taking place in the cul-de-sac itself. "Sac Parties," as they came to be known, had cases of beer stacked in the back of shiny SUVs no matter the weather, white kids hooking up in the bushes, and the Goldmans in house number six eventually calling the cops on us. In a way though, Jessica was right—once we had cars and later curfews, there were places we went that allowed me to shed, even if momentarily, the hatred of my body.

One night junior year while we danced in a warehouse in neighboring town, a skinny dark-skinned kid with a baseball cap trailed me with his eyes from a far corner of the scuffed wood-floored hall. "Damn. You are *fine*," he whispered as I walked past him to leave. I paused to look at him. The boys I knew didn't say "fine." I smiled, an invisible flush rising fast to my cheeks.

HIS NAME WAS Jason. Jason and I kissed and talked on my sun-drenched bed in the afternoons while my parents were at work, tiny particles of dust suspended in the bright light above us which then fell in stripes on his lithe, muscular, mahogany legs. His mouth had hints of peppermint even if I hadn't seen a stick of gum for hours, and he sometimes left a trail of vivid fuchsia welts down my neck to my collarbone along with his scent of baby powder and musk. These bits of him anchored me at times, stymieing my disappearance. But with all that was being spun around us, they proved too slippery to hold.

Jessica showed a picture of him to her mother one day. "Mom, look at the guy Chaya's going out with!" she said. "He's really hot."

"Woooo," Cheryl let out a low whistle as she took him in. "Chaya, he looks nineteen! And how handsome . . ."

She was one of the girls for a moment. Jason had a sly half-smile and lean biceps peeking out from under the sleeves of his white T-shirt—he *was* handsome. But as Cheryl held the photo between her French-polished fingertips, I felt the flicker of her morphing back into a Briarcliff mother, and, seeing him through her eyes, I grasped something I had foolishly disregarded: looks, among other attributes we had learned to covet, mattered little in this case. I sensed a stiffening in the air around us, the obvious tension of words unspoken, but since I was not really her daughter, she kept whatever she was thinking to herself.

My mother was not one of the girls. If she was around when I had friends over, she made us Swiss Miss vanilla hot chocolate in a maroon kettle, repeating "wanilla-wanilla-wanilla" in a singsong lilt because her accent brought endless amusement. In sweatpants and with a bindi punctuating her round face, she danced around in the syrupy glow of the kitchen, her long hair swinging limply below her butt.

"Your mom is *so* cute," Jessica would say, laughing, whenever my mother came up in conversation. Even if I had said something like, "My mom was being such a whore today and told me I can't stay out past midnight," she somehow always fell within the realm of cute. For me, though, seeing as that my mother had gone to medical school at sixteen and come to America alone to do her residency in Brooklyn before it was *Brooklyn*, and that these days, after long hours checking babies who may or may not have been born with HIV, she spent her evenings changing my grandfather's diapers, "cute" was not really the descriptor that came to mind.

So I hid that photo as well as any other evidence of my tryst with Jason because it was easier that way. But I ought to have known there were things one could not escape. My sister, distant as she was then, living on a college campus down South, made sure I knew he didn't count. "Black guys like anybody," she said.

"Fuck you," I responded.

WHO GETS TO claim innocence or righteousness, beauty or truth? Who gets to be good? These are the questions that have haunted me since leaving Briarcliff after high school. The Post-it happened years later, when I was home for a weekend in my twenties. And it was only then that I began to understand the deceptions of the cul-de-sac—to try, ever so slowly, to find upright in the crooked room. The failures I knew more intimately, namely because I had, for as long as I could remember, been inseparable from them. That its carefully engineered perimeter might not hold all of us, our dreams, but moreso the wretched, closeted beasts of our human grief and rage, was not something one considered upon choosing such handsome real estate. We thought only of its charm, never of its ugliness. We saw what we wanted.

But then, of course, the distortions were of our own making.

And these were the memories. They cannot capture the whole of our lives at Briars Corner, but there is something waiting to be revealed to us in the indelible. "Scars have the strange power to remind us that our past is real," Cormac McCarthy wrote. For someone whose realities were hazy, whose gaze was elusive and its objects evanescent, the grit of a memory that endures is the gift of knowing you were, in fact, here.

An early memory stays with me.

Jessica had a mole that covered the entirety of her knee. It was brown and uneven around the edges. When we were still small, three or four, a doctor cut it out and sewed together the pale skin of the surrounding area, leaving a flat, beige, waxy caterpillar of a scar in its place. I did not wonder what happened to the dark scrap that had been ripped away; that it was dangerous had been a given.

After the removal, she wore a soft canary-yellow brace around her leg while the incision healed. This was her uniform: a high ponytail sprouting from one side of her head with a scrunchie, an oversized T-shirt featuring the large, speckled face of a leopard, its whiskers glittering with rhinestones, and the mesh brace. We climbed onto the bed one day in the guest room at my house, where the carpet was a vintagey shade of rust and a checkered sheet covered the mattress. We hadn't been jumping for very long when the stitches popped. Blood soaked the brace and then the sheet and Jessica screamed and her mother was there, from across the cul-de-sac, before I could see anything but red.

"You know she shouldn't be playing rough! How could you be so irresponsible?" Cheryl demanded, looking down at me, as she cradled Jessica through her wailing. It was a brief but bitter scolding and then they were gone. My own tears of shock from the bleeding and of merciless badness that possessed me never came.

My mother? She's absent from the frame that lives doggedly in my mind.

NOW, MOSTLY EVERYONE has left, the families clearing out one by one for the next round who can benefit from the schools and let their children play unsupervised in the cul-de-sac. My parents, now eight miles away in a sparkling new riverfront complex in Tarrytown, have replaced the flimsy bedroom doors and finally begun to gut the kitchen, but only piecemeal. My mother refused to acknowledge the definitively retro look of it—and not cool way, its microfloral linoleum flooring conjuring an era that may never be fashionable again—but as realtor after realtor explained that rich people only like stainless steel appliances, she begrudgingly succumbed. A gleaming brushed-nickel oven and granite countertops meet the glossy beige cabinets she once assaulted twice daily with a damp paper towel.

Upstairs, the room I shared with my sister appears shrunken—the walls are impossibly closer together and the slanted ceiling lower despite my not having grown since the seventh grade. I catch my fishbowl reflection in a spherical track light above, the space sprawled out 360 degrees around me. Still. Empty. Skylights catching dots of dust floating in luminous squares of white. In fairness to my mother, the whole place is surprisingly well kept; if not for the style, it could pass for just a few years old. "We lived lightly," is how I always put it. Stayed inside the lines.

The knurly branches of the cherry tree are stripped from the autumn chill, and there's a fifteen-foot-long dumpster sitting in the driveway near an orange basketball hoop with torn netting. I hoist myself up to look at the carnage, see what ephemera comprises the casualties of downsizing to a townhouse. Beneath mounds of trash, mostly papers, I glimpse the smeared ink of my young handwriting on finely ruled cards—track titles. The mixtapes. I think of jumping in to salvage them, but weeks of rain water and the weight of our lives' belongings piled on top tells me it's no use. I jump down, let the color rush back to my knuckles and sigh, helplessness a noose that dangles at my periphery whenever I meet the bend in the ashen curb that opens to the cul-de-sac.

"This house won't sell because you don't want it to," I say to my mother, back inside. Karmic knots, energetic cords, things like that. The Meyers' house, a near exact replica of our own, sold quickly and for a reasonable sum.

For someone who let go of so much at so many different turns, she's holding tenaciously to Number Four.

My parents never told us what they left behind. But over the years I gleaned it was big. I wonder what they erased in order to embrace the existence Briarcliff invited them to call home, and whether severing parts of ourselves is a compulsion we learn or inherit. And on the train back to the city, when I come upon a video Jessica has posted on Facebook of her and Rekha doing a choreographed Roger Rabbit/running man sequence to C + C Music Factory on a wooden stage in an unknown Westchester auditorium, copied from the VHS tapes Cheryl has saved through moves and deaths and other rites of change, I tell myself that what we keep and what we forsake rests not on what we love or long for, but rather on what we ourselves were once given.

Esmeralda

Mia Alvar

That morning you are woken by an airplane, humming so close overhead it seems to want to take you with it. The clock says five—an hour ahead of your alarm. You've lived close to two airports for almost two decades. You're used to planes. They even show up in your dreams. In last night's dream, you died; your body crumbled into ash. Before you could learn what came next, before you could see where your *soul* went, a machine—some giant vacuum cleaner, which in real life was this plane—came down to sweep you off the earth like dust.

After today, you'll never hear a plane in the same way again. But you don't know that yet.

The boy whose bedroom you sleep in is now a man. He moved out long ago. His mother, Doris, keeps his room the way it was when he lived here: school pennant, baseball trophies, dark plaid bedspread. You pay low rent, and have agreed to leave this room and sleep out on the sofa when the son visits. (He never does.)

You know you won't fall back asleep, so you switch on

the lamp. Because the years of work have given you a bad back, bad knees, and bad feet, you like to pray in bed. A wooden Christ Child and Virgin Mary live inside the nightstand drawer. You lay them on the pillow next to you like shrunken lovers, wrap a rosary around your wrist. You interlace your fingers, shut your eyes, and squeeze your lips against your thumbs as if kissing His feet.

The God that you imagine looks like Father Brennan, the man who baptized you: tall and Irish, with white hair and kind blue eyes, shooting a basketball in black vestments on the parish playground. The Virgin is one of the nuns who ran the adjoining schoolhouse: a spinster with a downy chin, her veil a habit. Old and sacred words, they taught you. You would not invent your own any more than you would try to build your own cathedral. *In the name of the Father, and of the Son, and of the Holy Spirit.* Bead by bead, you whisper the same words Saint Peter spoke in Rome, the same words spoken today by all believers in São Paulo and Boston and Limerick and Cebu:

He rose again from the dead.
Lead us not into temptation, but deliver us from evil.
Blessed art thou among women and blessed is the fruit
of thy womb.
As it was in the beginning, is now, and ever shall be, world
without end.

You pray by heart the way you'd plow a field of soil, the way you push a mop across a floor. One foot before the other. After looping your way around the rosary, you coil it in its pouch. You tuck Mary and the Santo Niño back into their drawer, thanking them for the strength to rise another day, on two aching feet.

"LIKE THE GYPSY," John said, the night he asked your name.

You weren't listening. "*Eee, Ess, Em, Eee,*" you started spelling in reply, as you changed the trash bag from the can beside his desk.

"Mine's John. Not quite as fancy as yours." He held out his hand.

"Pleased to meet you." You stared at the freckles on his long, pale fingers. When he didn't pull them back, you wiped your latex glove, still damp from the dustrag, on your uniform. Then, embarrassed, you snapped off your glove and tossed it in the mother trash bag hanging from your cleaning cart. His hand was moist and smooth. The hand of a man who studied numbers on a screen and now and then picked up the phone.

He had the kind blue eyes of a priest. His hair was white (though he had all of it), his face almost as pale, but pink in sunburned places. On his desk, three computer screens folded outward like a panel painting at church. A woman with gold hair and green eyes, probably his wife, smiled in a frame beside his keyboard.

This new night job had just begun. You were still learning the floor, along whose windowed edges sat men like John, who had their own offices. These men stayed later than the ones who worked in open rows along the middle of the floor. You'd notice, over time, that John stayed latest out of everyone.

SINCE DORIS IS still asleep, you hold off on the vacuuming and step into the kind of fall morning that really does remind you of a big apple, bright and crisp. You buy skim milk and grapefruits, whole wheat bread and liquid eggs that pour out of a juice box and have less cholesterol.

Nineteen years of Tuesdays you have shopped and cleaned for Doris. Longer than her son lived in the room you rent for two hundred a month. On Wednesdays you clean the apartment under you, for the Italian landlord and his wife, whose children you have watched grow up and have their own. Thursdays you are in the city early, cleaning Mrs. Helen Miller's loft downtown. And Fridays you clean uptown, for the Ronson family, who own a brownstone top to bottom. Saturdays your fingers smell like pine oil from polishing the wood pews of the same old church that found you Doris and her extra room, those nineteen years ago. And in between you've cleaned for other people, one-time deals—after a party, or before somebody sells or rents out their apartment, or as a gift from one friend to another—never saying no to an assignment. Nineteen years of cash in envelopes, from people who never asked to see your papers as long as you had references and kept their sinks and toilets spotless.

The other day you pulled a knot of Doris's white hair from the shower drain, trying to remember when those knots were brown.

Now that you're no longer hiding, you have one job on the books, at night, in the tower where John works.

The living room TV is on when you get home. "Good morning," you call out, unloading bags onto the kitchen counter. Doris doesn't answer through the wall. She likes to do Pilates—counting bends and raises, panting—to the news.

Putting the milk away, you hear a sob.

"Doris?"

She isn't doing leg raises. You find her on the sofa, eyeballs red, fist covering her nose and mouth.

"Did Matthew call?" you ask. Over the years, her son has said things on the phone to make her cry.

She shakes her head and reaches for your hand. "Oh, Es." Her other hand points at the TV screen. A city building, gashed along the side and bleeding smoke. You almost fail to recognize it. You never see it from this angle anymore: the air, the view on postcards and souvenir mugs.

A pipe or boiler must have burst, you think, watching the ugly crooked mouth cough flame. You think, *A man in coveralls will lose his job today*. There's an Albanian gentleman whose name you know only because it's stitched across his shirt. *Valdrin*. You never speak to one another. He bows as you pass him in the staff lounge; he blows kisses as you leave the elevator.

You're wrong. They show a plane, show it and show it, flying straight into the tower's face and tearing through the glass.

"What if this happened late at night?" says Doris. "Es, thank God you're here."

She weeps as you two watch, again, the black speck pierce the glass, the smoke spill from the wound.

Trying to count floors, you stand. "I have to go."

"What? Absolutely not."

"I'll clean when I come back."

"Forget about that. Jesus! What I mean is, you're not going anywhere."

"I have to see about . . . my job."

But Doris will not hear of it. "No one's working now. Not your boss and not your boss's boss. You've been spared, don't you see? You're staying here. End of story."

"OK." You sit. "I'll get your coffee, then." You stand and

go into the kitchen, think. You pour Doris's coffee and bring her the cup. "I have to try to call my boss, at least."

In Matthew's room, you lock the door. You change into your panty hose and uniform, as if it's afternoon. Beside the bedroom door, you hold your shoes, a pair of hard white clogs a nurse friend from your church suggested for your troubled feet, and listen to the wall. As soon as you hear Doris go into the bathroom, you tiptoe through the kitchen. You grab your bag and jacket from the closet by the door, race downstairs, and slip into your clogs outside.

A BOOK SAT open on John's desk, the next time you walked in.

"Aha!" he said. "There she is." He pointed at the page and read aloud. "*La Esmeralda. Formidable name! She's an enchantress.*"

You thought about hiding inside the cart, between the toilet paper rolls.

He stood and came around his desk, still reading. "*Your parents never found that name for you at the baptismal font.*" He closed the book and smiled. "Where did they find it, Esmeralda?"

"Not there," you said, pointing your chin at the book. (Your parents would have used a book that size for kindling.) "They liked the sound of it. Or liked somebody with the name, maybe."

John wanted to know, if you didn't mind saying, where you were from.

"So I was right," he said, when you told him. "My wife's nurses are Filipina."

"Your wife is a doctor?"

"No." He looked down. Darkness, like the shadow from an airplane overhead, passed over his face. "A patient."

"Oh." The woman with green eyes and gold hair, smiling next to his keyboard, looked healthy, but you didn't say that.

Before John—and this is terrible to say; you'd never say it, but—the lives of Americans with money were not very interesting to you. Even the troubled ones, their troubles did not seem so hard. You'd ask, "How are you?" and they'd heave a sigh, winding up to tell you some sob story: how much they worked, who had it in for them, the things they'd wished for and were not getting. *Try hunger. Try losing your house*, a voice inside you, that would never leave your mouth of course, wanted to say.

But John's trouble—that moved you. Enough to ask, "Your wife is sick? What kind of sick?"

"The kind you don't come back from," John said. She'd been sick for fifteen years. The photograph beside his keyboard was how he preferred to remember her. Before nerve cells inside her brain began to die, before the tremors started, before her muscles stiffened and her spine curled in. Back when she could walk without losing her balance, back when she could eat and use the bathroom on her own, without John's help, and then a Filipina nurse, and then a second one for nighttime. Before she started to talk slowly, like the voice in a cassette recorder on low battery, and then stopped talking altogether. Back when she still knew who John, her husband, was.

"I'm sorry."

"I am too," he said. "It started fast, and now it's ending slowly. When you love someone you never think a time will come when they're a stranger." He looked and must have felt alone. But the photo that you kept at home, on Matthew's nightstand, was your brother's baby portrait. Long before the lies, the cruelties, the face scarred up beyond recognition.

John's family was Irish, and he grew up in a harbor town where his brothers still lived. "All five of them," he said. "All firefighters, like our father. Or policemen, like our uncle."

"You are not a fire- or policeman," you said.

John shook his head. "Did you ever hear of a family where the finance guy's the rebel? Me, and my cousin Sean, the priest. Plus we're the only two who didn't have kids. No sons to raise into cops or firefighters, either. I guess I never grew up dreaming I'd be some hero. No, I just looked across the bay at this skyline and thought, *I'll work there someday.* "Plus"—he tapped his wedding ring against the picture frame—"*she* wanted to work in publishing. No better place for that than in this city. And we decided that if one of us was gonna work in books, the other better work in money."

He asked after your family. You told him that your parents raised coconuts, coaxed copra oil from them, sold gallon cans of it to men who came in boats once a month. That you had just one brother. "Pepe."

He said, "You're not a farmer."

"No. I'm not."

"Are you and Pepe close?"

The first time Doris asked you this, you shook your head. *Almost nine thousand miles.* She laughed. "I don't mean close on a map," she said. "I know he's far away. I mean, how *distant* are you? Your relationship." This threw you. How "distant" could the blood, running through your own veins, be? "So you *are* close," Doris said. You learned to keep it simple with Americans who asked you after that. *Yes, very close.*

But here, with John, you answered like some old and lonely bag lady, whose cart was filled with stories, waiting for an audience.

"I never had a doll when I was small," you said. "So Pepe—I was ten when he was born—was like my parents' gift to me. He had the whitest skin. Almost as white as yours. And he didn't know anything! He have to be protected all the time. One day I'm cleaning eggs: he took one from the basket and bit it. Like an apple. I heard a scream and I see Pepe there, with blood and yolk and shells and dirt and feathers in his mouth."

You yammered on. About the dreams you had for Pepe. A boy that fair could finish school, grow up to star in movies, run for office. Being a girl—a poor and dark one, no less—you wouldn't dare dream these things for yourself. You left school at thirteen, to help with the coconuts and Pepe's chances.

John looked so much like priests you'd known, there might as well have been a penance grille between you. Is that another reason you said all this to a stranger?

"Even seven, eight years old," you told John, "Pepe slept with his knees up, his fist like this on his mouth, like he still wanted to suck his thumb."

"I was not my brothers' doll," said John, with a laugh. "Their football, maybe."

MAIN STREET LOOKS different early in the morning. The jade pendants and roast ducks have not shown up yet in the Chinese shop windows. A strip of orange tape is stretched across the top of the stairs you would have taken to catch the train.

A nearby cop confirms. No service. Not today.

But there has got to be a way into the city. There was a way nineteen years ago, wasn't there? When the Guzman family brought you with them from Manila to New York, only to send you back? *I wish we could afford to keep you, Esmeralda*, Mrs. Guzman said, once she had learned just how expensive New York was. *People in this city do it for themselves*. She handed you a one-way ticket back to Manila and the number of a good family there who needed a maid. You found a way to stay then, and you will now. In your bag you hook your thumb into the chaplet, whose gold-plate knobs have been rubbed black from years of prayer.

You turn and walk south underneath the rusty, quiet elevated tracks.

City people pride themselves on walking everywhere. "We're more like Europe than like the rest of America that way," Doris has said. John says his brothers live inside their cars (an insult). *My nieces can't go ten blocks in the city without whining*. What's wrong with cars? you'd like to know. Your clogs crunch over pebbles, twigs, and broken glass. Your feet are rioting already, every pain you've been contending with for years fired up. The pinpricks—quick and sharp along your arches—started at sixteen, the year you left your family's farm for Manila, to nanny and clean house for a city cousin who had married well. The bruise between your third and fourth left toes—a swollen nerve, your nurse friend tells you, but to you it feels round, like a pebble in a horse's hoof—grew the year that cousin moved to Qatar and bequeathed you, like a car or a perfectly good table, to the Guzmans. The L-shaped tendon from your right shin to the instep has been sore for six years, as long as you've had your green card. Since meeting John, you've noticed both your big-toe knuckles have gone numb.

Farther down the avenue, the Chinese characters turn into spoken Spanish in the streets. Small children in blue uniforms stream out of school, canceled today. At first they laugh and babble, as kids do when they get a taste of freedom. Then some look up at their teachers, smell their parents' fear.

"Why aren't you at work?" says one girl to the father who's arrived to pick her up.

You know some words in Spanish; you know *trabajar* and *nunca* and *mañana*.

One boy starts to cry. You think of *carabao* back home, who'd snort and stamp and know to head inland before a storm. One girl drifts from her class to join the crowd a block away. They're gathered at the window of an electronics store, watching the news, again and again, on screen after screen after screen.

Only because you know a bit of Spanish do you catch the words *la segunda torre*. You would not, less than two miles back, have understood these whispers in Mandarin or Cantonese.

"*Otro avión*," they're saying.

"*Ocurrió otra vez*."

OFTEN, WHEN YOU came in, he'd be reading. His screens would have gone dark, with white and red and green and blue windows that grew in size as they flew closer— meaning he hadn't touched the keys in a while, and his computer was asleep. And he didn't like just any book.

He liked them thick as cement bricks, and probably as heavy: books to prop a steel door open. With tiny print on thin pages that crackled as he turned them. When a colleague knocked, John moved his mouse to send the flying windows away and hid the book under his desk, next to his shoes.

Or else he'd be typing away: an email in a white window, so many lines of words that looked like they could add up to a thick book of their own. He'd click his way out of them when a colleague came, the way he'd hide his book.

He was writing to his family, his wife's family, the doctors, lawyers, all the people needing answers about her, and what he planned to do. "It takes me so long to say things," he said. "I don't know why. The irony is, *she* was all about the phone. She always said she could take care of something in a two-minute call that I'd spend an hour emailing about. She thought I was long-winded. She'd look over my shoulder and say, *No one's gonna read all that.* She thought most everyone was long-winded, including God and Tolstoy. I'm the crusty old one—I like novels long enough to age you while you read them. *Ninety-nine percent of books should have been thirty-three percent shorter,* she would say. She quantified a lot of things. Sometimes we wondered if the wrong one of us ended up in books and the wrong one in money."

You bowed your head while changing out his garbage bag, his wife's picture like an altar you'd just passed.

"Wow. That's a lot I spewed out, Esmeralda. Let's talk about you. You must email all the time. With your family so far?"

You shook your head. "I don't have a computer," you said, thinking with pride of all the ones you've bought for people in your village. "I type too slow. My mother doesn't know how to email."

"You get home to her much?" he asked, which set you off again. You, Esmeralda, whom nuns and priests and parents always praised for being such a quiet child. Doris likes to say, *Nineteen years under one roof and that is news to me*, whenever she learns anything about you.

"I always thought that once we bought the land," you started, "I'd go home for good."

But once those 1.6 hectares were all paid for, the dirt floor needed wood; the tin walls needed cinder blocks. Of course, a house that sturdy should also have faucets and a flush toilet. And even when the house was finished, there was always family to think about. Pepe ran off, but others came to need things in his place. Cousins had babies, who grew up to go to private school and college. Aunts and uncles got sick, needing medicine. And when they died, it cost money to bury them. Then there was the larger family: the village, and they knew about you too. The church could use a new roof after Typhoon Vera tore it off. Who else would pay for it? Who else could they depend upon? Not the sweet plantation daughters who ended up dancing go-go at Manila bars. Not the men who gave up looking for jobs in the capital and hunted scraps from garbage dumps instead.

"A trip home costs a lot of money," you told John, "and time off work. My family needs some things more than I need a vacation."

"And your brother, what does he do?" John asked.

You thought about it. "He gets into trouble."

"What kind of trouble?"

"All the kinds."

You told him about Pepe in grade four, sniffing glue

and paint thinners with older friends. About his disappearance from the farm at twelve, and his return, months later, with a motorcycle. How he'd paid for it, no one could tell. About the accident on that motorcycle that scarred his face for good. About the botched electronics-store robbery that landed him in jail.

"He's at the farm every few months," you said. "He stays one day, a week, two weeks before he disappears again. If I stopped sending anything, who knows when my mother would see him?"

"I'm sorry." John gave you the same eyes Doris did, when she asked if you got tired of supporting all those people. *Doesn't it get heavy, Esmeralda—the weight of the world?*

You shrugged. "I think having no one to lean on you is worse." Sometimes it did get heavy, sure. But then, you did get to go home, each week on Sunday, to the one House and one Father who were never far away. Each day, His Book reminded you—chapter by chapter, verse by verse— what joy it was to serve, to bear another's load. Those loads weren't heavier than a crown of thorns, were they? No heavier than a cross.

THEY'VE CLOSED THE bridge's westbound lane. Everyone else is streaming east out of the city, as far from the smoke as they can get. Not all of them move fast. Some stop at the pink cables and snap pictures. Even if you had a camera with you, you wouldn't need to. You will not forget the way the towers look today. Like chimneys of a house the sea has swallowed.

At the river, cops are waving west the only cars allowed into the city: ambulances and their own.

But there has got to be a way into the city.

Desperate, you remember a man you once overheard, in a deli, talking to his friend. The man had sworn off all American women. "They're just so *hard* on you," he said. "The foreign girls appreciate what we can do for them."

His friend had doubts about finding a wife abroad.

"Just try it, man. I like FilipinaFinder-dot-com. Or WorldWideWed. Be careful, though. A lot of them these days are *business* women, if you catch my drift."

He meant that some women would play a man—or many men, that is—for fools. They made a job of visiting and being visited, their schedules all booked up with fiancés who paid their passage back and forth to different cities, meeting future in-laws who would plan and go to weddings where the bride didn't show up.

"They always say they're nursing students," said the expert. "What's nicer than a nurse, right?"

I was right, John had said. *My wife's nurses are Filipina.*

You look down at the clogs your friend at church swears by, and at your pale blue skirt. On any other day, you wouldn't dare. You wouldn't cross the street. You wouldn't stand at the plaza's edge, or wave at the ambulance approaching the mouth of the bridge.

May God forgive you, Esmeralda.

It slows. An EMT rolls down the passenger window.

"Elmhurst, right?" he says. He nods at your shoes and blue uniform, sees what he wants to see.

You nod back once.

"There's room for one more in the back."

JOHN MUST HAVE gone to a meeting, or the men's room, the night your dustrag came too close and moved his mouse an inch or so across his desk. This happened sometimes, and not just with John. The screens woke from their floating windows and filled up again with numbers. Or sometimes, in John's case, words. An email he had yet to send, in its white window. You didn't read them—weren't supposed to, didn't want to, and would never have, that night, except your eye caught on the one word you could not ignore.

Your name.

Esmeralda—when's the last time you heard such a chintzy, soapy, froufrou name? Ridiculous.

You froze, looked at the door. You kept your gloved hands, with their Windex bottle and their dustrag, where they were, and moved your eyes down quickly, in case he came back.

. . . Thanks for taking time with me the other night. Not sure (don't want to imagine) where I'd be without someone to talk to about this, and I'm hoping—trying—not to need much more than to talk about it.

It comes down to the vow, right? In sickness and in health. Not "in health, and some amount of sickness I can bear."

Even the setup's a bad soap opera: "I met someone" (even the words sound pitiful to me, a married-man cliché). And of all people, the woman who cleans my office every night. Who even HAS a name like Esmeralda anymore? Esmeralda—when's the last time you heard such a chintzy, soapy, froufrou name? Ridiculous. And yet. I met her, I went home, I turned the bookshelves upside down to find *The Hunchback of Notre Dame*, to keep the name in my head. To have something to say to her the next day.

I can't remember the last time I stayed up late to read

a book, the last time I cared what happened next. But now I sneak them in at work, an addict. I still read to Anne—she would have wanted that, I think—but not those long old books. I started off with those, to tease her. And I thought, superstitiously, that more pages would keep her alive longer. Then it got to where I couldn't tell if she could hear the words, take any of it in. I know *I* stopped hearing them. Now I read her magazines and children's books. Is that sick, am I trying to get rid of her, without knowing it?

Meanwhile I bring *Hunchback* to the office, wait for openings to read it to the cleaning lady.

This woman—Esmeralda—has a story. Sad one. No money, very little love. Some luck, I'll give her that—some priest took pity on her the day she was supposed to go back to the Philippines, gave her a job cleaning his church on Barclay Street. But if you add it up—all the shit she's eaten, from the dirt floor she was born on to the village that's been leeching off her all these years, I think she wins, between us, despite Anne. But I feel happy hearing it from her. Is that fucked up? I hear about her hopeless junkie brother and my heart feels lighter, knowing someone else out there loves someone who doesn't exist anymore, though he's there, the same and not the same. It's not just that—not just, her story's like my story and "we get each other." It's that I'm thinking about stories, other people's, in a way I haven't since before Anne got so sick. I ride the elevator, look at passengers, consider lives outside of my own misery for once. I pity Esmeralda, and other people—I hear Anne's voice: *that's patronizing*—but it's a refreshing alternative to pitying myself. I watch her—Esmeralda, cleaning windows—and she's opened something, let some air and light into the sickroom.

There's the animal part of it too. No doubt about it.

173

You've spent your life proving it can be turned off, kept under control—no sympathy from you on this front, I get that. But it must be said, so you don't think I'm making high-minded excuses. It's about sex, for sure—but also survival. I keep thinking about being close to someone who's *not dying*.

We're all dying, I can hear you saying. Maybe. Remember being young, in summer, our first jobs—how dusk, the 5 or 6 or 7 p.m. hour—used to feel? The best part of the day—possibility, freedom—starting. Fifteen years now it's meant something else for me: getting ready to go home to Anne, the beginning of another long night. Now Esmeralda comes in, between 5 and 6, and part of me is punching out of my shift at the Y again, at quitting time.

I think of Anne, of who she was, of who we were to each other—two best friends in love—and I can't see her saying, "Don't. You signed a piece of paper." Too dickish? Too convenient? Does every lowlife think of his situation as the one technicality? The person I would ask about this can't answer now. Lucky you . . .

You panicked. Turned away from the screen and started dusting, anything—a file cabinet, even the wall, then looked over your shoulder, like a fugitive. You wish you'd knocked his coffee down, the picture frame, instead. Those things could go back to their places. But this screen, this window—you couldn't put it back. You heard the words inside your brain, even when you shut your eyes. Embarrassment, a slippery disgust slid through you, as if you'd seen a naked photograph he meant to hide. Or found some private trash inside his bin. You sprayed the screens and wiped, as if Windexing the words away.

And the screens did darken; the little windows floated back. It worked!

When John returned, you made sure to be far from his computer.

"Es!" he cried. You could have fainted.

Confusion, like an illness, tied you up inside. You vowed never to come near the lip of his desk again. Seeing your name, yourself, in his words, as he saw you—*froufrou, dirt floor, cleaning lady, of all people*—you winced. And yet, these words too: *happy, air and light, the best part of the day.* For weeks you couldn't clean his office without flushing at the cheeks, feeling a mist above your lip. What kind of school-girl silliness was this? You cursed him for it. Called up every dirty word you'd ever learned from fights or movies, here or in the Philippines. *Fuckshitjerkoffthedevilsonofawhore!*

You started to save him for last, hoping he might have left by the time you came to his door. But he was there, almost always. Calling out, "There she is!" Calling you Es.

ALONG THE EMPTY bridge, the driver turns his sirens off. You've taken the third seat, next to a woman wearing scrubs. The man to her right wears your clogs, in black. You sit Manila jeepney-style, six knees in a row—as if you're riding home from Nepa-Q-Mart once again, your cousins' children on your lap, the week's meat thawing at your feet, while strangers pass their fare through you up to the driver. Except there's a neat, unoccupied gurney in front of you. Static and the voice of a dispatcher come through the driver's radio, but you can't listen.

You twist the chaplet on your thumb, catching your finger on the first knob. *I believe in God, the Father Al-*

mighty . . . You close your eyes and move your lips. On any other morning, traffic might have taken you through all fifty Hail Marys, but the streets are empty now. You've just begun the third Sorrowful Mystery when you open your eyes to the back windows of the van, which is already racing south past the courthouse where you took your oath.

Doris had told you of an amnesty five years before, signed by the President. And though you feared it was a hoax, a way to smoke illegals from their hiding holes, she helped you fill out the forms and get your card. REGISTERED ALIEN. Five years later, you rolled all ten of your fingers through black ink and filled ten squares with your ten prints. The lines that cut across the rings told you how many years had passed since you arrived from Manila with the Guzmans. The oath itself took five minutes. Your mind, so trained by prayer, has held on to every word.

> *I absolutely and entirely renounce and abjure all allegiance*
> *and fidelity to any foreign prince.*
> *I will support and defend the Constitution.*
> *I will bear true faith and allegiance to the same.*

Afterward, some students at a table outside the clerk's door registered you, right then, to vote.

A couple, coming out of City Hall, asked you to photograph them. They weren't young, but the white daisies that the bride clutched in her hand were. A few of them she'd plucked and pinned into her hair. The air had dust and August grit in it, but on that day to you it was confetti. Every pigeon in the park looked like a dove.

"Our witness had to get back to the office," said the bride. "Will *you* celebrate with us?"

You'd barely answered when she took your hand. "I found our wedding party, hon!" she told the groom, and ran. Your other hand grabbed Doris's. Cars honked, but in a friendly way, at the jaywalking four of you. "Congratulations," people on the sidewalk slowed to say.

At a bar close to the water, the newlyweds ordered lemon pound cake—*the icing's white*, they said with a shrug—and champagne.

"Which one of you's the bride?" flirted the bartender, popping the cork.

"I am." She pointed at herself. "But pour Esmeralda's first. Today she's an American."

The golden fizz filled your glass to the lip. He poured the bride's, then Doris's, and then the groom's. The newlyweds insisted he, the bartender, drink too.

"Cheers," said Doris.

"To love," said the groom, winking at his bride.

"*Mabuhay*," said the bartender, winking at you. "Merlita taught me that. She cleans this place at night."

It went, as they say, straight to your head: cold bubbles star-bursting from your tongue and throat to your brain and your eyes, ringing the room with light.

"Now tell me it's still 'a piece of paper,'" said the bride to her groom. "Tell me you don't feel different."

"I do," he said. "It feels like . . . solid ground, where there was water. Right?" He put an arm around her.

"Drink to that," said Doris, so you did.

"And you," the groom asked, "what will you do first, as a full-fledged Yankee?"

The bride: "Besides get drunk with three other Americans."

"She's looking for a real job," Doris said.

"In an office," you said.

You meant the kind of job you did get, nine weeks later, cleaning offices in a city building where thousands worked. But the husband said, "Trust me. It's overrated."

"I want to send a postcard home and write an arrow," you said. "*See that building? That's where Esmeralda works.*"

They drank to you.

The newlyweds stood halfway through the second bottle and settled the bill. "We need to relieve the babysitter," they said. "But will you stay and finish this for us? Promise you will."

"No need to ask me twice," said Doris.

"All the best to you two," said the bride. Her eyes glassed up with tears. She squeezed your hand, and Doris's.

Doris swiveled her barstool to you. "You know they think we are a *we*, don't you?"

You swiveled back to where the newlyweds had gone. You didn't get it. Then you got it, blushed, and thought you ought to chase the bride and let her know the truth. But you'd drank more that afternoon than ever, couldn't feel your feet to stand. You opened your mouth to protest, but all that came out was a hiccup.

Doris giggled. So did you; you couldn't stop. You raised your glasses, clinked, and sipped again.

"Congratulations, Esmeralda," Doris said. "Now you'll get jury duty like the rest of us." But she beamed with pride.

You hiccuped, laughed some more, and then you kissed her, on the lips, just long enough to smell the powdery perfume and see the feather-colored down along her cheek. You thought of angels. Thanks to Doris, you were here. She was wearing lipstick for the occasion, and when you turned back to the bar mirror, so were you. The kiss was brief and sweet and overpuckered, like the one between two Dutch boys in a Delft figurine you dusted once. A souvenir. It said, below the boys' feet, AMSTERDAM.

"America!" you shouted at the mirror. That set you both off giggling again.

Today, seeing the park outside of City Hall get smaller from the ambulance, you think that when you see John next, you'll tell him this story. You will insist on what that bride insisted on. Demand that you and he stop hiding, walk out into the sunlight and the traffic and the pigeons and the parks together. "I am good at oaths," you will tell him. *So help me God.*

FOR WEEKS HIS smile, his chirpy greetings, shamed you. *There she is!* One day you'd had it. Maybe the piece of paper had turned you more American after all. Americans loved bringing secrets out. Discomfort didn't kill them. One day you turned to him, hands on your hips.

"It's wrong no matter what."

"I beg your pardon?"

"It's wrong no matter what. No need to ask your cousin who's a priest, because you know already."

You had heard, in many houses, wives beg their husbands for the truth after seeing something they weren't supposed to see. You must have sounded like them now, confronting him.

"I don't know what you mean," said John. His eyes jumped sideways to the screen. The husbands in those houses gave themselves away like this, too.

"You made a vow; that means always."

"Es," said John, "I really have no clue what you are saying." He stared at you.

You could have said, *Oh never mind*; or said something

in broken English. You once wrote off a week's pay from Helen Miller, because you couldn't bear to shame her for her slipping mind. With your own money you replaced the Ronsons' crystal tray, to keep their clumsy daughter out of trouble. And yet, something stopped you from protecting John.

"I saw my name on your computer."

"You had no right to look there," he said, sounding like those caught husbands again, "but I have nothing to hide. Please, be my guest." He rolled his chair wheels back. "Show me what you saw."

"I know it's not there now." You went to him, cloth and Windex still in hand. "I was here, doing my job." You mimed dusting around his files and keyboard. "I moved this thing by accident."

He didn't deny it then.

"It's wrong no matter what, John."

He'd said your name so often. This, your first time saying his, felt like stepping off a high ledge without looking.

He placed his long fingers on the keyboard. "I know that," he said. "I agree."

"It's wrong no matter what." Your voice had lowered into someone else's.

He looked so sad, so tortured by what he knew to be the right thing. Would Doris, Pepe, anyone you knew—even yourself, a day before—have ever guessed you'd be the one to touch him first? You remembered sitting in the church, years before, not knowing what came next but hoping for some kindness. You placed a hand on his shoulder. You felt a shaking from inside him—not a lot, not a "tremor," but enough to make you think he needed more warmth, another hand, which you then placed on his other shoulder.

You waited, then stepped forward. His hands descended on your hips. He dropped his forehead to the highest button on your dress, above your breasts—bone against flat bone. His short breaths blew the fabric back and forth.

And yes, if you'd stopped there, it might have been a hug, no more—an awkward hug, between two people, not quite friends. If either of you had moved any faster, any sooner, you'd have fled the scene, spooked like a horse. But John's hand went so slowly from your hip, down to your knee, under your skirt. Any rougher and you might believe it all happened against your will. You looked through the window at squares of light in other buildings, tiny other people, tiny desks and chairs. His hand shifted against you, inches up and inches down, till sounds came out of your throat. You leaned back, seeing pores in the foam ceiling tiles before you closed your eyes.

NEXT TO THE churchyard, where he parks, the driver of the ambulance stops you. "Hey, wait."

You almost run, prepared to force your way into the building before he can ask for your ID. He doesn't. He just tosses you a hard hat and paper mask before he walks off, putting on his own.

You smell, right then, the burning. Sharper than all other fires you have known. You put the hat and mask on and keep walking. Flames crackle from a broken car window, its alarm whooping. You haven't seen a car aflame since Manila in the early eighties, the riot town the Guzmans were escaping. Two nurses pass, a coughing man outstretched between them, his big arms hanging on their small shoulders. The cops and firefighters move so fast. You realize you're searching for a pair of blue eyes, wondering if John's brothers are here too, working, trying to find him. If this had happened late at night, would John search the faces of these nurses in blue? Their pale uniforms really do match yours. Only the skirt sets you apart. You couldn't sit down on the curb, as one nurse does now in her blue scrub pants, and weep into your knees.

The worst typhoon your village ever saw began while you were in a tree. The tallest one on the plantation (Mahentoy, you called it, after the giant in a folktale) let you see as far as the bay on one side and the next village on the other. You were looking for your father. You didn't know that he had hitched his way already to Manila, where the taxis needed drivers and cafés needed busboys regardless of the weather; or that you would not see him again. You thought there was still time to tell him that a Red Cross tent inland had food and water.

"Come down, Esme," you heard your mother say. Pepe wasn't with her.

You shimmied down. The water, when you landed, reached your knees.

"Where's the baby?"

"Darna brought him to the tent this morning."

But you'd already seen Darna, your neighbor, from high up in the tree, head inland with *her* children—three of them, all her own, and no more. Your mother trusted people who had never wished her well.

"All right." You walked her to the flooded main road and put her on a rescue boat. Then you turned, the water thigh-high now, and ran back to the house.

"Esme!" your mother called. "You'll drown."

The wind whipped at your face; the water slowed your legs down like a dream of running. The house was far enough away you had a chance to look at it, still standing, and feel proud of your papa, whose own hands built it, while scraps of other houses were sailing through the storm. One tin sheet could have sliced you clear in half, but missed. Falling coconuts hit the water with louder splatters than their sound on soil. You ducked. And underwater, it was dark and quiet. You could move faster. You swam until your fingers touched the door.

You prayed for love, not just acceptance, of God's will: even if that meant finding Pepe already bloated with floodwater. Farm girls saw their share of death, both animal and human: stillbirths, yellow fever, malnutrition. And who could blame God, anyway? Looking down on perfect Pepe, how could He not want him back in heaven for Himself?

Inside the house, the water nearly reached your ribs. And there you found him, floating in the wooden trough that had become his cradle. He cooed and gurgled, reaching for his toes. Not a scratch on him.

JOHN WAS THE closest you had ever come to an addiction. As a young girl, you never even longed for sweets. Each morning you sipped coffee next to Doris, but you never *needed* it. Smoking and drinking struck you as a man's vices, and a waste of money besides. Gambling, too. But nights with John—the stars in your brain, the beggar that sex made of your body—gave you a taste of it, that life, those forces that held Pepe at their mercy.

You walked into the walls of houses you'd cleaned for years. You broke a vase that had belonged to Helen Miller's mother. "Esmeralda! What's with you?" said Mrs. Miller. She docked you for it, as if money could replace a priceless thing. *I'm sorry, ma'am.* You went into his office that same night. Watched his reflection grow taller behind you as you wiped the windows. As he trapped you in his arms and closed his mouth over your ear.

If this was anything like what Pepe had felt, you couldn't blame him. You could understand almost everything your brother had done over the years, the lengths he went to for his appetites.

But Pepe, at this time, was trying to change. He'd checked himself into a rehab center in the north: the Farm, residents called it, which caused confusion for you and your mother on the phone, between discussing home and Pepe's rehab. The men there lived like soldiers. Their commander was a former *shabu* addict, who'd found God in jail, was now a priest, and lived by the old proverb about idle hands. His soldiers rose at dawn, cleaned the grounds, made and mended their own clothes, and cooked food that they had grown or raised themselves. Only after chores and Mass and meetings could they spend one hour every evening on the one leisure activity allowed: wood carving. They learned to shape blocks of *kamagong* wood: first into planks, then into spheres. The men who mastered those would build the planks into a cross, the beads into a rosary. The veterans learned figures—Mary and the saints, and, finally, to put all previous skills together, a crucifix with Christ on it. Pepe sent his handiwork across the ocean to your nightstand drawer. The priest did not like to rank residents, but Pepe thought he noticed his quick mastery of figure after figure, saw him linger on his work for longer than he did on other men's.

On the phone, in these months, Pepe spoke with all the fire, all the fever, of the new convert. He seemed to know what you were up to, in spirit if not form.

"Women your age forget what God expects of them," he said. "Once they're past childbearing and still not married, they stop guarding their virtue."

He used words like *fornication* and *adultery*, words you hadn't heard spoken this way since your days in the one-room parish schoolhouse. You almost felt his spittle through the phone line, landing on your sinful cheek. He said he had thought about becoming a priest.

Now you know you should have praised him more. Should have told him how much you looked forward to a crucifix made by his hands. But at that time you had your own urges to answer to. Sometimes you stopped listening, didn't write him back. You fell asleep on the train home, too tired even to pray for him before bed.

You're right, Pepe, you should have said.

In another time, another country, villagers would have stoned you to death.

YOU DID NOT expect to see shoes in the street, high heels that women kicked off as they ran. You think of hallways inside dark apartments, shoes and neckties and discarded bras forming a trail into the bedroom, sounds of muffled laughter and unbuckling, people so distracted by excitement sometimes they forget to shut the door. In those apartments, you've been trained to help and be of use no matter what.

And so, along your way, you stoop and start collecting them. The shoes, computer parts, and paper. As if this wave of people walking toward you has just left the party: you are here to clean up after. This much you know how to do. Your left arm gathers what your right turns up: shoe, shoe, battered keyboard, paper, paper, paper. Where will you bring them, Esmeralda? The wastebasket on the

corner? People might want them back. EARNINGS RE-
PORT, one paper says—no doubt something important.
Some of these shoes cost more than your rent. And some
are not in bad condition. Nicked and dusty, perhaps a bit
charred at the heels. You can restore them, bring them to
the lost and found. Those nice men at reception held an
umbrella for you for two days when you forgot it.

So much turns up that you unzip your tote to carry it.
It's possible that you look crazy, heading straight toward
disaster, scavenging for scraps, but you don't care. The
heaps grow higher the closer you get. One shoe, a patent
leather pump, gives you more trouble than the others.
You pull harder, then drop it. It's too hot. Your fingertips
have swiped into the dust a shiny band of leather that
reflects your face. Something inside the shoe has weighed
it down. Your eyes move, slowly as the cold blood in your
veins, from the shank, over the slender, melted heel, to
the ankle. A woman's ankle, dressed in nylon panty hose
like yours.

You cross yourself. Start digging through the rubble.
You'll bear any sight—a bone, a face—to close her lids for
her, in case she left this world with her eyes open.

ONE NIGHT YOU fell asleep inside John's office and woke
up at two.

"Did I snore?"

"A little," he said. "I'm sure I did too."

In the basement, you didn't know enough to skip the
time clock, go straight home, pretend that punching out
had slipped your mind. Someone like Pepe would have
known. Instead, as you had done five nights a week for six
months straight, you fed your time card to the clock and
listened to it bite.

Thirteen days later, the supervisor's call almost went to voice mail. You were coming back from the Laundromat with Doris's clothes.

"I'm doing payroll and your card says two-thirteen," the supervisor said. "Which means you either took too long to do your floors, or tried to steal time from the company. Which is it?"

She had a pretty accent. *Stealing time*, you thought: how strange, to imagine you could hold minutes in your hand and hide them in your pocket. Had Pepe thought of such a scheme yet? *Time is money.* People said that.

"Which is it, Esmeralda? Are you slow, or do you steal?"

You tried to think: which was the worse disgrace, in your profession? Neither one was true. You could turn the foulest six-stall ladies' room into a lab, in minutes flat. You'd never lifted so much as a slice of bread from someone's pantry.

"I can't hear you, Esmeralda."

By the age of twelve or thirteen, Pepe could spin great yarns of where he'd been and when. He hid things under the wooden floor slats. He sent lists of books and supplies he needed money for, long after he had stopped going to school.

Because you'd met this supervisor only once, barely remembered what she looked like—someone else had trained you—the woman you imagined on the other end had gold hair and green eyes. John's wife, *her* time—you'd stolen that. Ashamed, you chose the other lie.

"I have problem with my feet, ma'am," you told her. Broken English in a broken voice. You, Esmeralda, who'd never griped to an employer in your life—even when you stayed late and earned nothing extra.

"I suggest you get them checked, then. There are doctors just for feet, in the big city. Now that you have medical, you can. Not many cleaning jobs around that give you medical, are there, Esmeralda? That's why there's always applications on my desk."

"Of course," you said.

"I hope the doctor helps you, Esmeralda. But if you can't continue due to problems with your feet, I need to know. You understand—don't you?"

"Of course."

She went on. Words like *unacceptable*. Like *verbal warning*.

So you checked yourself into your own kind of rehab. That night, when John turned his chair to look at you, you headed for the window, far from him. The glass squeaked as you rubbed at fingerprints that weren't there.

"Es?"

"My boss. She could have fired me," you said. Your night reflection faced you, checkered by the squares of light from other offices.

"That's my fault," John said. "I should have woken you. It won't happen again."

"No." A line from *Annie*, which the Ronson children loved, came back to you. Miss Hannigan putting her girls to work until the orphanage shone *like the top of the Chrysler Building*. It takes a cruel master to keep cities clean. "It can't happen again."

"Es—"

"You know already," you said, "all the reasons we must stop."

For many nights his eyes still followed you. To work, with your head down, while being looked at in this way, took more resolve than anything you'd ever given up for

Lent. More will than your first graveyard shift. Your hands shook, as you pushed the vacuum down the corridor, and headaches almost split your skull in half. In time, though, he gave up. In three weeks you were back to nods. *Hello* and *thank you.* In another three weeks you were nothing but two workers, in one tower.

WHEN THE SPLINTERING happens—or the splinterings, a million pieces cracking into millions more—when the clouds come pouring through the street, you stare at them for longer than you should.

Your mouth and nostrils burn. A thousand knifepoints prick your skin. Something like sand rattles your hat. But you keep looking till the dust chalks up your eyes.

And then you close them.

The world grows quiet inside you, and outside time, slow as the center of a storm. You hear only your breath against the mask, the way John must have heard his on your dress, that night.

You clutch the shoes and papers to your chest like things you love. As if they're what you came to save. The bodies running past you, left and right, are a commotion you're not part of. You're prepared to let the monster swallow you.

And now you know why saints crave suffering, invite all kinds of pain so they can feel in some small way what Christ, whom they love, felt.

The flood had risen to your neck when you carried Pepe out of the house. So many of the trees had fallen. Those that hadn't yet were bowing to the ground as if to tell the wind, *You win.* You sat the baby on your shoulders and marched forward as the water reached your chin.

And then you heard the fibers come apart. Mahentoy, that old giant you had scaled to canvass for your father, started breaking at its base, and just missed you before falling like judgment's sword. It cleaved your home in half, where, not a minute earlier, you'd found Pepe. You ducked and ran, underwater, for both your lives.

Now two arms grab you by the ribs, knocking your breath out. You are yanked back into time and through the ash on someone else's feet, your own dangling. You cough, either from his grip around your lungs or from the soot that's gathered in them. Your hearing's back. And now it's clear this roar is bigger than those typhoon sounds from home. The breaking trees; the thunder in the sky; the helicopter's gun-like patter as it dipped to drop food sacks beside the rescue tent you reached with Pepe, by some miracle; the wave that rose fifty feet high and almost ate your hometown—those are smaller, even taken all together, than this roar, this day.

Your rescuer slams you into an iron fence. His badge is on your shoulder blade, his back a shield against the hail.

The world grows dark. You wonder if you've fainted, but you're fine. You're conscious. Night has, in fact, descended on this morning.

"Come on," the voice over your shoulder says. His hand and flashlight lead you down a set of stairs. He has you stand against a wall. Something like a cloud climbs up your windpipe. When the flashlight shines into your face, you think your eyeballs might ignite.

After Pepe crashed his motorcycle, he woke up remembering some Good Samaritan who'd held his head in her lap and pulled the bits of gravel from his face. She left him when the ambulance arrived. *My angel*, Pepe said, *my ghost*. He could not forget her voice or her fingertips.

"You'll be all right down here." With that, your savior's flashlight, and the portion of his black sleeve you can see, are gone.

You know you're not alone. The coughs and sobs and choking sounds of others echo off the station walls. They find your hands and lead you up the platform in the dark.

"HE'S GONE," YOUR mother said.

The rehab farm had released Pepe with a certificate and a kit of wood-carving tools. You'd bought him an apartment in the city, two hours from the plantation. But Pepe never showed to get his key. The rehab priest discovered money missing from his vault. Weeks later Pepe called your mother from Manila.

"He went to see about a business venture there," your mother said, "with friends."

"And you allowed it?" you said. "Don't you know what *business venture* means with Pepe?"

"He said replacement parts for small electronics. You don't think it sounds legit?"

"Do you?"

Your mother isn't half as dumb as she pretends. "You think I could have stopped him?" she said. "You wouldn't think so, not if you'd been here these years. He was a child when you last saw him. He might weigh next to nothing now, but there's no making him do anything."

That week, the lies you'd told the supervisor came true. Your feet clanged with such misery at work, you might as well have been stepping on glass. The bleach and toilet paper felt like bricks you had to push uphill. Even friends at church noticed a limp. That nurse you knew told you to toss your Keds for clogs that got her through her double shifts. You did. They didn't help.

John waited by his door that Tuesday night. "You've looked so tired," he said. "Can I help?"

You stepped back, fearing he might reach for you.

"I know I'm not supposed to care," he said, steering you to the sofa. "Or act on caring, anyway. You don't have to tell me why you're sad, either. I have an idea, though: you rest here. I'll clean the office."

You almost laughed. "I don't think so." And yet the leather felt so cool against your back. Your eyelids sank watching him take the handles of your cart.

Twelve minutes later, you woke with your feet up. John had finished at the window. He stared at the buildings.

"No one builds castles or cathedrals anymore," he said. "I read that skyscrapers are how cities show off, in our time."

The next night he was standing by the door again. The next night you removed your shoes. Each time, you fell asleep and woke to John dusting his cabinets or replacing his trash. These naps never lasted more than twenty minutes, but calmed you more than your own bed at night. You lay there—Esmeralda, daughter of the dirt, born to toil in God's name till your hands or heart gave out—reclining like an infant or a queen, a hundred levels aboveground. Priests had promised you this kind of peace in heaven.

You shall feast on the fruits of your labor, and your works shall follow you.

One of those nights you dreamed about your work. The office floor had thickened into soil, and you were pulling the cleaning cart behind you by your teeth. As the cart grew heavier, you turned and saw Pepe, dropping his woodwork and tools and motorcycle and replacement parts for small electronics into your garbage bag. Your heart rejoiced:

you hadn't seen Pepe in years, and here he was. Visiting you! How did he find you? Still, it dawned on you in this dream that you had to keep walking and could not stop. And Pepe could not follow, only wave goodbye and shrink behind you as you carted his burdens away. You woke in tears, sitting straight up and swiveling your legs as if you'd just remembered an appointment. John was on his knees, dusting the table by the sofa. His gloved hands caught your stockinged feet before they hit the floor.

"Are you all right, Es?"

You shook your head. "I have a problem with my feet."

He nodded. He didn't speak, only pressed his thumbs along your instep. You were silent too, letting the sore bones and stiff muscles speak for you. You looked up at the cratered ceiling tiles and closed your eyes. His forehead touched your knees, bone against flat bone.

"I missed you," he said afterward—his suit, your uniform, stretched across the table like ghost bodies.

Months after he'd disappeared, Pepe turned up again at the rehab farm. *Relapse,* said the once-addicted priest, *is just part of the process.* His rule for returning men was *three strikes and you're out.*

EMERGING FROM THE darkness underground a few blocks north, you hobble to the river, coughing clouds of dust. On the grass a rescue worker tears a white sheet from a gurney into strips. Red tears rain down his face. You think again of saints. You collapse to your knees, a park bench for your prie-dieu.

You'll catch your breath here, that's all. Before you head back south. John's tower stands, without its twin, still smoking in the distance. He's still there. You're sure of it.

Why shouldn't you expect a miracle? You found Pepe, fine and floating in his cradle, didn't you? What could have killed him didn't, because you were there.

But Pepe was a child, and without sin, some voice reminds you. God's book does not mince words about what happens to a man who does what John has done, what a woman like you deserves.

Is today a judgment, then?

God doesn't say.

And so you offer what you would have offered on the day you were prepared to find your brother dead.

Take me.

You'll walk into this river, wash away your sins. And if he lives, you'll see to it yourself that he lives right. You'll walk into this river and you won't come out.

You know that bargains aren't prayers. This kind of pagan trade isn't what Jesus meant by *sacrifice.* Today, though, you'll try anything.

And when you hear the second rumbling, you don't run. When smoke, the second night in one bright hour, again snuffs out the morning, you kneel and wait, elbows on the slats, hands clasped at your brow, stubborn as a statue while the glass and dust and paper coat the town.

You've come this far. Why wouldn't you go back for him? You came into this world with few advantages, but faith is wealth, and you, Esmeralda, are rich with it.

FOR ONE WHOLE year you both avoided the word *love.*

For one whole year you never talked about the future.

What you discussed, what kept you listening to each other all those hours in his office, was the past.

"I almost didn't stay here in this city," you told John.

"Get out of here," he said. By then you knew what this expression meant.

You were playing the game that lovers play, when lovers can't believe their luck. What if John had worked for that firm and not this one? What if the cleaning company had sent you to a midtown building? You never would have met. And further back in time, and further: what if John became a fireman or cop, like his brothers? What if you never left the Philippines?

"It's true," you said. "Mrs. Guzman, the one who brought me, couldn't keep me. She said she didn't know that living in this city was so hard. She bought me a plane ticket and called up a family she knew in Manila."

You told John about shopping for souvenirs at the airport. The T-shirts: so expensive. Snow globes you shook to watch the salt-shaped crumbs fall on the mini-skyline. People on the farm would ask about the snow—what would you tell them? That you hadn't stayed long enough to see it? You looked at yellow-taxi postcards, bright red apple magnets. People would ask about the skyscrapers. Had you ever climbed to the top of one? What would you say?

"I kept thinking of this rhyme that day," you said to John. "The Guzman kids liked it."

Because John's head was in your lap, your hand combing his white hair, you sang it.

If I were a spoon as high as the sky,
I'd scoop up the clouds that go slip-sliding by.
I'd take them inside and give them to Cook
to see if they taste just as good as they look.

"I never learned that one." John smiled. "How would the sky taste, do you think? If we got close enough?"

"Soft but crunchy," you said. (You had wondered too.) "And good for breakfast; just a little makes you full."

You told him somehow you weren't finished with the city. Something kept you here. The city wasn't done with you.

"It's brave, what you decided," John said. "When you think about it."

"But I wasn't thinking, not at all." You laughed. "Is it brave, or crazy? If I was thinking, I'd go home. I had no job. I had no place to live."

The job that brought you to him, to this building, was still eighteen years away that day. There would be lucky accidents and Doris and a change of laws and many other rooms to tidy in between. But as it happened, when you backtracked through the gate, and spent some of your last bills on a taxi back into the city, on a crisp, clear day like this one, you came very close to him and didn't know it. You just didn't know exactly where to go.

As far as towers went, you hadn't even been in this land long enough to know the difference between *tall* and *high*.

"I want to see the highest building in this town," you told the driver.

So he brought you here.

Love Poems for the Border Patrol

Amitava Kumar

I am trying now to remember when it was that I stopped thinking of myself as a new immigrant.

Was it after three years? Five? Fifteen?

I have a narrative in my mind that is teleological—I think the word for this, from my graduate-student days, is Hegelian—and it culminates in my becoming a writer. A writer of immigritude. There is something else. I cannot put a date to it but I suspect that the rawness of always feeling out of place, of not belonging, that fighting sense I had of forever being on edge, diminished or even disappeared once I reached the understanding that I no longer had a home to which I could return. Which went hand in hand, and this is part of the Hegelian schema I'm inhabiting here, with my finding a home in literature.

I arrived in the US for graduate study in literature in the fall of 1986. I was twenty-three. After a year, I began to paint even though I had come to the US with the intention of becoming a writer. I painted small canvases, abstract forms which sometimes had words, often in Hindi, written on them. Why did this happen? Maybe because one day in the college bookstore I had seen a coffee-table book that had the word INDIA printed on it in large letters. It was an expensive book but it had a discount sticker on it and I bought it. Inside were the expected photographs of the Taj Mahal, busy streets, people playing Holi, a Rajasthani shepherd wearing a bright turban. There was also a section on art. I saw the reproduction of a painting by S. H. Raza. On the left side of the canvas, at the bottom, were the words in Hindi: "Ma lautkar jab aaonga kyaa laoonga?" (Ma, when I come back, what will I bring?) Abstract art had never pierced me thus.

The real change that happened soon after that time was that I began writing poems. My poems were about India; they were political and of little aesthetic value. But they allowed me to imagine scenes from the life and the landscape I had left behind. The moon, voices in the dark, a village path, a fire. Which is to say, I had carried my memories with me when I left home, and after a while they found expression on the page. I haven't looked at these poems for a long time. They speak to me of a missing wholeness. I brought two bags from home, but I left a third behind. / Bags, passport, my shoes crossed the yellow lines, something was left behind. / Here I am, a sum of different parts. Travel agents sell ads for the parts left behind.

IN THE POETRY of immigrants nostalgia is as common as confetti at parades and platitudes at political conventions. In my case, I've got to say, my nostalgia was simply the clear bottle in which was stored an explosive rage. This was a rage directed against the figure of the immigration official. I wasn't lying when I had been asked at first if I was planning to return; but later, things changed and I didn't know what would happen in the future. There was the sense that it was I, and not the person interrogating me, who had paid a price by leaving home. I deserved sympathy. A part of me also felt that I belonged in this new country where I had lived for, say, a decade or more. But there was no chance of having an honest discussion about this with the immigration official. It all seemed an exercise in bad faith.

OTHER PEOPLE, UNLUCKIER than me, have suffered definite traumas. Famine; dictatorships; bombed cities; families wiped out. No such horrors in my past. All I had experienced was ritual humiliation at the American embassy in Delhi and at the immigration counters in several airports and land crossings in the United States. The poems I started writing after a few years in this country were accounts of such encounters. "Poems for the INS" (the acronym stood for Immigration and Naturalization Service, a name which changed in 2003, with the agency subsumed under the newly created Department of Homeland Security) were a series of poems I wrote offering vignettes that staged imaginary conversations between the narrator and the official at the visa counter. "You can't trust them," one officer says. / I'm prepared to bet he is from Brooklyn. / There is no response from the other one. He is not angry, / just sad that I now work in his country. / This quiet American has pasted Hindi alphabets / on his left, on his right there is a proverb from Punjab. / "You just can't trust them," the first one repeats, shaking his wrist to loosen his heavy watch. / The one sitting down now raises his weary eyes. / "Did you, the first time you went there, / intend to come back?" / "Wait a minute," I say, "did you get a visa / when you first went to the moon? Fuck the moon, / tell me about Vietnam. Just how precise / were your plans there, you asshole."

Writing as revenge. Fantasy in the purest form. Fantasy tethered to the hurt of the real. Now, with the distance of more than two decades, I feel a distance from that rage. And I also feel some tenderness for the person who was trying so very hard to inscribe an idea of himself against nullity. How else to understand this desperate stance? The cigarette smoke lingered / in the blue Minnesota chill / as my friend said, "I'd like to talk / to you of other things. / Not politics again things like / whether you are lonely." / "What could be more political than the fact that I'm lonely, / that I am so far away / from everything I've known?

Tenderness also for the humble inventory provided to the immigration official after the applicant is asked if he has any property in India, or relatives, anything: the list included the yellow of mustard blossoms stretching to the horizon, the old house with its damp walls and his sister's laughter, the smell of spices over a naked fire. But here's the crucial thing: in drawing up this inventory I was already moving away from who I was when I had arrived in the US. In remembering what I had lost, I was filling my mind with memories. These poems became the screen behind which my past receded.

AFTER TEN OR fifteen years, certainly by the time I had published *Passport Photos*, the confusion and loss of my early years had been replaced by a self-conscious construction of an immigrant self. I'm calling it a construction because it was an aesthetic and a textual idea. I was taking pictures of migrant life; I was reporting on novels and nonfiction about immigrants; my own words were an edited record of what I was reading. An eclectic mix of writers: Frantz Fanon, Aimé Césaire, June Jordan, Jamaica Kincaid, Hanif Kureishi, Salman Rushdie, Marguerite Duras, Guillermo Gómez-Peña. Reagan was still president when I came to the US. The Iran-Contra hearings, and not the O. J. trial of a decade later, was my introduction to televised spectacle. Gap-toothed Ollie North and his proclamations of innocence, the volume of hair on his secretary Fawn Hall's head, reports I read of Reagan declaring, "I am a Contra." I had consumed all of this as an innocent—and by writing poems I began issuing my declarations of independence. While writing this piece, I went back to read a long poem I had written in the midnineties, "Trotsky in the Park." I was on a postdoc fellowship at Stony Brook University and living in a sublet apartment in the East Village. I recognize what I'm doing in the poem: I'm drawing a map of a part of New York City in those lines, and placing people and their talk on the streets where I had seen or heard them. In other words, as an immigrant, I'm making myself at home, if that's the phrase I want, by writing myself into the urban landscape before my eyes.

Recently, I was reading the lectures that the novelist James Salter delivered at age ninety, at the University of Virginia, shortly before his death. In one of them, he quoted the French writer and critic Paul Léautaud (1872–1956) who had written: "Your language is your country." Salter had added: "I've thought about it a great deal, and I may have it backwards—your country is your language. In either case it has a simple meaning. Either that your true country is not geographical but lingual, or that you are re-

ally living in a language, presumably your mother tongue."
When I read those words I thought of my grandmother
who died a few years after I came to America. She was the
only person to whom I wrote letters in my mother tongue,
Hindi. On pale blue aerograms I sent her reports on my
new life in an alien land. Although she could sign her own
name, my grandmother was otherwise illiterate and would
ask the man who brought her the mail in the village or a
passing schoolchild to read her the words I had written.
And when my grandmother died, I had no reason to write
in Hindi again. Now it is a language that I use only in
conversations, either on the phone with my friends and
relatives in India or, on occasion, when I get into cabs in
New York City.

At another point in his lectures, Salter told his audi-
ence that "style is the entire writer." He said: "You can be
said to have a style when a reader, after reading several
lines or part of a page, can recognize who the writer is."
There you have it, another definition of home. In novels
like *A Sport and a Pastime* and *Light Years*, the sentences
have a particular air, and the light slants through them in
a way that announces Salter's presence. All the writers I
admire, each often different from the other, erect struc-
tures that offer refuge. Consider Claudia Rankine. You are
reading her description of a woman's visit to the new ther-
apist. The woman has arrived at the door that is locked.
She rings the bell on the front door. The therapist opens
the door and yells, Get away from my house! What are
you doing in my yard? The woman replies that she has
an appointment. A pause. Then, an apology that confirms
that what just happened actually happened. If you have
been left trembling by someone yelling racist epithets at

you, Rankine's detached, near-forensic writing provides you the comfort of clarity that the confusion of the therapist in the story doesn't.

THIRTY YEARS HAVE passed since I left India. I have continued to write journalism about the country of my birth: this has allowed me to cure to some degree the malady of distance. Writing journalism, with its open-ended exploratory questions, its demand for encounters with people and places, has been a gift to me. The tone of my writing has been primarily observational and I've reflected a great deal on the literature that is suited to describe or engage the conditions in the country of my birth. But I have also known for long that I no longer belonged there.

DESPITE THE LONG years here in the US, I have explored little. My journalism, while extending to, say, South Asian immigrants jailed on charges of terrorism, hasn't been extensive. I haven't reported in grand detail on rituals of national life, or road journeys, or malls, or the death of steel-manufacturing towns. I think this is because I feel a degree of alienation that I cannot combat. I've immersed myself in reading more and more of American literature, but no editor has asked me to comment on Jonathan Franzen or Jennifer Egan. It is assumed I'm an expert on writers who need a little less suntan lotion at the beach. I don't care. Removed from any intimate connection to a community or the long association with a single locale, my engagement with literature is now focused on style. Do my sentences, in their simplicity, their plain descriptive quality, reveal once again the voice of the outsider, a mere observer?

Do I detect a trace of self-pity or sadness in the questions above? I don't mean to convey that impression. The world is what it is. And, in any case, there are degrees of estrangement. I contemplate my solitude, which is actually a luxury, with the fate of others. Let me give you an example. In a cemetery that is only a few miles away from my home in the Hudson Valley is the gravestone of an Indian woman. "Anandabai Joshee M.D. 1865–1887 First Brahmin Woman to Leave India to Obtain an Education," reads the inscription. Joshee was aged nine when she was married to a twenty-nine-year-old postal clerk in Maharashtra, and twenty-one when she received a doctor's degree in Pennsylvania. A few months later, following her return to India, she died of tuberculosis at the age of twenty-two. Her ashes were sent to the woman who had been her benefactor in the US and that is how Joshee's ashes found a place in Poughkeepsie. Joshee had already achieved so much, and against such great odds, by the time she died. I'm aware that when she died, Joshee was younger than I was when I left India for America; involved in medical studies, and living in a world that must have felt immeasurably more distant than it does now, she probably didn't have time to write poems or worry about style. I read in a publication recently that earlier this year a crater on the planet Venus was named after her. It made me think that brave Anandabai Joshee now has a home that none of us will ever reach.

Blue Tears

Karissa Chen

If the Communists swim ashore, they'll slit our throats in our sleep and cut off our ears. That's what some of the other men say. The Communist generals wear belts of ears around their waists, the cartilage and skin turned black, curling into themselves like dried fungus.

Nobody sleeps on the beach, not even the areas where there are no mines. Nobody except me. I volunteer for all the night sentinel posts, stationed in that little tower overlooking the sea. After my shift is over, instead of heading back to my bunk, I sleep out on the sand. I tell people it's because I like looking at the fading stars. My commander, Colonel Li, never stops me.

You're a lunatic, he says. But a brave one. I like that.

KIMMUI, JINMEN, GOLDEN Gate, island of shit. I've been stationed here three months and have yet to find the gold the name speaks of. When I slept in the bunks, I never slept well. The humid air hung around me beneath the useless mosquito nets; the fucking vampires still needled around my ears. The hollow whooping call of some native bird kept me from ever completely resting. Now when I sleep outside, those same birds shit on me. The sun darkens the skin around the shit so that I walk around permanently with pale shit-stain-shaped blotches on my arms. It's better with the sea breeze, though. At least the air moves out here.

Out on this island, there's jungle and dust and sea and barracks and an omnipresent blanket of heat, and near nothing else. An unfriendly island meant to keep out unfriendly people, one of the lieutenants always jokes. I know when he says "people," he means the Communists, who fire on us sporadically, but by the way some of the local Jinmenese won't meet my eyes when I walk through town, I can't help but think they might believe it means us.

THE SEA IS wide and gray and smells of brine, just like it did back home. I can't tell how deep the water goes, but on the clearest of days, I can see the shoreline of Amoy, the city of my birth. It's the closest I've been to home since I left over four years ago. If I squint, I think I can see people going about their day. I think I can see folks haggling at market, buying vegetables, stopping to gossip with neighbors. I wonder if there's anyone I know. I wonder if I squint hard enough I'll be able see the road that would take me back to our village, back to my home.

It's two kilometers from where I stand to that swath of land. A man can swim that distance in an hour on a good day, if the current isn't too strong and the water isn't too cold, if the man is a strong swimmer and isn't prone to panic.

Of course, we're told that the only things on the other side of the gray strait that divides us are Communists. No markets, no tea shops, no small stands. There's probably nothing left on that shore but artillery, tanks, men who want us dead.

I WRITE A letter to you every night, wrap it around a stone, and throw it into the sea. One truth for every lie: Dear Mother, I am well, they are feeding us. Dear Mother, I'm a good shooter and I've learned to fight; I no longer cry easily when I'm bullied. Dear Mother, We're winning the war and will be home any day now. Dear Mother, I know you would tell me not to scratch my mosquito bites, but I can't help it—itch can drive a man insane. Dear Mother, You'd be proud of how brave I am, even when the artillery shells come. Dear Mother, I'm married now, don't worry about me dying alone. Dear Mother, From my shore, I can see yours and sometimes I think you might be able to see me waving.

MY ARMS ARE getting stronger. I can feel the ropiness of my tendons when I clench my fists, the hard ball of muscle when I press my arms to my side. The commanders are brutal: they make us toil in this heat, carrying heavy sacks of rice and equipment from one shore to another; they row us out to the middle of the sea, throw us in and tell us to swim back. If we fail, we squat. If we fail, we run. If we fail, we're berated and reminded of how the Communists will slit cartilage from skull when they catch us. Remember our comrades who died two years ago, fighting for your right to go home, they bark. Think you could protect us the way they did? If the Battle of Guningtou happened today, you punks, we'd all be dead.

I don't resist anymore. Four years and I've learned not to resist. Instead, I do extra push-ups and pull-ups after drills, run an extra two laps when I wake up from my morning sleep. Colonel Li tells me he's impressed with my progress. He winks and tells me I deserve a promotion. You'll be a KMT officer yet, he says.

THEY TELL US it's treasonous to miss home. Almost as bad as desertion, which is punishable by death. We *are* home, they remind us. Jinmen, Matsu, Taiwan. This is still China, and we are still home. It's only a matter of time, they say, until we're reunited with the Mainland. It's only a matter of time until we take the Mainland back.

They said that last year, and the year before that, and the year before that, and the year before that.

LAST WEEK, XIAO Su, my favorite teahouse girl, shook me awake. You were calling for your mother, she said. You were yelling. Her face looked weary as she blotted out my tears with a handkerchief. I turned my head away. Don't be embarrassed, she said. You're not the first one to miss his mother in his sleep.

She lay down on her side, one fist propped under her cheek, as if she had done this hundreds of times before. Stroking my arm, she said, Tell me about her.

I didn't want to. I didn't want to invoke my memory of you. The way you smelled of fish and kumquats. The way your hair was going gray at your temples. The way you hid your teeth behind your hands when you smiled because you were shy about how crooked they were.

Another day, I said, pulling on my pants. My time here is nearly up.

AT DUSK, THE anti-landing barricades sticking out of the beach look like the skin of a spiny lizard, something fantastical and to be feared. Imagining the whole island as merely the back of a mythical creature makes me think of the stories you used to tell me: of a world propped up on a turtle's back to prevent collapse, of a little boy who flew through clouds on the spine of a golden dragon to save his mother from the moon, of two sisters who transformed into a giant moss-covered rock and its surrounding lake to protect themselves from men who chased them. In all these stories, the world—its magnificence, its beauty—is created from long-suffering, from the sacrifice borne from love.

Be selfless, be brave, be filial, you said whenever you finished telling me the stories. These were the morals to your tales. These were the qualities you most wanted me to embody.

I'm trying, Mother. We are fighting for a free world, they tell us. We are fighting for our countrymen still trapped behind the Communist borders. But every day we're reminded that the Communists might sneak up on our shores and cut us down in our sleep. Every day we're told today might be the day we die. The unexpected rounds of fire, the mines that go off by accident, the terrifying loom of a China that is both home and enemy, the mosquitoes, the shit, the wetness and sand loitering in every crack of my soul—what is any of it for? They tell us and tell us but to be honest, I'm long past believing in the world my suffering is meant to build.

When the sun sets purple and red upon the glittering dark seas, there's always a moment when Amoy looks like it's burning.

EVERYONE MISSES HOME of course, even if we don't say it. I see the way Ah Lin fingers the small patch of fabric—not quite a handkerchief—that the others say he sleeps with under his pillow. I catch Min Min staring at a photograph that he always keeps in his breast pocket. Jiu Di grumbles often about how bland the food is, missing the chili peppers that dotted his food back home. Wei laughs as he tells us stories about the trouble he and his trickster brother used to get into, his body shaking until tears stream freely down his face.

As far as I can tell though, I'm the only one who can see his home from the coast. I've told no one but they probably already know. Maybe it's my Hokkien accent, the fact that sometimes I slip and speak in my mother tongue with the locals instead of the Mandarin we're all supposed to use. Or maybe it doesn't even come to that; maybe the way my gaze always drifts toward the sea is enough to raise suspicions.

IN MY DREAMS, you say the same words you said to me right before I left.

Be careful. Be brave.

Your face is blurry at the edges.

I'll burn a light for you, so you can always find your way home.

Three nights ago, I told Xiao Su about these dreams. Her face went pale. Don't repeat that story to Jinmenese, she said. Here they burn little lanterns outside their homes to guide the spirits of their dead ancestors. They'll find it inauspicious that your mother would do this for you while you're still alive.

I didn't tell her that was one of our superstitions too.

She looked worried, bit her red-painted lip. I hope she's stopped doing that, she said.

I know you. You haven't stopped lighting the candle. Maybe it's because you haven't given up on me yet. But once Xiao Su voiced her concern, I wondered if maybe it's possible that you already believe I'm dead.

IF YOU SEE anyone in the waters, you shoot, we're reminded over and over by our commanders. Doesn't matter if it's ours or theirs. Doesn't matter if they're coming or going. If you see them in the waters, they've already become our enemy and they cannot live.

I patrol the wall with its loopy barbed wire. I stare through the little notched windows of the tower. I see nothing but black sea and more black sea. Somewhere out there is our village, but it might as well be space, it might as well be air. Something I know exists but have no proof of.

I hold my gun through the slot in the tower and practice my aim. I stare at the words painted on the wall: If you cannot see, do not shoot. If you cannot aim, do not shoot. If you cannot hit, do not shoot.

But we know what they mean: what you can see, you shoot to kill.

THERE ARE RUMORS circulating that if you can find a local Taiwanese girl to marry, you can get off this wretched island, get sent back to Taiwan. Those who still have friends stationed in Taiwan keep writing them, asking if maybe they know of someone whose family might be more open-minded about marrying a KMT soldier. A comrade's girlfriend's friend, perhaps. A friend's sister. They long for families, for someone to write them a letter lightly scented with perfume, for someone to weep and burn money at their graves if the Communists kill us. They are thinking of legacy, of sons, of someone to carry on their family names. They're lonely.

I've even heard some of the slightly older officers, the ones who left behind wives in their hometowns, ruminating on whether or not they should find a good woman here. Perhaps we'd feel more at home, they say. These same men who tell us we'll be taking back the Mainland soon. They've finally begun to give up hope.

But I don't want to put down roots here. I don't care if it's treasonous to think this: this isn't my home. Decades could pass and I still will never forget where I come from.

SOMETIMES TOWARD THE end of my shift, when the early sun rakes through the clouds, I think if I stare at Amoy's coastline hard enough, if I bulge my eyes out of its sockets, I could separate my spirit and find my way back home. I could watch you as you are in that very moment, going about your morning chores: feeding chickens, splashing water on the steps, stirring a pot of peanut soup for breakfast. I could wait as Little Sister—forever nine in my mind, forever apple-cheeked—emerges grumbling and rubbing sand out of her eyes.

I could even drift out the door, past our neighbors' houses with their bowed roofs, and find that the same familiar routines of my childhood are still playing out:

Uncle Lim tying baskets of vegetables to a donkey cart; Auntie Zhay humming Peking opera as she dries oysters on her bamboo mat; Ah Kong, mouth smiling with betel nut, selling fresh meat buns from his stall; Old Tan crouching barefoot in the dirt with his small clay zodiac figurines, muttering: Where is the cat? Where is the cat?

If I follow the path far enough, if I continue toward the stream, would I still find Father, shirt off, back muscles rippling, enjoying his morning swim? Would his hair have gotten grayer, his body softer? If I picture his fuzzy features hard enough, will his narrow, sloped eyes—my eyes—twitch, will his large shell-shaped ears—my ears—ring? Will he know I am thinking of him?

I circle back to you, standing in the kitchen, cleaver in your palm. My thoughts of home always come back to you. Sometimes I think if I only imagine with enough sincerity, the slight breeze will seize your heart into stillness. Your hands will drop listlessly onto your cutting board, vegetables momentarily forgotten. You will know, then, that I am alive.

The visions dissipate but my spirit still lingers across the sea. If only you knew to turn your gaze toward this island. If only you knew I am standing right here.

AT AROUND THREE in the morning, the night is darkest. I know people think it's at midnight, but I swear, the night is darkest at three. On the island, all the windows are covered, the lights are out, and everything that isn't curtailed by curfew moves under the quiet of night. I can see nothing across the water; it's as if Amoy has been swallowed up by the ocean.

On certain nights, if I'm lucky, wisps of the shore begin to glow blue, an unearthly electric color, like someone in the sea has a flashlight and is shining it upward. Sometimes they glow in the snaking shape of the coastline. Sometimes they pool in circles. Sometimes they ripple outward. Sometimes they simply speckle across the expanse of the sea. Once, they created a trail, like the wake of a boat had left a path of blue smoke behind. Blue tears, they're called. The glow of some sea flora I don't understand. I've never seen anything like them before, but they are mesmerizing. The nights that they appear are the only nights that I forget, for a moment, how miserable I really am.

LAST NIGHT, SOME of the men confided that they thought we might never be going home. The Communists will never let us return, Jiu Di said. They'll kill us all before we can go back. Min Min said, It's been six years since I saw my fiancée. Do you think she's forgotten me? Wei laughed, quietly but without malice. I think it's time to settle down here. Find a nice new girl, not that brothel girl you always go to see, but someone you can picture raising your children. I don't want to, I said, glancing at Ah Lin who nodded. I'm not ready. Jiu Di put his hand on my arm. Aren't you sick of being homeless? he asked. Wei tossed back the rest of his beer. I've begun forgetting what my mother looks like, he said. She's right. I'm a terrible son. He laughed but I saw the tears brightening his eyes.

ON SOME NIGHTS I imagine what story you'd come up with about the blue tears. Maybe you would say they were supernatural, that a little boy could jump in them and be transported to another universe where he would be a wuxia hero. Maybe you would say they were the tears of an ocean god crying for the loss of his only daughter; touch them and you'd be turned into sea foam. Maybe you'd say they were a potion for eternal youth, and to drink them would mean one could live a thousand years without aging, without sadness. But I can't find the morals in these stories, not like the morals you might have told me. I wish you could see this wonder with me, explain to me whose suffering created this beauty, what sacrifice was required for us to have this gift.

AN UNEXPECTED ROUND of artillery fire hits the island during the day. Just a warning from our friends on the other shore, our commanders joked grimly, since the shells mainly landed on the beach, but flying debris still hit several buildings, injured some of our men. Ah Lin's arm caught some of the shrapnel while he was patrolling and had to be amputated. I saw him biting down on the ball of his fabric scrap to keep from screaming as they carried him to the medic.

If it had been nighttime, it would have been me. I would have been sleeping on that beach. I would have been hit. My brains would have been splattered across the sand, bits of my flesh thrown in the waves for fish food. Or maybe I would only have been injured, like Ah Lin, and I'd be missing a leg now, or an arm. Maybe my face would have been burned off, and I'd become unrecognizable, to you, to myself, to anyone. Without my face, without my legs, would you still know me when I came home?

This is the recurring nightmare I have, one I have

even when I'm awake: I walk up our path, I knock on our door. I am ready to hold your arms, ready to collapse with relief at finally being home. But instead you stare. You stare and stare and then you murmur, You must have the wrong house. Or, You look nothing like my son. Or, You must be mistaken, my son has long since passed away. And you close the door in my face, leaving me standing alone.

Thinking twice about sleeping on the beach yet? Colonel Li asked me, once everything calmed down a bit. You're going to die out there if you don't stop acting so crazy.

TONIGHT AGAIN, THE water glows blue. The other men have gone to bed early, sober despite the extra beers we all ingested. Everyone rattled by the day's events. In the quiet of the night, I watch the blue tears undulate in the water. From up here in the tower, they look like a necklace cuffing our land.

Jiu Di, put on duty for extra security tonight, has fallen asleep. I know because I can hear his snores loud from his post. He doesn't stir when I leave the tower, when I skirt along the wall and down the steps, doesn't even notice me when I step out onto the beach.

I want to touch the sea, I want to see if I can cup the tears in my palms. But like any magic, it dies when it's disturbed. The water is normal in my calloused hands. It tastes like regular salt water against my tongue.

Across the sea, with the little bit of light from the blue tears, I think I can see a pinprick of light where Amoy could be.

I let the water drip from between my fingers.

I don't want to die here, Mother. Don't let me die here.

IT'S A LIE, the thing I told Xiao Su. You never said you'd wait for me, never said you'd burn a light. That happens only in my dreams, even though it happens every night.

I don't remember the last thing you said to me. I don't even remember the way you looked the last time I saw you. Maybe you were wearing that indigo cotton shirt you liked best. Maybe you had an apron on. I wish I could remember, I keep trying to remember.

I was walking in the fields, on my way back from town. I had purchased a cup of rice, a bag of oil. I was supposed to go home immediately, but I'd dawdled, had enjoyed watching the hustle and bustle of the city, so different from what it was like in our quiet little village.

And then the KMT army marched past, a ragged group of men. I watched them, taking in their gaunt faces, their torn-up uniforms, the sour stench of sweat and grime wafting around them in a cloud. I thought to myself how sorry they looked, how I hoped the war would end soon. I started to turn away, away from my discomfort and pity, when a dull pop cracked the back of my skull, and I went sprawling to the ground. I opened my eyes and saw the muzzle of a rifle prodding me to get up. Then I was marching in line with them. Mumbling through the words of army songs I did not know. The oil and rice dropped somewhere behind me. I had no chance to turn back. No chance to tell you goodbye.

I was fourteen.

Maybe your last words to me were Be careful. Maybe, as you stashed the money into my hands and retreated back into the kitchen, you called out, Hurry home soon.

THE SEA ISN'T as cold as I expected it to be. It's relatively warm. My arms are slicing through the water at a steady pace, like a knife through the night. I can't see Amoy but I know it's there. I know you're there. I know, too, the possibilities: that I might drown, that I might be caught by the Communists and become nothing more than a pair of ears, that I might be caught by my own men and shot before tomorrow morning.

But none of that matters. Behind me is that bastard island, Kimmui, Golden Gate. I've left my rifle, my helmet. I've left the other men, those who miss home as much as me. Behind me are the blue tears whose glow I can no longer see, though maybe I've already caught their magic, maybe their iridescent molecules are clinging to my hairs, buoying my skin. The sea welcomes me, it cleaves a path for me. I'm riding on the back of a water dragon, I'm coasting on the shell of a tortoise.

Two kilometers separates me from home. Beyond this sea is beach and land and road and a light that will guide me home. Beyond this sea sleep the donkey and the stream, Ah Kong and his buns, Old Tan and his lost cat. Beyond this sea are Father and Little Sister with their faces I don't know if I know anymore. Beyond this sea is you, and you are waiting for me. Less than two kilometers. If I keep going. If I keep going.

Tigress

Rowan Hisayo Buchanan

How does a man become a beast? Kishi Chikudo became a tiger.

IT STARTED WITH the 1893 Chicago World's Fair. Japan spent $650,000 on their exhibit, about sixteen million in today's dollars. They built a pavilion and employed the finest sculptors, painters, and ceramicists to ornament it.

Chikudo was head of the Kishi School, founded by the renowned tiger painter Kishi Ganku. In this tradition, Chikudo painted a tiger. But it wasn't good enough. He tore it up.

Actually, it started before the World's Fair. Forty years earlier, Commodore Perry's warships broke into Japan. The new kaikoku ("open country") policy eased trade relations. Waves of bowler hats, paper money, cable cars, record players, and railway lines slopped into Japan. The turmoil was enough to send any man mad, but Chikudo stayed sane.

The tigers arrived in boats: tigers lying on dirty straw,

flea-eaten tigers, hungry tigers, real, live tigers. Try to un-learn the tiger. Unlearn the weight of her. Forget the soft curves of her ears and the deceptively gentle scallops of her paws. What would it be like to see her for the first time? Chikudo saw his first tiger when he was already in his sixties. To see her only a few paces away, a distance of less than a leap? Even behind the bars of a cage, what would it be to see the black V-stripes sweeping up her belly like migrating geese? What would it be to meet her hay-yellow eyes? This was what Chikudo tasked himself to capture.

He tried a second tiger and soon tore it up. More than replicating light falling on a striped pelt, for Chikudo painting the tiger was an act of empathy. He wanted to capture the essence of this foreign beast.

For centuries, images of tigers had made their way to Japan on plates and scrolls. Painting a tiger was like paint-ing a dragon—one followed conventions. Every tiger was a copy of a copy: a Japanese artist copying a Chinese art-ist or a Japanese artist copying an older Japanese artist copying a Chinese artist. Many imitation tigers resembled crooked-tailed tabbies. For these artists, to imagine the tiger as sinew and fur was as hard as it is for us to imagine Chikudo.

Chikudo advised his students to follow the principle of 写生, shasei, copy life. This might seem obvious; it is easier to draw a thing if you have seen it. But shasei does not just mean to use life as a template. It means to look for the essence of the living thing and to represent that in its truest form. Chikudo visited the tigers again and again. He looked at ribs that were larger than his wrists. He ex-amined their bellies, soft and white as camellia petals.

Four times, Chikudo painted a tiger and tore it up. He worked without pencil. Each stroke had to be perfect. Some marks had to be darted into wet paper. A dry dot of color might be added days or weeks later.

By the time he began on the painting that would hang in Chicago, he had at last reached something in the tiger that was behind the two-tone green and yellow of her eyes. 心持ち, kokoro mochi, is an aesthetic standard to which a painting can be held. One in which the primary criterion is the empathy the painter feels for the subject, so that he in some way becomes his subject. Literally, heart holding.

We cannot observe Chikudo. We know that he probably painted kneeling upon the floor, not standing up like Western painters. But did he drip ink on his sleeve? Did he let the black spread in spots and stripes? Or was he too adept for dirty sleeves? We cannot see at which stroke the madness crept up the horsehair brush. We cannot listen to him shout to an apprentice to bring him more ink. We cannot hear the growl rolling up his throat. But we can understand loving a subject so much you become it. We can feel in our own eyes the ache in his: the longing to honor himself, his country, and this greatest beast.

ON VISITING THE World's Fair, the *Century Illustrated Monthly* called Chikudo's *Tigress* "a marvel of Japanese realism." He had succeeded. But Chikudo could not know this. Chikudo was no longer an artist. He had stared and stared. He had felt the way muscle folded around bone. He knew the rush of air into great lungs and the beat of a one-kilogram heart. He had felt the tiger's scorn for the small, bald creatures who caged her. His hands had blurred into her haunches. His ears had curved into a tiger's semicircles. Chikudo was a tiger. To paint her, he had become her.

The *Century Illustrated Monthly* reported his state as "temporary mental derangement." Three years later, Chikudo died. There is no record as to whether he was man or beast at the time.

Chikudo's *Tigress* is in private hands, but for a few months in the spring of 2015, she emerged for an exhibit at the Japan Society. She laughed openmouthed at the Americans admiring her pelt. Behind her long teeth rested a tongue, dark as new blood. Is it not a glorious thing to be a tiger?

The Stained Veil

Gaiutra Bahadur

Ramchand's death, in Connecticut in his late sixties, was unexpected. He was a diabetic, but one who watched what he ate, strictly monitoring his calories, and who walked every day at the same hour, clocking his time precisely. He retired even earlier than usual that evening, complaining of indigestion. When his wife, Rani, followed an hour later, she found him gasping for air on her bed. They slept in the same room, but they had not slept together for many years. Later, the emergency room nurses found thousands of dollars, in immaculate one-hundred-dollar notes, stuffed into his trouser pockets. Ramchand distrusted banks. His account had been seized by the government when they fled their country, so he kept a substantial amount of cash hidden in their bedroom in Bridgeport. Even Rani didn't know where. Although Ramchand had gone into cardiac arrest with no history of heart trouble to warn him, somehow he understood that his time had come. He understood enough to lie on that bed, hers not his, with enough money on his body to bury him.

At the funeral home, she betrayed little emotion as she received the procession of relatives who had come to pay their respects. They had come from up and down the East Coast and a few from as far away as Florida and Toronto to say goodbye. As they filed past, they registered her otherworldly quiet, an eerie halo encircling her as she sat in the front row. A niece knelt beside her to whisper a consoling memory of Ramchand, the year he was mayor, riding around on a bicycle with a basket in front to meet his constituents in the little market town near their village. Remembering how seriously he had taken to his role, Rani smiled to herself. He had been a figurehead, really, a token Indian in the ruling African party.

"Uncle Ram gone," she said, squeezing the girl's hand.

There was only the slightest quiver in Rani's voice. Her children did not know what to make of her composure. Over the years, they had seen her entire body shake with emotion, during almost epileptic breakdowns. Perhaps the antidepressants had numbed her. Even at the crematorium, as the mechanical maw closed around the coffin and their son flipped the incinerator's switch, turning on the wails of the women in the room along with the flames, Rani shed her tears silently.

In the car, on the way back to the house, she told her son-in-law how pleased she was with the memorial service. So many people had come from so far away—and once she reprimanded their eldest grandchild who didn't want to deliver a eulogy, the young woman had complied, finding between grief and shyness a few words of strangled tribute. Her granddaughter had done her duty as the firstborn, and this had satisfied Rani's sense of dharma. If the girl had not found her voice, Ramchand would not have liked it.

After this terse expression of approval, Rani retreated back into herself, humming. She looked out the window, beyond the narrow streets and the row of houses leaning together for support, beyond the squat city of ruined factories and empty warehouses where they had spent the last twenty years, their American years. The song she was humming took her back to a place where she could be alone with the task of remembering Ramchand.

The turning point in their marriage had happened before they emigrated. While at first he could not ration his glasses of rum, in later days he was frugal to a fault, counting closely the coins he earned as a shopkeeper as well as the affection he gave as a husband. Ramchand had gone from excess to austerity, and each had been cruel in its own way.

As a young man, he had been fond of racehorses and drink. Sometimes, he lost himself in it so deeply, he threatened violence. On too many afternoons, dread was coiled in their house on Cloud Nine Avenue, like a cobra that had somehow stolen in.

To keep him from the rum shop, their eldest daughter would lock herself in their bedroom with his clothes. When he was forty-one, he quit drinking, yet the attention he paid Rani was no less measured out. He transferred his fervor from the bottle to Hinduism, clasped his faith with the same desperate logic and need for solace as his daughter used to clasp his clothes behind a barred bedroom door. From the moment that Ramchand found the gods, for the rest of his life he would be their devotee, just as Rani was and would continue to be his.

She had spent almost all of her own life by his side. All her years, except the first sixteen, had belonged to Ramchand, to his shop, to his children—the three who survived and the four who didn't. Grief would collect beneath her bones in layers, a still but gestating thing, gathering and sedimenting with each infant's loss. This kind of mourning, this slow and silent unbecoming, wasn't one she could ever have imagined in her first sixteen years.

THOSE YEARS HAD unfolded in the shelter of a father enlightened enough to let Rani stay in school, just long enough to learn to read and write and count—skills that later served her well as a shopkeeper's wife. She had been the cosseted darling, the youngest and the prettiest of the Mohabir daughters, the one who most gracefully wore the dainty shoes, respectable handbags, and store-bought dresses that were the relics of her family's faded prosperity.

In those sixteen years of rooted innocence, she had known place and its boundaries intimately. There was her family's rice mill, where cattle moved in circles in the yard, crushing paddy underfoot around a threshing pole. On Saturdays, she would go to Miss Evie's bungalow—Miss Evie who taught her to sew and knit, whose son, Esau, would one day become a composer of classical music in another country. Once, she'd peeked through a back window of the Kali temple down the road, only to run home sick to the stomach at the sight of the blood of a sacrificed goat. That was the extent of her transgression and thrill.

The village sat unassumingly on the edge of endless rows of flowering cane, but hidden in its tall quiet, it contained well too much drama for the good of its inhabitants. Too much story, coiled like snakes in the cane. Her father used to say in rounded and swaying dialect, while observing his girls in some fracas, some private disagreement that had embroiled them: "Ayu get too much o' story wid ayu self."

That's what it was like in Lovely Lass.

Rani crossed the boundaries of this world for the first time when she married Ramchand. Whim, his village, was a half-day's journey from hers, near the next big sugar estate down the coast. Her father had chosen for her a young man from a devout family, high caste but humble before god. What Rani had noticed was how handsome he was, his features symmetrical and angular, his face cut with precision, like a dark jewel. He was as dark as she was fair.

When, decades later, she and Ramchand left for America in late middle age, she would remember this first migration from her father's home to her in-laws'. There was nothing that could match it for daring. It was the most routine, inevitable thing a girl could do. And the most terrifying. After that, what move could possibly be as bold?

Rani didn't understand it at the time, but ever since she was a child, the older women at work in the rice fields and the kitchens were singing her fate just as they sang their own. So many of the folk songs they taught her had been about a bride going to her in-laws' house, and a stained veil had often featured in them. It would be her destiny as it had been theirs.

Their in-law songs, those sasurals, held a heroine's fear and wonder on crossing an unspeakable threshold. The songs had featured in the Bollywood movies screening at the Astor, the cinema house in New Amsterdam, the town nearby. Of course, Rani was not there to see Meena Kumari as the courtesan in *Dil Hi To Hai*, crooning "Laaga Chunari Mein Daag," with eyes that mourned, yet feet that stamped and hips that pivoted. The boys in the village would skip school to catch the pivoting hips, but that was their privilege. As a girl, how did she dare? She wasn't at the matinees, as the boys were, over and over again, to hear the sensual tragedienne sing: "How will I go to my in-laws with a stained veil?"

A good girl from a good family, she would never settle into a scarlet-cushioned seat next to boys who might wonder how precisely the veil had become stained: Was it from sex or violence? Did they know yet that the two could exist together, in the same moment's loss?

The image had come from Kabir, a saint-poet from the land that her ancestors had left generations ago. As Rani sewed in the yard, or helped her mother grind dal in the kitchen, she would chant:

You must leave your home forever
Putting on a veil you will go to meet your beloved
You must leave your home forever

This veil of yours is stained
The neighbor women jeer—

These words written some four centuries earlier would fly away from her as she formed them, their meaning difficult and strange. When she was big enough, the old women tried to tell her how to make sense of the poems. Imagine the father's house as the world we know, the earth, they said—and trust that the husband's house is a higher reality, the mystical. Trust was their instruction and refrain. When you go to your marriage bed, they explained, the stain will be the spot that proves you are pure; but know also what Kabir knew, that the besmirched veil is the physical world, the impure body that we must all cast off in death. Rani was perplexed. Kabir didn't seem to know the difference between a dirge and a bride's ballad. Did death and marriage call for the same song? Rani might have been forgiven for wondering, as she intoned:

> *You will never escape this body's betrayal,*
> *Wrinkling and bunching with time.*
> *You must leave your home forever.*
>
> *Kabir says: when you seek to understand*
>
> *You will always fail.*
>
> *Kabir says: any song your body sings*
> *Is a death song*
> *What bride wears her veil*
> *In the presence of her beloved?*
>
> *Cast it off.*
> *You must leave for your real home.*

WHEN RANI ARRIVED at the little white house standing on stilts, so like the bandy-legged egrets that alighted in the rice fields, her in-laws were kind. They were not the cruel ones foretold in so many sasurals, the ones where mothers-in-law slapped their daughters-in-law for failing to make perfectly round rotis, or fathers-in-law loomed with the rancid smell of stale bush rum on their breath. Ma and Pa doted on her. Ramchand was both loving, and not. It was easy to admire him. He looked like a matinee idol, with thick, oiled curls and a cocksure grin that betrayed his knowledge of just how convincing his jawline was; on his face light and motion played, in eternal boyishness. What dealt the final blow, making him irresistible, was the vulnerable undertow in otherwise scampish eyes.

Ramchand's father had sweated in the cane fields, and so had his mother. They wanted better for him—and Rani was definitely that. Her family had some position. Their business, though struggling then, had once been robust. As early as the thirties, Mohabir Enterprises was exporting rice overseas, all the way to the islands; they had an office in New Amsterdam, and it even had a telephone.

At eighteen, what did Ramchand have, besides his ambition and eyes that seduced? When she arrived, with a spangled chunari well too proud to be stained, he had Rani. To have her, as his wife, was one path to the prosperous world that his confidence had marked as his own. Success was rightly his. And when he removed her veil that first night, it was with a tender kind of possessiveness. Whose woman was she? She and all that she represented was his, to do with as he pleased.

It's hard to know how he learned what he pleased to do that night. He could not have learned it from the Bollywood movies at the Astor, with their strategic cutaways, leaving kisses suspended in the imagination, somewhere between intention and execution. There were no scripts for it there, nor in the songs that Rani was taught. Or perhaps she just hadn't known how to decode them. She knew only that she liked Ramchand and wished to please him. She knew, too, that blood rushed to her shoulders when he took her by the hand and led her into their bedroom. The sensation was bewildering, a strange kind of levitation, as if she were both anchored in her body and floating outside it.

"Come," he had said.

The command was gentle. And he spoke softly to her, admiring her beauty, expressing wonder at the depth of innocence in her eyes, telling her how proud it made him to nuzzle a nose as sculpted as hers. Her fair shoulders, again, blushed. He undid her blouse to reveal them, a few shades less scarlet than her sari, and instead of turning those innocent eyes away, she looked directly into his own. They had a liquid quality that made her dissolve, but in that instant they crystallized with purpose, as if before him lay an impossible target that he had to apply every muscle and all his wits toward hitting. It was that single-minded look, fixed with determination on his sudden goal, that she would most remember about their wedding night.

This stalactite quality in the eyes would appear again during the course of their marriage. It was there when, on the edge of orgasm, lying on top of her, he yanked at her hair, giving her an unexpected thrill. And it would be there the time he had her on her hands and knees, and she looked back over her shoulder to hear him express an intention that she could never have imagined him expressing, much less with such blunt, profane brutality. Then his eyes became something darker, fired by entitlement, stunned by disbelief, as she said no and turned over. How dare she deny him? In a fit, faster than either of them could register it, he completed an act that he would, much later, recognize required forgiveness.

It wasn't Rani that he ultimately asked for forgiveness. In prayer, seeking quiet in his conscience, he acknowledged to himself: "She said no, but I turned her back over and took it anyway."

It provided some comfort to him to remember that,

afterward, he had held her, stroking her hair as if she were a bruised child. He had been, at once, her violator and her protector. And she, like him, would for a long time afterward tether and untether feeling to fact: her pride in who she was to what she had allowed him to do, her adoration of him to what he had been capable of doing. How could she have fought him? Wouldn't resisting have made his actions even more wrong, his character even more compromised? And how untethered would she have been then?

Under his spell, she had gone to a place where ego had not mattered. She had climbed down into the unconfessable cave of what it meant to be in love: to be willing to submit, even to choose it. Was she mirroring what the world told her she was, as a woman? Was she choosing a psychological prison like the many legal and physical ones that society had constructed for her? What he did that night wasn't a crime. They were married, after all. And he never did it again. Once he had asserted his right, he never again exercised it. The world was what it was: Paddy did not grow without flood. Sita did not let Ram go into exile alone—no, a good Hindu woman never abandoned her husband. Nor did she refuse him. Love was its own dictatorship. Of this, she had no doubt.

WHEN THEY CAME to America, Rani and Ramchand were running from a political dictatorship which they had resisted in modest ways. When the police came to his shop and tried to seize his goods as contraband, Ramchand jumped on top of the counter to stop them. He had performed many such acts of bravery, shopkeeper's bravery, during the days that flour, potatoes, and imported brands were banned. In the end, their greatest act of resistance was to leave. Like everyone else, they had queued outside the American embassy. Sponsored by their daughter in Connecticut, they waited long, drowsy years for their green cards.

Driving home from the crematorium in Bridgeport, Rani traveled back to the day that finally convinced them it was time to go, the day of Ramchand's first brush with death. Flashbacks often found her there, remembering how a bullet found its home beneath his left shoulder blade.

When the robbers arrived at Cloud Nine Avenue, Ramchand was pulling shut the shop's wide, barnlike doors to reveal the faded Pepsi-Cola ad painted across them. The bandits came with guns in the middle of a crime wave, a spree of what the papers called "choke-and-rob." The opposition parties, in the underground pamphlets they pressed secretly into receptive palms, declared petty Indian shopkeepers the targets, and the dictator the prime mover behind the scenes.

The family responded as if they had expected their turn at any moment. Rani was in the back of the house, in the kitchen, attacking dough with a rolling pin, and the children were upstairs at their evening routines, the girl ironing her school uniform and the boy cradling his shortwave radio, his ear cocked for the cricket scores. When she heard the gunshots, and the screaming, the girl undid her golden earrings shaped like bells, placed them gingerly on her tongue, and hid behind the clothes hanging in her mother's wardrobe, as terrified of swallowing the jhumkas as of being discovered. The boy slid under the bed, pressing his rail-thin body into a corner, trying to make himself even smaller than he was. Rani had run out into the front yard with her rolling pin still in hand, raised as if to defend her family. She was in time to watch Ramchand reach beside the shop door for the cutlass that always waited there, its long, curved blade too rusty to be any real threat to the six armed young men she saw encircling him.

"Coolie man, nah even try da," one warned, drily.

Even though they wore red kerchiefs with white polka dots across their mouths, Rani recognized the robbers as village boys, barely out of their teens. The one who cautioned Ramchand with such composure was the son of the bowlegged policeman at Whim station. And the one who shot Ramchand was the old lady Winifred's nephew, the light-eyed one everybody called Hazel. The first Sunday of every month, at four o'clock, Rani went to Winifred's house to receive phone calls from her daughter in the States. Had Hazel overheard Rani talking about the black market flour and Enfamil formula hidden behind the parlor cases displaying pine tarts and Chinese cakes? Had he been there when Rani described the baby bangle, a slender, fretted rope specially ordered from the goldsmith for her first grandchild, born in America?

It was Hazel who fired when Ramchand grabbed the machete. The slur had made her husband act the hero. She was sure of it. The insult must have wounded him as deeply as the bullet. His attackers didn't address him as Mr. Maraj or Uncle Ram or Mayor, or even Bicycle Uncle, as the village boys sometimes mockingly called him. Instead, as he reeled from the bullet's impact, Ramchand heard: "Coolie man! Nah man! Keep de cutlass fo' you wife."

His entire life, Ramchand had been belittled by that

epithet. He had inherited the hurt from his parents, who had been branded the same by plantation overseers. Ramchand couldn't seem to save—or marry or Brahmin—his way out of the shame of it. Not even joining the ruling party had helped. And it didn't seem to matter that he sold the banned wheat flour to Winifred too, to Indian and African alike. He was from cane country, a son of indenture lacking high school or Christ, town ways or creolized polish, and no one was ever going to let him forget it, certainly not his neighbors who had come to rob him. As he lay there bleeding and humiliated, just another coolie with a cutlass in his hand and a bullet in his back, the bandits shot his sister to death. She had bolted out of her house next door, yelling bloody murder from her veranda when the first shots rang out.

Rani was too stunned to scream. In her trance, the men took easy charge of her, disarming her of the belna before taking her by the elbow and leading her into the house. "Where de gold, auntie?" Hazel asked.

All Rani could see as she took him to the room where her jewelry and the last of her children were secreted was Ramchand collapsing. His eyes were open when he hit the ground. Where, she wondered, was the stalactite in them then? That afternoon, the robbers almost added another layer to Rani's grief. Among the things they carried that night were her wedding jhumkas and mangal sutra, the necklace of sovereigns that her mother had thrice pawned when the family rice mill had failed, the bangle for the baby in Connecticut, jute bags filled with flour and sugar, and all the petty cash in the register; but they did not succeed in taking Ramchand's life.

In the years to come in America, whenever the illness

that never stopped growing inside seized her, she would ransack every room searching for lost jewelry. The police had ultimately rounded up the thieves and recovered the precious necklace strung with pound sterling coins, a rarity from plantation days, and the rest of the stolen goods—everything but the money. Rani remembered going to the station to identify the young men and her things, but it had done no good. The police released the robbers and kept the jewelry.

Afterward, whenever depression took hold, she would hunt madly for bangles that were exactly where she had left them. She would phone her children, accusing each in turn of taking the jewelry without asking. Rani repeatedly acted out the loss of what she still possessed, as intensely as if she were mourning the proud man cut with precision who once made her shoulders blush, as if the robbers had in fact stolen her dark jewel that day, as if he had departed long before he lay down on her bed to die.

When his soul was actually about to depart, his ashes in an urn on her lap, she found herself returning to those two other thresholds in their lives. As she remembered leaving for marriage half a century before and for a new country more recently, she sang of stained veils. It seemed appropriate. Had there not been blood, both times? Weren't both migrations tarnished with violence? So Rani sang the verses that the old women had taught her. *The bride cries, she must go to her lover's. She cries because she must go.* She was an old woman now. *My love will beat me with a bamboo rod. My love will hold me by the neck and beat me.* Finally, she understood what the words meant.

She hummed to herself until she saw before her eyes Ramchand, wearing jhumkas and a red chunari with golden beadwork. He looked young again, his curls blue black and glistening under the veil, his eyes rimmed with kohl, a bride before the gods, ready to go to his last home. His lips moved, forming the words "laaga chunari me daag," and he danced with bells on his ankles, the spark coming from his hips, the grace from the nimble flight of his hands. Their coquette's tracery framed his eyes, those eyes that had always contained want and wrong and the fire of this world. The vision tossed its head. *How will I go to my in-laws / With a stained veil.*

Ramchand threw off the veil, slowly crossing over to another realm.

And Rani, forgiving the body's betrayal, let him go.

I'm Charlie Tuna

Jason Koo

I'll be sitting at home, eating a tuna salad sandwich,
      when the awareness kicks in: *Well* this *is a little sad.*
The 2 p.m. light, weak through the trees, the crooked
      cloth napkin on my lap, crusted stains in the creases:

sad. The lunch looks almost professionally made:
      wheat bread lightly toasted, pickle perfectly placed,
just the right smattering of BBQ chips to fill out
      the gap of plate, but still I am conscious of a blight

on it all, something that makes me stop my chewing
      and notice the minute dirt speckling the carpet,
the cat hairs clinging to the couch, all the fine grains
      of my slovenliness. I feel too grown for my chair.

I am attacking my sandwich, really wolfing it down.
      Look at this barbecue pollen on my fingers. What is it
about lunch alone in my apartment that makes me
      feel I am not evolving into my life but becoming

sweepable, material for a dustpan? I can hear my mom
    in the silence: *None of my friends asks about you anymore.*
They all feel sorry for me; they think you're a failure.
    Where did you get that shirt? You look like an orphan.

Hard to disagree as I watch myself picking lint
    off my sweater and dropping it on a small helipad
of books to my left, licking the orange microbes
    from my fingertips and dipping them right back in

to the chips. Not my solitude but my narrowness
    bothers me, how eagerly my mind takes to this
focal field, delighting in the thought process
    of sandwich, pickle, chip, sandwich, pickle, chip,

then the variants, chip, pickle, sandwich, sandwich,
    chip, pickle, sometimes studying one of the components
at a slower chew, the tender, watery seeds tattooed
    on the inner skin of the pickle, the pockmarked canyon face

of a chip, when it could be studying the face
    of a man, looking for the inner skin of him, the seedbeds
there beneath the deadgrowth, combining that face
    with other, far-ranging things of the world in a process,

opening out from the cell of my apartment, taking in
    the Pentagon and penguins, car bombs, marriages,
mudslides and satellites, helicopters disintegrating—
    already I can see the details thinning as my mind reaches

its limits. But would there be any limits if I were living
    differently? If I let more people into my life, even those

I couldn't stand? People who act as if they've never had
    a feeling, never experienced a single moment

of transcendence—already I am doing it, keeping people out.
    I like to think I am generous, a jazzy Falstaff
to the world, but the dirt and silence of my apartment
    read like an indictment. My mom calls, I don't pick up.

Jason, are you there? Are you there? Jaaaay-son. I know you're there.
    Why don't you call *us once in a while, let us know we have*
a son. Gee. I finish my lunch, look at what I've left
    on my plate: dimpled pool of pickle juice, breadcrumbs,

splinters of chip. Part of me just wants to shut down,
    staring at that plate, feeling the pressure each small thing
is putting on it, asserting its last life before being swept
    by water down the drain. I don't know how my plate

manages it, holding so much scrappy smallness up,
    not just the smallness but the lame air above it, polluted
by my exhalations, unleavened by the light, but it does, it
    takes the weight, just as the table below it takes *its* weight,

the floor below the table, the table's, the whole apartment
    below me, the floor's; so that I *can* get up, clean my plate,
feel the majesty running in my veins again, gift of so
    much water from an unknown source, walk confidently

down the hall into the other room, type *Hello hello*
    at the top of a new page, beginning to get past myself,
the privilege of my emotion, this grainy actual window
    lacquering my vision: into the world ongoing

and vociferous, my fingertips tapping on the keys
        as on the smooth foreheads of cats, releasing me
into alleyways and nooks, the shade of tanks, prying open
        all the cabinets and closed doors, poking into trash.

Bon Chul Koo and the Hall of Fame

Jason Koo

Boston to Cleveland, ten hours with Dad in the car,
    and I'm thinking, How am I going to get through this,
remembering the last time we took a road trip,

    ten years ago, stadium-hopping through the Carolina League,
Class A ball, Kinston, Winston-Salem, Lynchburg
    and, of course, Durham, back in high school

when I was writing The Great American Novel
    about a starting pitcher on the Kinston Indians (which
began, "Ball four," and went on for 147

    single-spaced pages) and told him I needed to do
some on-site research, getting the exact dimensions
    of fields, the colors of uniforms, the feel and flavor

of local crowds, as well as a few good player names
    (such as Wonderful Monds, outfielder for the Bulls),
and he surprisingly agreed to take me, only to get

food poisoning on the second day of the trip
and spend the rest of it lying down in the backseat
	of the car or, if he had space, right there in the bleachers,

never saying, *Let's go home*, but not happy either,
	sighing every few miles we'd drive in silence, as if to say,
I'm barely able to eat a nacho, going to all these stupid games

	and still I cannot talk to my son, and even though I knew this,
I didn't break the silence, not even to say, *Thanks,*
	Dad, I appreciate what you're doing or *How're you feeling?*

and when he would break it, finally working up the courage
	to ask me a question, as if I were a famous poet
and he a lowly MFA student at a post-reading Q&A,

	articulating it in his head beforehand, getting the English
right, making slight clicking noises with his mouth
	as he prepared to speak, building up the right tension

of tongue against teeth, he would go for too much,
	asking, *So, Jay, what do you see yourself doing in ten years?*
or *How come you hate your mom?* and I would react badly,

	almost violently, and he would go back to sighing again,
and I would drift away. I don't want to repeat that
	silence yet don't exactly want to make the effort to talk,

would, truthfully, much rather be driving alone
	listening to one of my favorite bands, the music coalescing
with my mind over the landscape, my body going weightless

with speed, so I feed Dad questions about Korean
political history, our family, subjects I know he can talk about
    with pleasure and authority (and that I, now, am

genuinely interested in), letting him apply the gas
    to the conversation while I steer it with just a light grip
of thumb and finger, enjoying the opening space

    of two drives, and he's supplying me with dates, telling me
he was born in 1945, went to high school in the early
    sixties, served in Vietnam in the early seventies, married Mom

in 1973 and moved to America in 1974, none of which
    I knew, exactly, until now, growing up as I did not just
with gaps in my knowledge of family history

    but a whole obliterating fog, and as he talks I realize
how greedy I am for this knowledge, the simple facts
    of my past, notched in dates, the credentials of a twentieth-century

personal history, as if my self were a hole finally filling
    with the proper topsoil of information, the featherweight
seeds at the bottom abruptly catching into life,

    and I feed him questions at greater speed, with more reach,
asking about the Korean War, how badly our family
    was affected by it, whether we had to flee our homes,

whether anybody fought or (gulp) died, slightly afraid
    that he's going to reveal a whole substrata of slaughter
and suffering beneath my level of consciousness,

but he says, *No, our family was lucky, the war never reached us.*
Daegu was the last line of defense and it was never crossed.
Grandpa was a police chief so he didn't need to fight in the war.

And I'm thinking, Whew! but at the same time, Is that it?
wondering how I managed to evade history even in a country
literally split in half by it, almost disappointed

by the narrative, musing, This is not the Korean
American Experience publishers are looking for,
"may you never remember and may you never forget,"

that sort of thing, but digging Dad's no big deal attitude,
the cool way he recounts all this, the partly surprised
expression he wears on his face, as if he hasn't thought

about this stuff in years and is not exactly sure why
I'm asking. We're driving through New York State,
both of us feeling pretty good about ourselves, Dad damn near

chatty, but I start to feel that old familiar tug
toward silence again, the not-quite-ease of the conversation,
the buildup of so many previous car rides in silence

to and from the airport, school, violin and tennis lessons,
the silence more a father than my own father,
when he asks, *Do you want to go to Cooperstown?*

And my immediate reaction is No, not really, but I can
sense how much it means to him, how he's starting to believe
in the romance of the father-son relationship again

and needs to cement this feeling with a solid event,
and something tells me it's now or never, that if we don't go today
    we'll never go, and then I'll have to take *my* son,

so I say, *Sure—do we have time?* since it's Sunday, 3 p.m.,
    the museum likely closes at five and we still have a good
seven hours to go until home, and Dad needs to work

    tomorrow. He calculates, *Well, it's about twenty, thirty
minutes detour, and we have about thirty minutes to go before that,*
    which leaves us almost no time to see the museum

but we go for it, shooting through the countryside,
    and even though it's only supposed to be about a half hour
off our route, once we've made the turn for the museum

    it seems to take an eternity to get there, our car proceeding
more and more into nowhere, no cars before or behind
    us, and I joke, *What genius put the Baseball Hall of Fame*

way out here, trying to keep the mood light, since the landscape
    is no *Field of Dreams* (especially under a light rain
during the off-season) and I know Dad's sense of romance

    must be fading; but I think we're supposed to feel
we're moving back in time to a "mythic" America,
    leaving the evil of cities and the twentieth century behind,

though all I feel is anxious and out of place, the growing
    obviousness of our faces, and I'm half-hoping the museum
will be closed when we get there so we won't be seen.

But it's open. And Cooperstown itself is charming, all
the stores and restaurants baseball-themed—everything
        bats and balls!—and I can imagine this whole experience

would have been less threatening to me as a child,
        in the summer, in the sunlight. We approach the ticket
counter and I find myself bristling slightly at the man

        who addresses Dad in a louder-than-usual voice, *Hello, sir!*
How can we help you today? But I'm determined
        to feel welcome, so I smile, joke with him, ask

a few questions about the Hall in crisp English.
        Then Dad surprises me: *Could I have one adult, one senior citizen?*
At first I think he's trying to put one past this guy

        but then I realize he is that old, and for the first time
since coming home I look him steadily
        in the face, notice the skin is paler, blotchier

than I remember it, the already thin hair not just thinner
        but *weaker*, the scalp more glazed. We take the man's advice
and start on the second floor to make sure we see

        the permanent exhibition before the museum closes,
the window display of history from the nineteenth century
        to the present, all the browning artifacts, the long cool bats

of sluggers, Ruth, Gehrig, DiMaggio, the homerun balls
        notching a number, 60, 61, 714, the no-hitter balls all lined up
neatly together on a wall, some smudged and greasy,

others surprisingly clean, each bearing the whorled imprint
of its author somewhere in the cowhide and seams,
    the tightening of a grip, fastball, forkball, slider, erosion

of oil and saliva; but as I'm looking at all this I'm struck
    by how much effort of imagination it takes to get inside
the history, how groomed and clinical this history is,

    the objects mute, almost helpless in their Plexiglas cages,
robbed of movement, the real record of the game,
    the signature of each swing and delivery upon the air,

the weight shifts, positionings, balances, the digging
    of cleated toes into dirt, the pitch-to-pitch, inning-to-inning,
game-to-game, season-to-season accumulation of tension

    and release in memory—so that I want to dump this all
into stadiums, foul the objects off into stands,
    fleck them with beer, mustard, relish, the dirt and germs

from each grasping hand. Nothing feels organic, least of all
    me in my black leather jacket and shoes, leaning in to read
each accompanying paragraph of information (I learn

    a pop-up was once called a "skyrocket"), the objects
kept from me not only by the glass but by my image
    on top of the glass and then my glasses on top of that.

Dad falls behind, fussing with his camera. He catches up
    to ask if I can pry open the plastic packaging
on a battery and, when I can't, goes downstairs to seek out

scissors. He returns, triumphant, then has me move station
to station to create a storybook of our lives against
    the century: first, Cy Young (a Cleveland Spider),

Bob Feller (ace of the last Cleveland Champs
    in '48), Mickey Mantle (my favorite legend as a kid),
and then the Thurman Munson Yankees of the seventies,

    the team my parents followed when they lived in New York
and I was born. I think back to Cleveland, nights in the kitchen
    when Mom would let me listen to the game on the radio

while she cooked, going over the heroics of Guidry, Jackson,
    Lou Piniella (*When he came up, we'd all go* Loooooo), helping me
to believe in a possible immortality for my woeful Indians,

    a time when I cared about each game with an intensity
that made Dad scowl (*Jay, it's just* gayyym), praying before
    every Cory Snyder at bat (who hit .236), not wanting to leave

games until the final pitch (even the 17–0 rout we attended
    as a family), believing each missed moment took a brick
out of the next, that I could build out of baseball

    an edifice of meaning to house my lonely, unimportant self.
I would have given anything then for Dad to do
    what he's doing now, taking me to *Cooperstown!*

But he always just seemed to be annoyed with me,
    and Mom, if anything, was the more indulgent of the two,
and she was not indulgent. Now Dad needs this

more than me, and I try to wait patiently as he takes
one picture after another with his digital camera,
    often asking me to re-pose when the picture turns out

badly. I look too tall in all the images, overdressed,
    not awkward enough, and I start to wonder if it's too late
for father and son, the Hall closing, a long drive through the dark

    still ahead, but Dad looks so happy, oblivious to all
the disappointment dusting his shoulders, trusting
    in his camera to lock our experience into glossy rectangles,

that I can believe, for a moment, in the rightness of our presence,
    the confirmation of the country around us,
until a rude old woman comes up to me and says, *Sir, we're CLOSING*,

    as I try to catch a glimpse of the inductee plaques.
I say, *But we still have five minutes*, and she says,
    Don't you want to go to the gift shop? and I storm out

thinking—I can't help it—racist, small town, white trash,
    where the hell does *she* have to be at this hour, just wanting
to get in the car and leave—but Dad wants to take

    a few more pictures outside the museum. I stand there
stewing in the flash, thinking I'll say something when
    she comes out, like *Don't you understand going to Cooperstown*

is a pilgrimage? But when she does come out, we're still
    taking pictures, and she doesn't even look at us, just waddles
on her merry way home, and I look past her at the lights

twinkling the streets, the windowfronts softened by the rain,
and understand that confronting her would disrupt
    this quiet passage home she likely looks forward to every day,

the clean pine air fresh on her skin, a comfortable couch
    and a night of good television on up ahead, and the anger
of an Asian in this context just seems ridiculous . . .

    I turn back to Dad, smile sincerely this time, defiantly, trying
to hold it as he troubles over the angle, the background,
    and a car drives by and sees us Asians with a camera

Chicken & Stars

T Kira Madden

My mother is late. She is often late picking me up from school these days, but today she is later.

I am in the seventh grade, waiting outside under the palms. I have recently decided that I am depressed. I don't look like any other kids in Boca Raton—my black hair, high cheeks—and people tell me I smell like a Nike factory. I want to be white. I want to have a nickname, a skirt rolled up at the waistline, smooth knees. I want to be pretty enough to kidnap. Murdered in an act of passion. Worth that much.

I always tell my mother to *stay in the car* at dismissal, *don't ever, ever get out to look for me*, because more than anything else, I want to make friends.

Today my mother is later than late, and I think she must have fallen asleep somewhere. My mother and father have been in their Other Place lately—the place they go when the sweating glasses come out, the pipes and cigarettes that smell funny. I like to call them magic sticks, because it is only a matter of minutes between the blaze of the sticks and that Other Place, where my parents' voices change pitch and their eyes bulge with colors and their throats bob differently.

It wasn't always like this.

We used to have car rides, the three of us, clasped fingers on the center console. Music. Cigarettes flipped out the window in scabbed trails of light.

It was like that.

I saw one of the magic sticks in a commercial recently. In the commercial, two boys swivel around in office chairs, smoking. One of the boys accidentally blasts the other boy in the face with a gun. I asked, *Mom? Is marijuana one of your magic smokes?* She said *yes.* I said, *Did you know it is a DRUG and it will KILL you?* She said all commercials want to do is make everybody walk around the world looking the same, acting boring. A patty-cake world, she says. And there is no sameness about us.

The other stuff I learned about from Whitney Houston on the news. I ask my mother about this, but she says it's not the same thing. Sometimes she buys a white powdered ibuprofen from the pharmacy and mixes it into her ice tea. She says, *See? Look. Read the package, it's harmless. This is what you saw.*

I am beginning to know better.

MY MOTHER'S BLACK truck grumbles up around the corner. Her truck is not fancy. It has dents all over, a few of my horse ribbons sun bleached, tangled, hanging from the rearview mirror. My mother likes to call this car "Big Beau," petting the dashboard affectionately.

I use a suitcase on wheels as a backpack, because my spine can't handle the weight. I roll it over to her car, yank the handle of it when the wheels snag on the sidewalk cracks. I open the backdoor of the car, chuck the suitcase in, *It's about time*, slam the door. I open the passenger door and slide in.

My mother's face is battered, blue. Her bottom lip drags down as if an invisible hanger were hanging her clothes on it. Her eyes are almost entirely sealed shut. Purple marks the size of boxed chocolates cover her arms. She reaches for my hand and holds it.

There was a fight, she says.

HE'S ASLEEP ON the couch when we arrive home. This is his place in our house. My father has never been a bedroom father, a kitchen father, a backyard father, an office father, a roof father; he is a father of the living room couch. I wonder if he was always this way, with his other family, that other life none of us are supposed to mention. He keeps a worn photo of two boys in the slip of his wallet, boys in the sun, playing ball. Even though their faces are crinkled as petals, I can see that they have his nose.

Now my father is facedown on the pink, leather cushions and I sit down next to him. His left arm dangles. I lift it and let it drop. He feels dead to me. I love him more than anyone I've ever met.

Beneath his arm, on the floor, is his crown-sized ashtray overflowing with orange filters. It's almost beautiful this way, like an exotic flower or a Bloomin' Onion from Outback. When my father is too drunk to walk or drive, he lights each and every butt in the ashtray. He sucks at them between his fingers like he's drinking a milkshake through a cocktail straw. Around the couch are several empty vodka bottles, a cracked cobalt glass, one hundred dollar bills, a smashed mirror. My father doesn't move no matter how much I touch him.

I watch my mother fill a cup with water from the kitchen sink, holding steady to the counter. We use well water here. It smells like cheese water, the kind that collects in the refrigerator drawers, so we plug our noses to drink. My mother points over to our pantry, and I walk over to it. The white door hangs off its hinges like a loose tooth. The shelves inside are split perfectly in half, *That's where my face went*, all the screws yanked from the walls. I lift a can of Campbell's soup from the pile of them on the floor, *Chicken & Stars*, twist it around in my hand. It is easier to look at your favorite soup than it is at blood. Campbell's soup, my every meal, the first thing I learned how to make for myself. A can of Campbell's is exactly one pound, it says so on the label, and this is the measurement by which I weigh everything else in the world. I weigh eighty-one soup cans. My mother stares into the pantry, shaking her head. She sips slow and gently from her glass, careful not to spill.

What's all this? I say.

My mother points to each shelf and there are noises now—words coming out between each cry: *money, investment, snapped, pushed, and then, the soup cans, the money.* I ask her to slow down. She says my father has been binging on his special stuff and hasn't slept in over three days. The fight started in the kitchen, simple at first, before he took her by the wrists and didn't know what to do with all his love. She says things like this all the time lately, words like *love* to describe our suffering. She doesn't know if I'm old enough to hold the truth in my hands, to measure that.

I hug my mother at the kitchen sink, let her cry into my shoulder. She leaves black and blue and red there on my white, crisp uniform. I am only five two but we are the same size by now. From a slight distance, people mistake us for sisters.

I send my mother to her bedroom and tell her I will heat up two cans of Campbell's for dinner. I pluck them from the top of the pile. I crank the can opener till the aluminum exhales. I smash the pots and pans around, bang them into each other like gongs. The stove coils throb red. The stars boil. I open and close the dishwasher in a crashing swing, like I'm bowling. I want my father to wake up so badly, for him to tell me his side of the story, to bury his head in his hands, apologizing, changed. He doesn't move.

WHAT ARE WE *going to do?* my mother says, in the bathtub. It is one in the morning, and my father is still asleep. She has been in here so long the water's gone cold, and I turn the Hot lever every few minutes.

What do we do now?

I wash my mother's body with a sea sponge. I can see every vertebra of her spine like this, curled over, her head down. She holds her shins close to her chest as if to give the water more room. There are no more wounds to clean, nothing I missed, but I can tell the sponge is comforting to her. It's a quiet touch. I dab it across her shoulders, wring it over her midnight clumps of hair.

Please don't cry anymore, I say. *We don't have to do anything.*

Has he ever hurt you? she wants to know.

He hasn't. He has never touched either one of us before today. Not like this.

Once, when I was younger, he was in such a spell that he came after me and my mother with a wooden baseball bat. He said he would kill us. I think he thought we were somebody else, some other people who had hurt him. I think he hoped we were.

We ran into the bedroom and locked the door. My mother screamed, held me to her chest. He beat the door with the bat until the entire thing splintered into tooth-picks. He fell asleep on the tile floor outside the bedroom, the handle still in his hand. He woke up and yelled, *Who broke this bat? I paid for this!*

That night, I asked my mother why he even owned a bat—he doesn't play baseball.

He bought it to protect us, she said.

I don't bring up this incident.

WHEN MY MOTHER gets out of the bath I wrap a towel around her from behind. I dip Q-tips into the mouths of ointment bottles and make her wounds look glossy. I pull a T-shirt over her head, lift rose-patterned pants up and over her body. Her face is still, staring. I help her into bed, right foot, then the left, walk to the freezer, little fistfuls of ice in a grocery bag. I spin the bag, knot it, pass my father's body on the way back to her room.

I press the cool bag to her cheeks, her eyes.

I say, *It's okay, MomMom.*

This is a habit of mine. When I love somebody more than I've ever loved them, I repeat their name, double and triple it. I say it till it's somebody else's name. Years later, when my father dies, *Daddy Daddy Daddy My Daddy* is the only thing I will say.

My mother holds my hands against the ice against her face. She says, *You want to get out of here?*

MY MOTHER PACKS her bag, and I go into my room, pack my own. I don't have much to take: my diary, a book on witchcraft, a book on Drew Barrymore, my stuffed tiger, Tia, a pair of riding boots and spurs. I spill out a drawer full of underwear, silk pajamas. I drop all of my things into a black garbage bag. I have always wanted to run away. I have always wanted this rush, the swing of my arms around objects that I will pack to remind myself of the way things used to be. More than anything, though, I have always ached for the runaway's return home, like in the movies—parents with their outstretched hands, heavy blankets with which to wrap you, the home-cooked meal with plates warmed in the oven, the tired, grateful faces. I have always wanted the reunion.

My mother carries our bags to the car. She does not even look into the living room as she passes.

I walk to the couch, scoot my father's body over. The back of his neck looks like roast beef, hot to the touch. I run my fingers through his sandy hair. I say, *You made a really big mess this time. We gotta go.*

My mother honks Big Beau three times. I kiss my father on the back of his skull, set the alarm, and run.

MY MOTHER SAYS little in the car. She looks strong, her temples bulging, her chin up. She gets like this when things are at their worst: upturned, dignified. She looks the facts in the face, my mother. She hands me a map and a new highlighter from the dash, says, *Find the best route out of here.*

An hour later, she calls up my half brothers, the other boys, leaves a message: *You're on your own for the intervention. I'm gone.* I have never heard this word—*intervention*—and I ask her what she means. It is something that could save my father, she says, something they were planning for this week. My brothers were going to fly all the way to Boca Raton for this. They wrote parting speeches about missed T-ball games, flute recitals. They have what she calls *Bottom Lines* to offer. She repeats herself, over and over, like she is trying to believe it herself, *This will save his life, it will save him, it will.* This explanation shocks me because I never knew he was dying.

We make one stop on our drive to Seven Devils, North Carolina, where we will hide out on a mountain for one month. My mother feels too tired to go on, but I am awake. Somewhere near Jacksonville she pulls into a motel. She tells me to hush. She finds a metal gate to the swimming pool, lifts the peg from its hole. My mother says, *Go ahead, jump in, you have more clothes in the car. Tire yourself out,* she says. *We have a long way to go.*

Everyone knows I don't know how to swim but I have always loved the water. I like it here in the shallow end with my T-shirt bubbling up in a tie-dye dome. In the water, I can be a ballerina, a gymnast, anybody else. I can do things like balance on my toes. I swish around and flick the surface until my mother falls asleep on a lawn chair. She looks like she is sunbathing even though it is still dark out. Ripples of aqua light flick across her bare legs, her bruises.

I wonder if my father has woken up by now. If he has checked the bedrooms, the car.

I kick my legs as hard as I can in the water. Take a breath. There is nothing I love more than to sink to the bottom of a pool. See how long my body can keep itself from rising.

For Mitsuye Yamada on Her 90th Birthday

Marilyn Chin

They say we bitch revolutionaries never go out of fashion
Wearing floppy hats and huge wedgy shoes
A feather bandolera and a lethal python

Sometimes we wear a fro perm cause we hate our straight
    hair
Sometimes we wear it straight to the ankles like Murasaki

I bleached mine purple to look like Kwannon Psylocke
Maxine's beaming, like the Goddess of Nainai temple
A cross between Storm, the X-girl and Ahsoka Tano

We love our laser eyes, our Yoko granny glasses are dizzy!
Short women poets unite! Revolution ain't just style
It's destiny!

We will make a comeback, we always do
You and Nellie and Meryl making a rad film
Janice in a miniskirt testifying at Glide Church

Hisaye still svelte with her bluesy magpie clarinet
Wakako dancing to a Taiko drum and Sheila E
Rats! The FBI's rifling through your garbage again
Bastards are after your studded bell-bottoms and a *raison
d'etre*!

Boys, you can have them, even my embroidered hot pants!
We'll all drag it with Cher, sporting black bangs of
resistance
We'll emolliate our bras at the Atlantic City Boardwalk
Listening to Buffy Sainte-Marie and fusionist Jazz bash
Angela Davis and Ché, spinning revolution in our brain
When an album was a symphony
Not a blip on a Spotify Lumumba
We'll lip-sync to Marvin Gaye and mash to Soul Train

And stage a sing-along-sit-in with Odetta!
Forget about Dylan, he's a whiner
Where's Jamie Baldwin, where's Dick Gregory?
Soak our gall with bell hooks and Barbara Christian
Oh sweet Jesus! Allen G's chasing your nephew around
the Bodega

Imagine the long march with Mao or MLK or Harvey
Milk
Study the physiognomy of foreheads of twisted fate
I was a naïve girl-poet wearing wet nappies
While you were fighting the WRA
And Executive order 9066

Where is Manzanar, where is Topaz, where is Tule Lake?

Wherefore, Gila River and Heart Mountain?
Sound like vacation hotbeds
Where rich white retirees play bingo and waltz!

They whisked your father away deep into the night
Auctioned your house off to some sleazy Hollywood exec

Hell, nobody knew
We were sucking on the tithes of the early Renaissance

Drove a pink Buick to a poetry camp called Woodstock
Ate hashish with Sylvia Plath's ghost at an Irvine bus stop
Binged on Neruda's psilocybin odes at Bullfrog

(Meanwhile, let's mock a Whitmanesque praise poem at
    the Iowa workshop)
They say don't write political, girl, just hang yourself with
    abjection!

Let's bum rush a haiku party with conceptual artists
How long can you stare at a Urinal, for god's sake!

What's the difference between the old regime and the
    new regime?
The new one has lightsabers and a bona fide Wookiee

I confess, I was faking it, I was a revolutionary freak!
Did a hunger strike with Cesar Chavez cause he's sexy
Mao was a new crush, Marx whetted the yoni,
I was just a horny girl poet, please forgive me

I binged on duck noodles on Clement Street after sucking
    down a bong
Wrote ten thousand letters for Amnesty International
    high on shrooms

But I confess that on the second day of a relapse
I threw up alphabet soup all over my slutty girlfriend's
    Austin Healey
She thought she was a dykey James Bond, oh really!
I lied that the dog did it!

    For your 90th birthday, my dear Auntie Mitsuye
    I write you this silly poem
    not counting syllables, accentuals or diphthongs
    not making it sing or pulling a long conceit
    out of a colonialist' ass-
    anine simulacra, or trying to rap with the youngsters
    wearing a Compton cap. Or break-dancing
    for an endstop
    Jeremiad

    Not trying to make a hybridity lipidity sonnet
    the volta is loving   my vulva   lapping vodka   on the
        Volga!
    not a long religious rant about a pussy Jeoffry,
    nor dogging the doggy dogma dharma
    who left her yellow mark all over the doggity diaspora
    not lifting a hind leg   but squatting in the morning
        glory
    like a real Asian Diva

They paid you
20,000 for your civil liberties
A mule and ten acres of scorched paddy apotheosis

They slapped a cruel judgment on the new century
There will always be another brown girl to hate
Rape her village, burn her wedding veil, shoot her in the
    face
Plant a black flag on her sweet soul
Strap her down with a ticking heart-bomb and show no
    mercy

Auntie Mitsuye
No more redress, no more reparations, no worries about
    legacy
Let's live raunchily and have the last laugh

Somewhere in a faraway kingdom
We shall eat that magical pill of immortality

You and me and Emily D.
Gnawing ganja cookies, dreaming on our backs
And Bessie's crooning her heart out on a crappy 8-track!

The Faintest Echo of Our Language

Chang-Rae Lee

My mother died on a bare January morning in our family room, the room all of us favored. She died upon the floor-bed I had made up for her, on the old twin mattress from the basement that I slept on during my childhood. She died with her husband kneeling like a penitent boy at her ear, her daughter tightly grasping the soles of her feet, and her son vacantly kissing the narrow, brittle fingers of her hand. She died with her best friend weeping quietly above her, and with her doctor unmoving and silent. She died with no accompaniment of music or poetry or prayer. She died with her eyes and mouth open. She died blind and speechless. She died, as I knew she would, hearing the faintest echo of our language at the last moment of her mind.

That, I think, must be the most ardent of moments.

I keep considering it, her almost-ending time, ruminating the nameless, impossible mood of its ground, toiling over it like some desperate topographer whose final charge is to survey only the very earth beneath his own shifting feet. It is an improbable task. But I am continually traveling through that terrible province, into its dark region where I see again and again the strangely vast scene of her demise.

I see.

Here before me (as I now enter my narrative moment), the dying-room, our family room. It has changed all of a sudden—it is as if there has been a shift in its proportion, the scale horribly off. The room seems to open up too fast, as though the walls were shrinking back and giving way to the wood flooring that seems to unfurl before us like runway carpet. And there, perched on this crest somehow high above us, her body so flat and quiet in the bed, so resident, so immovable, caught beneath the somber light of these unwinking lamps, deep among the rolls of thick blankets, her furniture pushed to the walls without scheme, crowded in by the medicines, syringes, clear tubing, machines, shot through with the full false hopes of the living and the fearsome calls of the dead, my mother resides at an unfathomable center where the time of my family will commence once again.

No one is speaking. Except for the babble of her machines the will of silence reigns in this house. There is no sound, no word or noise, that we might offer up to fill this place. She sleeps for a period, then reveals her live eyes. For twelve or eighteen hours we have watched her like this, our legs and feet deadened from our squatting, going numb with tired blood. We sometimes move fitfully about, sighing and breathing low, but no one strays too far. The living room seems too far, the upstairs impossible. There is nothing, nothing at all outside of the house. I think perhaps it is snowing but it is already night and there is nothing left but this room and its light and its life.

People are here earlier (when?), a group from the church, the minister and some others. I leave her only then, going through the hallway to the kitchen. They say prayers and sing hymns. I do not know the high Korean words (I do not know many at all), and the music of their songs does not comfort me. Their one broad voice seems to be calling, beckoning something, bared in some kind of sad invitation. It is an acknowledgment. These people, some of them complete strangers, have come in from the outside to sing and pray over my mother, their overcoats still bearing the chill of the world.

I am glad when they are finished. They seem to sing too loud; I think they are hurting her ears—at least, disturbing her fragile state. I keep thinking, as if in her mind: *I'm finally going to get my sleep, my sleep after all this raw and painful waking, but I'm not meant to have it. But sing, sing.*

When the singers finally leave the room and quickly put on their coats I see that the minister's wife has tears in her eyes: so it is that clear. She looks at me; she wants to say something to me but I can see from her stunted expression that the words will not come. Though I wanted them earlier to cease I know already how quiet and empty it will feel when they are gone. But we are all close together now in the foyer, touching hands and hugging each other, our faces flushed, not talking but assenting to what we know, moving our lips in a silent, communal speech. For what we know, at least individually, is still unutterable, dwelling peacefully in the next room as the unnameable, lying there and waiting beside her, and yet the feeling among us is somehow so formidable and full of hope, and I think if I could hear our thoughts going round the room they would speak like the distant report of ten thousand monks droning the song of the long life of the earth.

LONG, LONG LIFE. Sure life. It had always seemed that way with us, with our square family of four, our destiny clear to me and my sister when we would sometimes speak of ourselves, not unlucky like those friends of ours whose families were wracked with ruinous divorce or drinking or disease—we were untouched, maybe untouchable, we'd been safe so far in our isolation in this country, in the country of our own house smelling so thickly of crushed garlic and seaweed and red chili pepper, as if that piquant wreath of scent from our mother's kitchen protected us and our house, kept at bay the persistent ghosts of the land who seemed to visit everyone else.

Of course, we weren't perfectly happy or healthy. Eunei and I were sometimes trouble to my parents, we were a little lazy and spoiled (myself more than my sister), we didn't study hard enough in school (though we always received the highest marks), we chose questionable friends, some from broken families, and my father, who worked fourteen hour days as a young psychiatrist, already suffered from mild hypertension and high cholesterol.

If something happened to him, my mother would warn me, if he were to die, we'd lose everything and have to move back to Korea where the living was hard and crowded and where all young men spent long years in the military. Besides, our family in Korea—the whole rest of it still there (for we were the lone émigrés)—so longed for us, missed us terribly, and the one day each year when we phoned they would plead for our return. What we could do, my mother said, to aid our father and his struggle in this country, was to relieve his worry over us, release him from that awful burden through our own hard work which would give him ease of mind and help him not to die.

My mother's given name was Inja, although I never once called her that, nor ever heard my sister or even my father address her so. I knew from a young age that her name was Japanese in style and origin, from the time of Japan's military occupation of Korea, and I've wondered since why she chose never to change it to an authentic Korean name, why her mother or father didn't change the names of all their daughters after the liberation. My mother often showed open enmity for the Japanese, her face seeming to ash over when she spoke of her memories, that picture of the platoon of lean-faced soldiers burning books and scrolls in the center of her village still aglow in my head (but from her or where else I don't know), and how they tried to erase what was Korean by criminalizing the home language and history by shipping slave labor, draftees, and young Korean women back to Japan and its other Pacific colonies. How they taught her to speak in Japanese. And as she would speak of her childhood, of the pretty, stern-lipped girl (that I only now see in tattered rust-edged photos) who could only whisper to her sisters in the midnight safety of their house the Korean words folding inside her all day like mortal secrets, I felt the same burning, troubling lode of utter pride and utter shame still jabbing at the sweet belly of her life, that awful gem, about who she was and where her mother tongue and her land had gone.

She worried all the time that I was losing my Korean. When I was in my teens, she'd get attacks of despair and urgency and say she was going to send me back to Korea for the next few summers to learn the language again. What she didn't know was that it had been whole years since I had lost the language, had left it somewhere for good, perhaps from the time I won a prize in the first grade for reading the most books in my class. I must have read fifty books. She had helped me then, pushed me to read and then read more to exhaustion until I fell asleep, because she warned me that if I didn't learn English I wouldn't be anybody and couldn't really live here like a true American. *Look at me*, she'd say, offering herself as a sad example, *look how hard it is for me to shop for food or speak to your teachers, look how shameful I am, how embarrassing.*

Her words frightened me. But I was so proud of myself and my prolific reading, particularly since the whole year before in kindergarten I could barely speak a word of English. I simply listened. We played mostly, anyway, or drew pictures. When the class sang songs I'd hum along with the melody and silently mouth the strange and difficult words. My best friend was another boy in the class who also knew no English, a boy named Tommy. He was Japanese. Of course, we couldn't speak to each other but it didn't matter; somehow we found a way to communicate through gestures and funny faces and laughter, and we became friends. I think we both sensed we were the smartest kids in the class. We'd sit off by ourselves with this one American girl who liked us best and play house around a wooden toy oven. I've forgotten her name. She'd hug us when we "came home from work," her two mute husbands, and she would sit us down at the little table and work a pan at the stove and bring it over and feed us. We pretended to eat her food until we were full and then she'd

pull the two of us sheepish and cackling over to the shag-
gy remnants of carpet that she'd laid down, and we'd all go
to sleep, the girl nestled snuggly between Tommy and me,
hotly whispering in our ears the tones of a night music she
must have heard echoing through her own house.

Later that year, after a parents' visiting day at school, my
mother told me that Tommy and his family were moving
away. I didn't know how she'd found that out, but we went
to his house one day, and Tommy and his mother greeted
us at the door. They had already begun packing, and there
were neatly stacked boxes and piles of newspapers pushed
to a corner of their living room. Tommy immediately led
me outside to his swing set and we horsed about for an
hour before coming back in, and I looked at my mother
and Tommy's mother sitting upright and formally in the
living room, a tea set and plate of rice cookies between
them on the coffee table. The two of them weren't really
talking, more smiling and waiting for us. And then from
Tommy's room full of toys, I began to hear a conversation,
half of it in profoundly broken English, the other half in
what must have been Japanese, at once breathy and stacca-
to, my mother's version of it in such shreds and remnants
that the odd sounds she made seemed to hurt her throat as
they were called up. After we said goodbye and drove away
in the car, I thought she seemed quiet and sad for me,
and so I felt sadder still, though now I think that it was
she who was moved and saddened by the visit, perhaps by
her own act. For the momentary sake of her only son and
his departing friend, she was willing to endure those two
tongues of her shame, one present, one past. Language,
sacrifice, the story never ends.

Inside our house (wherever it was, for we moved several times when I was young) she was strong and decisive and proud; even my father deferred to her in most matters, and when he didn't it seemed that she'd arranged it that way. Her commandments were stiff, direct. When I didn't listen to her, I understood that the disagreement was my burden, my problem. But outside, in the land of always-talking strangers and other Americans, my mother would lower her steadfast eyes, she'd grow mute, even her supremely solemn and sometimes severe face would dwindle with uncertainty; I would have to speak to a mechanic for her, I had to call the school myself when I was sick, I would write out notes to neighbors, the postman, the paper carrier. Do the work of voice. Negotiate *us*, with this here, now. I remember often fuming because of it, this one of the recurring pangs of my adolescence, feeling frustrated with her inabilities, her misplacement, and when she asked me one morning to call up the bank for her I told her I wouldn't do it and suggested that she needed "to practice" the language anyway.

Gracious god. I wished right then for her to slap me. She didn't. Couldn't. She wanted to scream something, I could tell, but bit down on her lip as she did and hurried upstairs to my parents' bedroom where I knew she found none of this trouble with her words. There she could not fail, nor could I. In that land, her words sang for her, they did good work, they pleaded for my life, shouted entreaties, ecstasies, they could draw blood if they wanted, and they could offer grace, and they could kiss.

BUT NOW—AND I think, *right now* (I am discovering several present tenses)—she is barely conscious, silent.

Her eyes are very small and black. They are only half-

272

opened. I cannot call up their former kind shade of brown. Not because I am forgetting, but because it is impossible to remember. I think I cannot remember the first thing about her. I am not amnesiac because despite all this *I know everything about her.* But the memories are like words I cannot call up, the hidden vocabularies of our life together. I cannot remember, as I will in a later narrative time, her bright red woolen dress with the looming black buttons that rub knobbly and rough against my infant face; I cannot remember, as I will soon dream it, the way her dark clean hair falls on me like a cloak when she lifts me from the ground; I cannot remember—if I could ever truly forget—the look of those soft Korean words as they play on her face when she speaks to me of honor and respect and devotion.

This is a maddening state, maybe even horrifying, mostly because I think I must do anything but reside in this very place and time and moment, that to be able to remember her now—something of her, anything—would be to forget the present collection of memories, this inexorable gathering of future remembrances. I want to disband this accumulation, break it apart before its bonds become forever certain.

She wears only a striped pajama top. Her catheter tube snakes out from between the top buttons. We know she is slipping away, going fast now, so someone, not me, disconnects the line to her food and water. The tube is in her way. These last moments will not depend on it. Her line to the morphine, though, is kept open and clear and running.

This comforts me. I have always feared her pain and I will to the end. Before she received the automatic pump that gives her a regular dosage of the drug I would shoot her with a needle at least five times a day.

For some reason I wish I could do it now:

I will have turned her over gently. She will moan. Every movement except the one mimicking death is painful. I fit the narrow white syringe with a small needle, twisting it on tight. I then pull off the needle's protective plastic sheath. (Once, I will accidently jab myself deep in the ring finger and while I hold gauze to the bloody wound she begins to cry. I am more careful after that.) Now I fill the syringe to the prescribed line, and then I go several lines past it; I always give her a little more than what the doctors tell us, and she knows of this transgression, my little gift to her, to myself. I say I am ready and then she lifts her hips so I can pull down her underwear to reveal her buttocks.

I know her body. The cancer in her stomach is draining her, hungrily sucking the life out of her, but the liquid food she gets through the tube has so many calories that it bloats her, giving her figure the appearance of a young girl who likes sweets too well. Her rump is full, fleshy, almost healthy-looking except for the hundreds of needlemarks. There is almost no space left. I do not think it strange anymore that I see her naked like this. Even the sight of her pubic hair, darkly coursing out from under her, is now, if anything, of a certain more universal reminiscence, a kind of metonymic reminder that not long before she was truly in the world, one of its own, a woman, fully alive, historical, a mother, a bearer of life.

I feel around for unseeable bruises until I find a spot we can both agree on.

"Are you ready?" I say. "I'm going to poke."

"*Gu-rhaeh*," she answers, which, in this context, means some cross between "That's right" and "Go ahead, damn it."

I jab and she sucks in air between her teeth, wincing.

"*Ay, ah-po.*" It hurts.

"A lot?" I ask, pulling the needle out as straight as I can, to avoid bruising her. We have the same exchange each time; but each time there arises a renewed urgency, and then I know I know nothing of her pains.

I NEVER DREAMED of them. Imagined them. I remember writing short stories in high school with narrators or chief characters of unidentified race and ethnicity. Of course this meant they were white, everything in my stories was some kind of white, though I always avoided physical descriptions of them or passages on their lineage and they always had cryptic first names like Garlo or Kram.

Mostly, though, they were figures who (I thought) could appear in an *authentic* short story, *belong* to one, that no reader would notice anything amiss in them, as if they'd inhabited forever those visionary landscapes of tales and telling, where a snow still falls faintly and faintly falls over all of Joyce's Ireland, that great muting descent, all over Hemingway's Spain, and Cheever's Suburbia, and Bellow's City of Big Shoulders.

I was to breach that various land, become its finest citizen and furiously speak its dialects. And it was only with one story that I wrote back then, in which the character is still unidentified but his mother is Asian (maybe even Korean), that a cleaving happened. That the land broke open at my feet. At the end of the story, the protagonist returns to his parents' home after a long journey; he is ill, feverish, and his mother tends to him, offers him cool drink, compresses, and she doesn't care where he's been in the strange wide country. They do not speak; she simply knows that he is home.

NOW I DAB the pinpoint of blood. I'm trying to be careful.

"*Gaen-cha-na*," she says. *It is fine.*

"Do you need anything?"

"*Ggah*," she says, flitting her hand, "*kul suh.*" *Go, go and write.*

"What do you want? Anything, anything."

"*In-jeh na jal-leh.*" *Now I want to sleep.*

"Okay, sleep. Rest. What?"

"*Boep-bo.*" *Kiss.*

"Kiss."

Kiss.

This will be our language always. To me she speaks in a child's Korean, and for her I speak that same child's English. We use only the simplest words. I think it strange that throughout this dire period we necessarily speak like this. Neither of us has ever grown up or out of this language; by virtue of speech I am forever her perfect little boy, she my eternal righteous guide. We are locked in a time. I love her, and I cannot grow up. And if all mothers and sons converse this way I think the communication must remain for the most part unconscious; for us, however, this speaking is everything we possess. And although I wonder if our union is handicapped by it I see also the minute discoveries in the mining of the words. I will say to her as naturally as I can—as I could speak only years before as a child—*I love you, Mother*, and then this thing will happen, the diction will take us back, bridge this moment with the others, remake this time so full and real. And in our life together, our strange language is the bridge and all that surrounds it; language is the brook streaming through it; it is the mossy stones, the bank, the blooming canopy above, the ceaseless sound, the sky. It is the last earthly thing we have.

MY MOTHER, NO longer connected to her machine, lies on the bed on the floor. Over the last few hours she suffers brief fits and spasms as if she is chilled. She stirs when we try to cover her with the blanket. She kicks her legs to get it off. Something in her desires to be liberated. Finally we take it away. Let her be, we think. And now, too, you can begin to hear the indelicate sound of her breathing; it is audible, strangely demonstrative. Her breath resonates in this house, begins its final cadence. She sounds as though she were inhaling and exhaling for the very first time. Her body shudders with that breath. My sister tries to comfort her by stroking her arms. My mother groans something unintelligible, though strangely I say to myself for her, *Leave me alone, all of you. I am dying. At last I am dying.* But then I stroke her, too. She keeps shuddering, but it is right.

What am I thinking? Yes. It is that clear. The closer she slips away, down into the core of her being, what I think of as an origin, a once-starting point, the more her body begins to protest the happening, to try to hold down, as I am, the burgeoning, blooming truth of the moment.

For we think we know how this moment will be. Each of us in this room has been elaborating upon it from the very moment we gained knowledge of her illness. This is the way it comes to me, but I think we have written, each of us, the somber epic novel of her death. It has taken two and one-half years and we are all nearly done. I do not exactly know of the others' endings. Eunei, my sister (if I may take this liberty), perhaps envisioning her mother gently falling asleep, never really leaving us, simply dreams of us and her life for the rest of ever. I like that one.

My father, a physician, may write that he finally saves her, that he spreads his hands on her belly where the cancer is mighty and lifts it out from her with one ultimate, sovereign effort. Sometimes (and this ought not be attributed to him) I think that his entire life has come down to this struggle against the palpable fear growing inside of his wife. And after she dies, he will cry out in a register I have never heard from his throat as he pounds his hand on the hardwood above her colorless head, *"Eeh-guh-moy-yah? Eeh-guh-moy-yah?" What is this? What is this?* It—the cancer, the fear—spites him, mocks him, this doctor who is afraid of blood. It—this cancer, this happening, this time—is the shape of our tragedy, the cruel sculpture of our life and family.

In the ending to my own story, my mother and I are alone. We are always alone. And one thing is certain; she needs to say something only to me. That is why I am there. Then she speaks to me, secretly. What she says exactly is unclear; it is enough, somehow, that she and I are together, alone, apart from everything else, while we share this as yet unborn and momentary speech. The words are neither in Korean nor in English, languages which in the end we cannot understand. I hear her anyway. But now we can smile and weep and laugh. We can say goodbye to each other. We can kiss, unflinching, on our mouths.

Then she asks if I might carry her to the window that she might see the new blossoms of our cherry tree. I lift her. She is amazingly light, barely there, barely physical, and while I hold her up she reaches around my neck and leans her head against my shoulder. I walk with her to the window and then turn so that she faces the tree. I gaze longingly at it myself, marveling at the gaudy flowers, and then I turn back upon her face, where the light is shining, and I can see that her eyes have now shut, and she is gone.

But here in this room we are not alone. I think she is probably glad for this, as am I. Her breathing, the doctor says, is becoming labored. He kneels and listens to her heart. "I think we should be ready," he says. "Your mother is close." He steps back. He is a good doctor, a good friend. I think he can see the whole picture of the time. And I think about what he is saying: *Your mother is close.* Yes. Close to us, close to life, close to death. She is close to everything, I think; she is attaining an irrevocable nearness of being, a proximity to everything that has been spoken or written or thought, in every land and language on earth. How did we get to this place? Why are we here in this room, assembled as we are, as if arrayed in some ancient haunted painting whose grave semblance must be known in every mind and heart of man?

I count a full five between her breaths. The color is leaving her face. The mask is forming. Her hand in mine is cold, already dead. I think it is now that I must speak to her. I understand that I am not here to listen; that must be for another narrative. I am not here to bear her in my arms towards bright windows. I am not here to be strong. I am not here to exchange goodbyes. I am not here to recount old stories. I am not here to acknowledge the dead.

I am here to speak. Say the words. Her nearness has delivered me to this moment, an ever-lengthening moment between her breaths, that I might finally speak the words turning inward, for the first time, in my own beginning and lonely language: Do not be afraid. It is all right, so do not be afraid. You are not really alone. You may die, but you will have been heard. Keep speaking—it is real. You have a voice.

Biographies

MIA ALVAR's collection of short stories, *In the Country*, won the PEN/Robert W. Bingham Prize for Debut Fiction, the 2015 Barnes & Noble Discover Great New Writers Award, and the Janet Heidinger Kafka Prize. Alvar has been a writer-in-residence at the Corporation of Yaddo, the Djerassi Resident Artists Program, the Lower Manhattan Cultural Council, and the Blue Mountain Center for the Arts. Her work has appeared in *One Story*, the *Missouri Review*, the *Cincinnati Review*, and elsewhere. Born in the Philippines and raised in Bahrain and the United States, she lives in New York City.

GINA APOSTOL's third novel, *Gun Dealers' Daughter*, won the 2013 PEN Open Book Award and was shortlisted for the 2014 William Saroyan International Prize. Her first two novels, *Bibliolepsy* and *The Revolution According to Raymundo Mata*, both won the Juan C. Laya Prize for the Novel (Philippine National Book Award). Her essays and stories have appeared in the *New York Times*, *Los Angeles Review of Books*, *Foreign Policy*, *Gettysburg Review*, *Massachusetts Review*, and others. She lives in New York City.

CHAYA BABU is a Brooklyn-based writer, journalist, educator, and organizer. She was a 2016 BuzzFeed Emerging Writers Fellow and a 2015 Open City Fellow with the Asian American Writers' Workshop, and her writing has also appeared in the *Margins*, *Racialicious*, the *Feminist Wire*, the *Wall Street Journal*, the *Sunday Guardian*, *India Abroad*, and elsewhere. Babu is currently pursuing her MFA in writing at Pratt Institute, and she is also editor at large at the *Brooklyn Quarterly* and a teaching artist with Community Word Project.

GAIUTRA BAHADUR is a Guyanese American writer. *Coolie Woman*, her narrative history about indentured women, was shortlisted for the 2014 Orwell Prize. Her essays appear in the anthologies *Nonstop Metropolis* and *Living on the Edge of the World*. She was named a Nieman Fellow at Harvard at thirty-two and has written for the *New York Times Book Review*, *Lapham's Quarterly*, the *Guardian*, *VQR*, the *Nation*, *Dissent*, *Ms.* magazine, and elsewhere. She has won fellowships from the MacDowell Colony, the New Jersey State Council on the Arts, the Barbara Deming Memorial Fund, and others.

ROWAN HISAYO BUCHANAN is the author of the novel *Harmless Like You*. She is British, Japanese, Chinese, and American—hyphenation and ordering vary depending on the day. She has a BA from Columbia University and an MFA from the University of Wisconsin–Madison. She was an Asian American Writers' Workshop fellow, and her short work has appeared in *Granta*, the *Guardian*, *Guernica*, *Apogee*, and the *White Review*, among other places. She has received residencies from the Gladstone Library and Hedgebrook.

WO CHAN is a poet and performance artist. Chan is the author of the chapbook *ORDER THE WORLD, MOM* and has received honors from Poets House, Kundiman, Lambda Literary, Millay Colony of the Arts, and the Asian American Writers' Workshop. Chan has been published in *VYM Magazine*, *Cortland Review*, 92 Street Y, the *Margins*, *No Tokens*, and elsewhere. Chan is a member of the Brooklyn-based performance collective Switch N' Play and has also directed the all–Asian American experimental theater piece *WHITEFLAG/WHITEFACE*, which debuted at the 2016 HOT! Festival at Dixon Place.

ALEXANDER CHEE is the author of the national bestseller *The Queen of the Night*. His acclaimed debut novel, *Edinburgh*, was published in 2001. He is a contributing editor at the *New Republic*, an editor at large at *VQR* and LitHub, and a critic at large for the *Los Angeles Times*. His essays and stories have appeared in *Best American Essays*, the *New York Times Book Review*, *Tin House*, *Slate*, *Guernica*, NPR, and *Out*, among others. He is winner of the Whiting Award and fellowships from the National Endowment for the Arts and the Minority Corporate Counsel Association. He is currently an associate professor of English and creative writing at Dartmouth College.

KARISSA CHEN is the author of the chapbook *Of Birds and Lovers*. Her fiction and essays have been published in numerous publications, including *Gulf Coast*, *PEN America*, *Guernica*, and the *Toast*. She was the recipient of a Fulbright Fellowship to Taiwan and is a Kundiman and VONA/Voices fellow. She currently serves as the senior literature editor of *Hyphen* magazine and is a cofounding editor of *Some Call It Ballin'*.

MARILYN CHIN was born in Hong Kong and raised in Portland, Oregon. She is the author of books of poems including *Hard Love Province* (winner of the 2015 Anisfield-Wolf Book Award), *Rhapsody in Plain Yellow*, *Dwarf Bamboo*, and *The Phoenix Gone, the Terrace Empty*, and the novel *Revenge of the Mooncake Vixen*. Her awards include the United Artist Foundation Fellowship, the Radcliffe Institute Fellowship at Harvard, the Stegner Fellowship, and the PEN/Josephine Miles Award, among others. She is featured in anthologies including *The Norton Anthology of Literature by Women*, *The Penguin Anthology of Twentieth-Century Poetry*, and *The Best American Poetry*. Chin is professor emerita of San Diego State University and currently the Grace Hazard Conkling Poet-in-Residence at Smith College.

MUNA GURUNG is a writer and educator based in Kathmandu, Nepal. She received her MFA from Columbia University, where she was a teaching fellow. Her fiction, nonfiction, and translated works have appeared in the *Margins*, *Himal Southasian*, *Words Without Borders*, *No Tokens*, *PIX Quarter*ly, and *La.Lit*. Muna was a 2015 Asian American Writers' Workshop Margins Fellow and is the founder of KathaSatha, an initiative that fosters a storytelling culture in Nepal.

KIMIKO HAHN, author of nine books, finds disparate sources give way to poetry—whether black lung disease in *Volatile*, Flaubert's sex-tour in *The Unbearable Heart*, an exhumation in *The Artist's Daughter*, or classical Japanese forms in *The Narrow Road to the Interior*. Rarified fields of science prompted her latest collections *Toxic Flora* and *Brain Fever*. Her most recent chapbook was *Replendent Slug*. Her honors include a Guggenheim Fellowship, PEN/Voelcker Award, and Shelley Memorial Prize. Hahn is a distinguished professor in the MFA Program in Creative Writing & Literary Translation at Queens College, CUNY, and is the President of the Board for the Poetry Society of America.

Born in Syria, **MOHJA KAHF** is a professor at the University of Arkansas. She is the author of the novel *The Girl in the Tangerine Scarf*, and the book of poems *E-mails from Scheherazade*. Her second book of poetry, *Hagar Poems*, treats the story of Hagar, Abraham, and Sarah. She is a member of the Syrian Nonviolence Movement and a Boycott, Divestment, Sanctions movement supporter.

ALICE SOLA KIM lives in New York. Her writing has appeared in publications including *Tin House*, the *Village Voice*, *Lenny Letter*, *McSweeney's*, BuzzFeed Reader, and *The Year's Best Science Fiction and Fantasy*. She is a winner of the 2016 Whiting Award and has received grants and scholarships from the MacDowell Colony, Bread Loaf Writers' Conference, and the Elizabeth George Foundation.

JASON KOO is the author of two collections of poetry, *America's Favorite Poem* and *Man on Extremely Small Island*, and coeditor of the *Brooklyn Poets Anthology*. He has published poetry and prose in the *Yale Review*, *Missouri Review*, and *Village Voice*, among others, and won fellowships from the National Endowment for the Arts, Vermont Studio Center, and New York State Writers Institute. An assistant teaching professor of English at Quinnipiac University, Koo is the founder and executive director of Brooklyn Poets and creator of the Bridge. He lives in Brooklyn.

AMITAVA KUMAR is the author of two novels and several works of nonfiction, including *A Foreigner Carrying in the Crook of His Arm a Tiny Bomb*, described by the *New York Times* as "a perceptive and soulful . . . meditation on the global war on terror and its cultural and human repercussions." His latest book is a novel, *Immigrant, Montana*. Kumar's essay "Pyre," in *Granta*, was chosen by Jonathan Franzen for *The Best American Essays*. He is a professor of English at Vassar College and was awarded a Guggenheim Fellowship for nonfiction.

CHANG-RAE LEE is the author of *Native Speaker* (winner of the Hemingway Foundation/PEN Award for Debut Fiction), *A Gesture Life*, *Aloft*, and *On Such a Full Sea*. Selected by the *New Yorker* as one of the twenty best writers under forty, Lee teaches writing at Stanford University.

T KIRA MADDEN is a writer, photographer, and amateur magician living in New York City. Her work has appeared in *Guernica*, *Black Warrior Review*, *Columbia Journal*, the *Kenyon Review*, and *Tin House* online. She is a recipient of fellowships from the MacDowell Colony and Hedgebrook and serves as the founding editor in chief of *No Tokens*.

Winner of 2015 Association of Writers and Writing Programs Intro Journals Award and the 2014 Intro Prize in Poetry by Four Way Books for his first full-length collection *The Taxidermist's Cut*, and recipient of a PEN/Heim Translation Fund Grant, **RAJIV MOHABIR** received fellowships from the Home School, Voices of Our Nation's Arts Foundation, Kundiman, and the American Institute of Indian Studies language program. His second volume of poetry, *The Cowherd's Son*, won the 2015 Kundiman Prize. He received his MFA in poetry and translation from Queens College, CUNY, where he was editor in chief of the *Ozone Park Literary Journal*.

MUHAMMAD AMIRUL BIN MUHAMAD is a Malay Singaporean student currently pursuing a degree in mass communication. He enjoys writing stories and listening to others when they tell him theirs. On his personal blog, *Spinning Stop*, he writes about a variety of things, including depression, love, nebulous apparitions, sex, and crying babies, among others.

FARIHA RÓISÍN is a writer living in Montréal. She has written for the *Guardian, Vice, Al Jazeera*, and the *New York Times*, as well as many other publications. She is also a cohost of two podcasts, Toronto International Film Festival's *Yo, Adrian*, and *Two Brown Girls*, which reflects on the intersections of race and pop culture.

SHARLENE TEO was born in Singapore and lives in London. She is completing a PhD in creative and critical writing at the University of East Anglia, where she received the Booker Prize Foundation Scholarship and the David T. K. Wong Creative Writing Award. She was shortlisted for the 2017 Berlin Writing Prize and holds fellowships from the Elizabeth Kostova Foundation and the University of Iowa International Writing Program. In 2016 she won the inaugural Deborah Rogers Writer's Award for *Ponti*, her first novel.

JENNIFER TSENG is the author of two poetry books, *The Man with My Face* and *Red Flower, White Flower*. Her chapbook, *Not so dear Jenny*, won the Bateau Press Boom Chapbook Contest. Tseng's debut novel, *Mayumi and the Sea of Happiness*, was a finalist for the New England Book Award, shortlisted for the PEN Robert Bingham Award for Debut Fiction, and has been featured in the *Boston Globe*, *Los Angeles Times*, *Huffington Post*, *Financial Times*, *Elle*, and elsewhere. She currently teaches for the Fine Arts Work Center's summer and online writing programs, and for the Martha's Vineyard Institute of Creative Writing.

ESMÉ WEIJUN WANG is an essayist, the author of *The Border of Paradise: A Novel*, and the recipient of the 2016 Graywolf Nonfiction Prize. Raised in the San Francisco Bay Area, she received her MFA from the University of Michigan and has been awarded the Sudler Award, Hopwood Award for Novel-in-Progress, and the Elizabeth George Foundation Grant. Her work has appeared in *Salon*, *Elle*, *Catapult*, *Hazlitt*, the *Believer*, and *Lenny Letter*.

WENDY XU is the author of *Phrasis*, winner of the 2016 Ottoline Prize, and *You Are Not Dead*. The recipient of a Ruth Lilly Fellowship, her work has appeared in *The Best American Poetry*, *Boston Review*, *Poetry*, *A Public Space*, and widely elsewhere. Born in Shandong, China, she lives in New York City and serves as poetry editor for *Hyperallergic*.

Acknowledgments

First off, to my dear contributors—we are honored to have you in these pages.

Thank you also to everybody who submitted to our open call. We received almost five hundred submissions and we were able to take on only a handful. There were so many brave and brilliant writers we were not able to accept. Thank you for your words and your time.

We believe this book is unique and necessary, but there are works that lit our way. Three anthologies in particular come to mind. *Aiiieeeee! An Anthology of Asian-American Writers*, edited by Frank Chin, Jeffery Paul Chan, Lawson Fusao Inada, and Shawn Wong, was the first great Asian American writing anthology. I remember flipping through the pages feeling a whole world open up to me. *Good Girls Marry Doctors*, edited by Piyali Bhattacharya, is a brilliant nonfiction collection of South Asian women writers. Piyali advised me when *Go Home!* was only a hope. She told me exactly how difficult and exactly how wonderful putting together an anthology would be. Without her guidance, I would not have known where to begin. *The Good Immigrant*, an essay collection edited by Nikesh Shukla, came out as I was editing *Go Home!* Seeing the work Nikesh has been doing with communities and to give voice to the unheard has been an inspiration.

This project couldn't have happened without the synergy of the Asian American Writers' Workshop and the Feminist Press. In 2015, AAWW adopted me as a fellow—little did they know

I'd never leave them alone again. In particular, thank you, Ken Chen and Jyothi Natarajan. When I suggested this anthology to them they were so open and enthusiastic. Jyothi read, edited, advised, and cheered this project at every turn. I could not have done it without her. Thank you, Clarissa Wong, for reaching out to me from the Feminist Press. Thank you, Jisu Kim, for adopting this project and working so hard to help it come to pass. Your support, editorial eye, and vision were so necessary.

I'd also like to thank the people in my personal life who aided and influenced the putting together of these pages. Thank you, Tony Fu, for always being there for me. Thank you, Kyla Cheung, for all our conversations. Thank you, Paul Hardwick, for the constant reassurance and kindness. Thank you to my brilliant agent, Lucy Luck, for all you do. Thank you to my family—my mother, father, brother, and in particular, to my grandmother, who fed, loved, and put a roof over my head so that I could be an AAWW fellow.

Permissions

"Mothers, Lock Up Your Daughters Because They Are Terrifying" by Alice Sola Kim first appeared in *Tin House*.

"My Grandmother Washes Her Feet in the Sink of the Bathroom at Sears" from *E-mails from Scheherazad* by Mohja Kahf. Gainesville: University Press of Florida, 2003. Reprinted with permission of the University Press of Florida.

"The Place Where I Live Is Different Because I Live There" from *You Are Not Dead* by Wendy Xu. Cleveland, Ohio: Cleveland State University Poetry Center, 2013. Reprinted with permission of the Cleveland State University Poetry Center.

"what do i make of my face / except" by Wo Chan first appeared in *Vetch: A Magazine of Trans Poetry and Poetics*.

"Aama, 1978" by Muna Gurung, first appeared in *No Tokens*.

A version of "Meet a Muslim" by Fariha Róisín first appeared as "Growing Up Muslim in a Post-9/11 World" in Broadly.

"Esmeralda" from *In the Country: Stories* by Mia Alvar, compilation copyright © 2015 by Mia Alvar. Used by permission of Alfred A. Knopf, an imprint of the Knopf Doubleday Publishing Group, a division of Penguin Random House LLC. All rights reserved.

"Tigress" by Rowan Hisayo Buchanan first appeared in the *Harvard Review*.

"The Stained Veil" by Gaiutra Bahadur was first published by Commonwealth Writers on www.addastories.org. Verses by Kabir translated by Rajiv Mohabir.

"I'm Charlie Tuna" from *Man on Extremely Small Island* by Jason Koo. Winston-Salem, North Carolina, 2009. Reprinted with permission of C&R Press.

"Bon Chul Koo and the Hall of Fame" from *Man on Extremely Small Island* by Jason Koo. Winston-Salem, North Carolina, 2009. Reprinted with permission of C&R Press.

"The Faintest Echo of Our Language," copyright © 1993 by Chang-Rae Lee, first appeared in the *New England Review*.

The Feminist Press is a nonprofit educational organization founded to amplify feminist voices. FP publishes classic and new writing from around the world, creates cutting-edge programs, and elevates silenced and marginalized voices in order to support personal transformation and social justice for all people.

See our complete list of books at
feministpress.org

Founded in 1991, the **Asian American Writers' Workshop** is dedicated to the creation, publication, development, and dissemination of Asian American literature. An alternative art space devoted to literature at the intersection of race, migration, and social justice, we see ourselves as a sanctuary space for the imagination. Covered by the *New York Times*, the *Wall Street Journal,* and NPR, we seek to invent the future of Asian American literary culture. We believe Asian American stories deserve to be told.